Contents

D0492911

Introduction

For those of us living in the colder parts of the northern hemisphere, the long months of winter sometimes stretch from October to April—nearly half the year. While green thoughts and nursery catalogues may sustain some plantsmen through this long period, others may seek a more practical outlet for their horticultural interests, or just the sight of greenery and flower colour in their home. And for those residing in towns, this yearning for a contact with nature lasts throughout the year. It is to all these that *The Indoor Garden Book* is directed.

Indoor plants provide contact with nature for they are living growing things, and interesting because of it; at the same time they will enhance almost any interior by adding natural forms, colours and fragrances. However, used at random they look messy and may be at odds with the decoration of a room. Professional designers are well aware of the decorative qualities of plants and how they can be used to complement a decorating scheme. But this skill in matching plants to interior decoration, and in placing them effectively in a room, can be easily learnt through practice and through an appreciation of the different decorative qualities of plants and flowers. This book sets out to show you how to get to know your plants and flowers and appreciate their shapes, colours, sizes, textures and seasons within an interior setting.

How to use your indoor plants

Begin your decorating by thinking about the sort of space you want to fill with plants. Do you want one large dramatic plant to act as a single focal point, or a smaller group of

A Victorian flavour
The classic late nineteenth-century interior is dark and cluttered with heavy drapery and over-stuffed furniture. Several large Kentia palms (*Howea belmoreana*) might be placed in the room, with gloxinias (*Sinningia* sp.) clustered on side tables. Here, a series of hanging baskets helps to break up the large expanse of window and lightens the gloom of the dark wooden panelling.

Period romanticism
A more romantic approach to the interior appeared around the turn of the century, combined with a re-appraisal of simple garden flowers. This torso is surrounded by a group of poinsettias (*Euphorbia pulcherrima*) whose lush flowers echo the colour of the sculpture; the effect is rich and voluptuous.

Traditional country-house style
Though modern, this room is a scaled-down version of a traditional, grand, country-house interior with bright colours, a fireplace, deep upholstery and an arrangement of garden flowers. Strongly coloured exotic house plants would appear alien in this setting, and although some orchids (*Cymbidium* sp.) have crept in here, their colour is sufficiently delicate to blend in with the decoration.

plants of contrasting shapes, colours or textures? Perhaps you only have space to use plants in a hanging basket, or trained round a piece of furniture, or round part of the structure of the room. Step-by-step projects in the chapter on *Plant Display* show you how to put these ideas and many more into practice. A simple arrangement of fresh flowers will immediately lighten the mood of a room and, in the *Cut-Flower Arranging* chapter, a selection of cut flowers and foliage, including commercially available material and garden varieties, have been used to create a series of seasonal displays. In winter, cut flowers are expensive, so it is worth considering the use of dried material in the home to sustain the colours and mood of summer and autumn. The chapter on *Dried-Flower Arranging* shows you how to make trees, wreaths and decorations as well as flower arrangements. In *The Plant Finder's Guide*, decorating tips are given on how to use each of the featured plants to best effect, while *The Room-by-Room Guide* shows how plants and flowers can be used in a variety of novel and exciting ways in different parts of the home.

Styling with plants

Never has there been such a range of styles for living as there is today. Yet all—even the most modern—are subtly influenced by the past. Recognizing the component parts of a style of décor helps to define the qualities you need in a plant to enhance that style. To illustrate this, and show how to approach your decorative schemes, I have chosen a selection of contemporary styles of decoration and analysed them, to show how plants contribute to the overall styling.

American colonial style
Another trend in interior decoration is one which is strongly influenced by the houses and artefacts of colonial North America. The early homesteaders were gardeners, and this is reflected in the way that herbs and vegetables, along with country flowers, are used for decoration in this style. The daisy bushes (*Chrysanthemum frutescens*) in rough wicker baskets used in this bedroom are typical.

Simple rustic style
In Britain, nostalgia for a rural past took another turn when stripped-pine furniture and small-print fabrics appeared in the 1960s. The style is comfortable and unpretentious, with much allusion to country pursuits. Country flowers, such as these daffodils (*Narcissus* sp.), and dried flowers find a place here.

The influence of the exotic
The hippy movement of the 1960s brought the east closer to the west, and fabrics, carpets and ornaments from the east have now found their way into many homes. The rich patterns and colours of many ethnic textiles suit the strong forms and bold colours of tropical and semi-tropical plants.

The history of indoor plants

Plants have been used indoors for many centuries. The Dutch interest in painting interiors and flower-pieces went hand-in-hand with an increasing interest, throughout the western world, in the cultivated plant. Again, the Dutch tulip craze of the 1630s must have influenced other countries, but travellers, since the returning Crusaders, would also have brought plants home and fostered them indoors prior to the advent of glass. We know, too, that herbs were used extensively indoors: for strewing, medicinal and culinary purposes. In the seventeenth century, orangeries, structures made of brick or stone with large south-facing windows, were built to shelter orange trees in winter. But it was not until the introduction of glass structures, which could be heated, that plants could be grown inside to any degree.

Tropical fruit was initially cultivated in primitively heated houses; pineapples, guavas and limes were grown—and also the first camellias. Later, there followed the date palm and banana. Succulents, such as the aloe and agave, were also raised for medicinal purposes and to decorate terraces in summer. During the nineteenth century, the conservatory became a standard addition to larger houses; house plant cultivation moved into the realms of fashion, with fern houses, palm houses, and houses for exotic plants being all the rage. Simple potted plants too began to escape from the conservatory to become the necessary accompaniment to the heavy, draped look of the late nineteenth-century interior—although the smoke from open fires did the plants little good. Floristry became a fashionable lady's accomplishment.

One reaction to this style was to seek inspiration from what

The influence of the 1930s
This contemporary bathroom looks back to the 1930s in its monochromatic colour scheme and the geometric form of the metal-framed mirror. The simplicity calls for plants with a strong form, and these dragon trees (*Dracaena marginata*) add softness and interest to a setting which might otherwise look clinical.

The oriental look
This modern interior is heavily influenced by the austerity of a traditional Japanese home. Colours are largely neutral and are offset by carefully positioned areas of bright colour—the pink leaf margins of the ti plant (*Cordyline terminalis*) in the foreground pick up the colour of the cushions. The bare branches are chosen for their linear forms.

Linear austerity
The evolution of the Modern movement in architecture and interior design was complex, with influences from Japan, Scandinavia, Italy and America. But it was typified by more severe linear forms, a lack of pattern, and "designer" furniture in laminated wood or metal and leather. This type of hard-edged interior is softened and enriched by the use of large plants, such as these Kentia palms (*Howea belmoreana*)— which here also help to link indoors with outdoors.

must have been a continuing, unsophisticated, cottage tradition of keeping temperate plants indoors to root or over-winter, and of hanging herbs from the rafters to dry. An alternative Modernist movement at the beginning of this century used specific plants in its interiors—the lily being a great favourite. But the real origins of the use of house plants lie in Scandinavia where, traditionally, plants were brought indoors to relieve the bleakness of a long winter; and it was not until after the Second World War that they really became part of the modish interior. It was then that house plants as we know them started to make their appearance, with species from Asia and Central and South America becoming available. Since then, new varieties have been bred which need less maintenance and, with central heating and correct management, they can be kept very successfully indoors.

Choosing plants

The plants which are or are not suitable for you will depend on the particular type of decoration you have, for currently there are a number of interior styles. Your selection will depend on personal taste and on what it is practical to maintain—given the specific limitations of day- and night-time temperatures, light availability, the presence of draughts, children and pets, and, of course, available space.

The industrial style
During the 1970s, a new style of design appeared which made use of industrial artefacts. The hard lines and strong colours of this style called for the use of large plants with distinctive shapes, and flowers with strong forms and colours.

A softer approach
In the 1980s, a softening of the high-tech style has occurred with the introduction of subtle pastel colours. In this interior, the rooms blend into each other to create a feeling of space and light, and large plants, such as these weeping figs (*Ficus benjamina*), can be used in an architectural way to link the spaces.

Classical eclecticism
Another current mood is a classic look characterized by discreet colours and patterning, and bold pieces of furniture which may be modern or traditional. Plant groupings are strong and simple; they are part of the overall conception of the room, but punctuate rather than dominate the setting.

·1·

THE DECORATIVE QUALITIES OF PLANTS

The photographs in this opening chapter demonstrate the astounding diversity of plant form—from striking architectural plants with bold foliage to relatively inconspicuous ground creepers. There is a tremendous range of growing habit, as well as leaf and flower size, shape, colour and texture. Cut flowers, too, provide a kaleidoscopic array of colours—rich and vibrant or subtle and subdued. The flower heads may be large or small, flat, spiky, spherical or more complex, and these shapes themselves may suggest an appropriate way to display the material.

Bear these decorative qualities in mind when choosing plants and flowers, so that their characteristics will enhance the mood of your home. Think about the form and size of a plant if you want it to be part of the landscape of your room, or link parts of the room which have different functions. When planning smaller groups of plants, or arrangements of flowers, consider their colours and textures in conjunction with wall colours and fabric textures, so that the display and its setting show a sense of overall harmony.

Infinite variety
One of the principal joys of using plants in the home is the diversity of decorative qualities they provide. Here, a random selection of freshly cut flowers, leaves and berries gives some indication of the range of colour, texture, size and shape available.

Plant form

Of all plant characteristics it is shape that probably creates the strongest initial impression. Shape is primarily to do with the general outline of the plant, but it also embraces other characteristics that contribute to the plant's overall form: the density of the growth, the size and number of individual stems and branches, the way the leaves or leaflets are arranged and the "weight" of the foliage. Of course, shape is always changing as a plant grows, but certain generalizations can be made and throughout this book I have used a system of classification that divides plants into eight different shape categories: upright, arching, weeping, rosette-shaped, bushy, climbing, trailing and creeping. These are the categories used in *The Plant Finder's Guide* and here you will find a plant to illustrate each one of them.

Coconut palm
Cocos nucifera (see p.169)
This plant has an *arching* shape, as do most of the palms and ferns; its sword-shaped fronds have a hard outline.

Japanese fatsia
Fatsia japonica (see p.181)
The overall shape of this plant is *bushy* but the large fingered leaves have a strong individual outline.

Creeping fig *Ficus pumila* (see p.193) With its spreading shape, this *creeping* plant resembles a green carpet when allowed to ramble; it can also trail or climb.

Sweetheart plant
Philodendron scandens (see p.188)
Plants usually combine different elements of
shape; this *trailing* philodendron has beautifully
shaped leaves as well as stems that trail
in an attractive way.

Algerian ivy
Hedera canariensis (see p.184)
The shape of its support will
dictate the overall shape of a
climbing plant, but individual
foliage will give an outline that
may be delicate or bold.

Stick yucca
Yucca elephantipes (see p.167)
Plants with *upright* growth and
spiky leaves have a simple
bold shape.

Ponytail
Beaucarnea recurvata (see p.171)
The soft shape of this *weeping* plant is created by
the mass of drooping, grasslike leaves.

Bird's nest bromeliad *Nidularium innocentii*
(see p.175) Most *rosette-shaped* plants
have a strong outline that demands attention.

Leaf size

In many fields successful design often relies on the simple repetition of elements of similar sizes. This principle holds good for the arrangement of plants but impressive effects can also be achieved by emphasizing differences in scale. For example, the delicate tracery of small climbing plants can be highlighted by juxtaposing them with broad expanses of leaf of an uncomplicated shape.

Dwarf coconut palm
Microcoelum weddellianum
(see p.170) Juxtapose these small slender fronds with other larger palms.

Kentia palm
Howea belmoreana (see p.170)
Display large plants on their own, or in groups with spiky-leaved plants.

Rosary vine
Ceropegia woodii (see p.201)
A plant which looks best on its own; allow the stems
to trail from a hanging basket or shelf.

Elephant's ear philodendron
Philodendron hastatum
(see p.187)
A large-leaved climber best
used as a feature plant or as a
foil for low-growing plants.

Sweetheart plant
Philodendron scandens
(see p. 188)
Use in a hanging basket or
arrange around a large-leaved
philodendron.

Leaf shape

Leaf shape is a very strong visual characteristic of a plant and a striking display can be achieved by concentrating solely on either contrasting or harmonizing leaf shapes. There is a great variety of leaf shapes to choose from—lance-shaped leaves, oval leaves, heart-shaped leaves, wavy-edged leaves and even leaves shaped like a violin. The shape of its leaves can be the most important feature of a plant or it can be a secondary charm.

Pothos vine
Scindapsus pictus "Argyraeus" (see p.188) Heart-shaped leaves with acutely pointed tips.

Swiss cheese plant
Monstera deliciosa (see p.187) The large oval leaves become perforated as the plant gets older.

Passion flower
Passiflora caerulea (see p.185) Fan-shaped leaves with many deeply cut lobes.

Grape ivy
Cissus rhombifolia (see p.186) The leaves have pointed tips and scalloped edges.

Fiddle-leaf philodendron
Philodendron bipennifolium (see p. 169) The young irregularly shaped leaves become violin-shaped when mature.

Asparagus fern
Asparagus setaceus (see p.183) Wiry stems carry triangular sprays made up of feathery branchlets.

Dumb cane
Dieffenbachia exotica
(see p.163)
The long oval leaves have wavy margins and a distinct point at their tip.

Weeping fig
Ficus benjamina (see p.171)
Small, slender, oval leaves with curved edges and pointed tips.

Stick yucca
Yucca elephantipes
(see p. 167)
Long, narrow, spiky leaves with finely toothed edges.

Silk oak
Grevillea robusta (see p.166)
The leaves are highly divided giving a delicate fernlike appearance.

Boston fern
Nephrolepis exaltata
"Bostoniensis".
(see p. 170)
The fronds are divided into narrow leaflets giving a graceful feathery appearance.

Finger aralia
Dizygotheca elegantissima
(see p.165)
Narrow leaflets with saw-toothed edges radiate like spokes from the top of each stem.

Leaf colour

The range of colour found in leaves is startling: from the variety of different greens to leaves with all-over colours from silver-white to deep purple, as well as those which are patterned or mottled with contrasting colours. Dramatic displays can be made with foliage plants by concentrating on the interplay between two, or at most three, colours.

Wandering Jew
Zebrina pendula (see p. 189)
The leaves are finely marked with two translucent green stripes.

Snakeskin plant
Fittonia verschaffeltii
(see p. 193)
Carmine-red veins traversing olive-green leaves create a dramatic colour contrast.

Angel wings
Caladium hortulanum hybrids (see p.182)
Paper-thin leaves with very delicate markings in combinations of red, pink, white and green.

Painted nettle
Coleus blumei
(see p.177)
Leaf colour and pattern varies, with rich mixtures of yellow, red, orange, green and brown.

Croton
Codiaeum variegatum pictum
(see p.164) Leaves in a range of warm exotic colours mottled with spots, blotches and veins.

Blushing bromeliad
Neoregelia carolinae "Tricolor" (see p.174)
Green- and cream-striped leaves which become suffused with red at flowering time.

Peacock plant
Calathea makoyana (see p. 165)
Leaves which look as if they
have been hand-painted with a
spectacular pattern of dark
blotches.

English ivy
Hedera helix hybrids
(see p.190)
The mid-green leaves have
darker green blotches and
cream margins.

Ti plant
Cordyline terminalis (see p.163)
The striped leaves are outlined
in a vivid pink.

Angel wings
Caladium hortulanum hybrids
This young leaf, from the same
plant as the leaf to its left, shows
the colour variation which can
occur on the same plant.

Silvered spear
Aglaonema crispum
"Silver Queen" (see p.164)
Beautiful dark-green leaves
heavily marked with silvery-
green blotches.

Eyelash begonia
Begonia "Tiger Paws"
(see p. 193)
The bright-red markings on the
undersides of the emerald-green
leaves show through as brown
on the upper surface.

Strawberry geranium
Saxifraga stolonifera "Tricolor"
(see p.190)
Olive-green leaves with a pink
margin and fine pink hairs.

Polka-dot plant
Hypoestes phyllostachya
(see p.179)
Dark olive-green leaves which
are heavily spotted with pink.

Leaf texture

There are as many variations in leaf texture as in shape, size or colour. Very few leaves have no textural quality and textures can vary from glossy to matt, from hairy to wrinkled, from ribbed to quilted, each variation giving added interest to the plant. Subtle displays can be made by juxtaposing plants with contrasting leaf textures.

Norfolk Island pine
Araucaria heterophylla (see p.166)
Tiers of needle-covered branches give an overall filigree lightness.

Cast-iron plant
Aspidistra elatior (see p. 165)
Distinctive ribbing marks run along the length of these leathery leaves.

Bird's nest fern
Asplenium nidus
(see p.173)
The lance-shaped leaves are extremely smooth and shiny with a central rib.

Emerald ripple peperomia
Peperomia caperata
(see p.180)
The heart-shaped, dark-green leaves have a corrugated surface with a waxy feel to them.

Painted-leaf begonia
Begonia rex-cultorum (see p.183)
The highly decorative foliage is covered in pimples giving it a curious rough texture.

Maidenhair fern
Adiantum raddianum
(see p.183)
Leaves have a soft filmy texture
and are arranged on gracefully
drooping fronds.

Purple velvet plant
Gynura aurantiaca (see p.191)
The toothed leaves are covered
in soft purple hair, giving them a
furry texture.

Staghorn fern
Platycerium bifurcatum (see p.191)
The antler-shaped fronds are
covered with fine, white,
feltlike scurf.

Red herringbone plant
*Maranta leuconeura
erythroneura* (see p.178)
Bright-red veins stand out from
the surface of the satiny leaves.

Columnea
Columnea "Banksii" (see p.189)
The dark-green paired leaves are
fleshy with a waxy texture.

Flower size

The beauty of flowers does not depend solely on their colour, although it is an important factor. Size contributes to the unique appeal of a particular bloom and is a major consideration when planning an arrangement. Use flowers which are in scale with one another and, when choosing a container, make sure that its size is suitable for your flowers.

Mimosa
Acacia longifolia (see p.212)
This evergreen shrub produces short-stemmed clusters of fragrant, golden-yellow flowers the size of peas.

Delphinium
Delphinium elatum (see p.217)
The tall spikes of these cut flowers are suitable for any kind of large arrangement.

Chrysanthemum
Chrysanthemum hybrids (see p.222)
These flowers, the largest
of the numerous cut varieties of
chrysanthemum, are the size of
grapefruits.

Poinsettia
Euphorbia pulcherrima (see p.178)
These striking house plants have large,
bright-red bracts which form a circle
around the insignificant flowers.

Cornflower
Centaurea cyanus (see p.217)
The single, small, round heads of
these cut flowers are the size
of golfballs.

Anemone
Anemone coronaria (see p.222)
These brightly coloured, poppy-
like flowers have heads as large
as tennis balls.

Flower shape

Flowers come in an immense variety of shapes from the simple petalled blooms of the primula to the exotic, petalless, globular flowers of the nodding pincushion. Successful flower arrangements depend upon an appreciation of shape, and the natural outline of the flower can be used as a key to the overall design. Use long, thin flower spikes for outline and rounded shapes for focal point in large displays.

Bells-of-Ireland
Moluccella laevis (see p.217)
These are long spikes of small white flowers surrounded by green cuplike bracts.

Tom thumb
Kalanchoe blossfeldiana (see p.196)
The small flowers of this house plant grow in dense clusters and may be cut and used in a vase.

Painter's palette
Anthurium andraeanum (see p.182)
These strange-looking blooms consist of a waxy, shield-shaped bract and a protruding cylindrical flower spike.

Baby's breath
Gypsophila paniculata (see p.213)
The loose clusters of tiny single or double flowers create a hazy effect which is emphasized by displaying them alone in a glass container.

Transvaal daisy
Gerbera jamesonii (see p.217)
These large single or double flowers come in vivid colours and provide focal interest in mixed arrangements.

Pansy
Viola wittrockiana (see p.213)
These attractive heart-shaped flowers have layers of soft, lobed petals.

Bird-of-paradise
Strelitzia reginae (see p.164)
These unusual flowers consist of a green bract supporting orange-and-blue flowers which stand erect like the crest of a tropical bird.

Zonal geranium
Pelargonium hortorum
hybrids (see p.178)
These rounded clusters of small flowers are available in a wide range of colours.

Orchid
Dendrobium sp. (see p.223)
These long-lasting flowers grow
in arching sprays that bloom
right down the stems.

Peruvian lily
Alstroemeria pelegrina (see p.213)
The trumpet-shaped flowers are
borne at the ends of the
long stems.

African violet
Saintpaulia hybrids (see p.175)
The single or double flowers of
these house plants grow in
clusters on a
short stem.

Gentian
Gentiana sp. (see p.217)
These small flowers are
shaped like a funnel.

Sword lily
Gladiolus sp. (see p.215)
These elegant cut flowers
have tall, one-sided spikes
of single florets.

German violet
Exacum affine (see p.178)
The flowers of this house plant
are small and saucer-shaped
with a single layer of petals.

Begonia
Begonia tuberhybrida
(see p.176) These house plants
carry both single and double flowers
which are large and roselike.

Nodding pincushion
Leucospermum nutans (see p.221)
These unusual globular blooms
are covered with protruding spikes.

Carnation
Dianthus caryophyllus
(see p.215) These double flowers
which grow on clustered stems have a
"ruffled" appearance.

Primula
Primula obconica (see p.181)
This house plant has clusters of
brightly coloured blooms on a
single stalk.

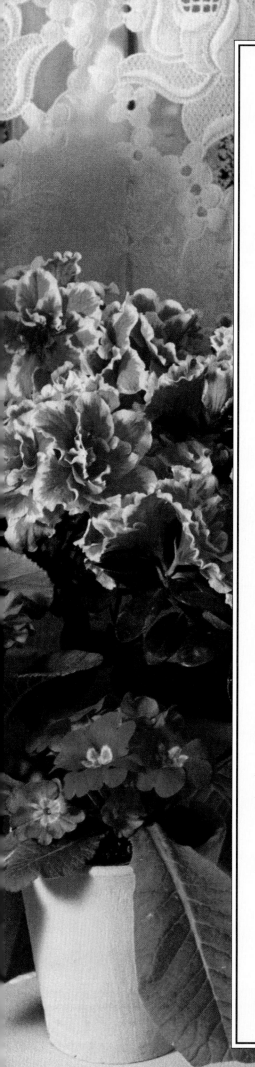

·2·
PLANT DISPLAY

The arranging, grouping and positioning of plants and flowers is an art, not a science. It is a matter of taste, and therefore not an area in which there are hard-and-fast rules. However, there are guidelines, and it is possible to give advice on what is likely to look good and what is not.

Perhaps the most important thing to remember is that every plant arrangement must be designed in context. This means taking into account not only the appearance of the plant itself, but also the container you intend to put it in, the background against which it will be seen, and the room features or items of furniture by which it will be surrounded. Arrangements may consist of a single plant in a simple pot, a formal grouping of associated plants, a jungle-like garden room or conservatory overflowing with greenery, a single vase of bright, colourful, cut flowers, or a mixed display that incorporates any or all of these elements. In each case, the first thing to do is to look at the plants and flowers themselves and see them in terms of the qualities described in the previous chapter. Only then turn to the choice of container and make your selection not just on the basis of choosing the right size for your plant's health, but also in terms of how the container can add to your display, and how it can enhance the mood you want to create.

Co-ordinating plants and containers
The colour of flowering house plants can be picked up, and reinforced, by the colour of their containers. Here, the colour of the containers holds the group together and, at the same time, because they are a less assertive pink than the flowers, attention is focused on the plants.

Matching plants to containers 1

The criteria to be borne in mind when selecting a container for your plant are many and complex, and for every rule formulated it is possible to show an example that breaks it successfully. In every case the decision will be tempered by personal taste and preference but it is worth setting down some basic guidelines.

The most important consideration is the proportion of the container to the plant. In general, the smaller the plant the more it should equal the height of its container. To find out what combinations will work together it is best to try various permutations of container with your plant, standing back to appreciate the result in each case. Having selected a container whose proportions suit the plant, make sure that both together will suit the particular place

in which you want to put them. This is fundamental to the success of the arrangement for not only the container, but also the plant inside it, must be suitable for the setting both practically and aesthetically.

It is essential to choose a style of container and a type of plant that will reflect and enhance the ambience of the room for which they are intended. The style of the container depends on the material of which it is made and on its shape, colour and texture. The style of a plant can be analysed in a similar way: for instance, the spiky-leaved yucca has a hard-edged modern look to it, while a begonia with lush flowers and a soft outline will suit a more traditional setting. So do not be tempted to buy a yucca in an aluminium pot if you have a period house decorated with chintzes.

Containers for different-shaped plants

Scarlet star
Guzmania lingulata

Pothos vine
Scindapsus pictus "Argyraeus"

English ivy
Hedera helix hybrids

Conical glass bowl
The crisp linear form of this bowl complements the red flowers and strong outline of these rosette-shaped plants.

Spherical ceramic pot
The trailing pothos vine hangs attractively over the edge of this rounded pot. The simplicity of the pot, both in shape and colour, shows off the silver variegation in the leaves.

Tall terracotta pot
An English ivy displayed in this way needs a tall pot to show off its trailing stems. A tall upright plant would look out of proportion in such a container.

Boston fern
Nephrolepis exaltata "Bostoniensis"

Button fern
Pellaea rotundifolia

Ponytail
Beaucarnea recurvata

Classical lead urn
The height of this imitation lead urn sets off the Boston fern's arching fronds. The combination has a formal look reinforced by the urn's classical design.

Round ceramic pot
The simple shape of this container sets off the delicate outline of the button fern's arching fronds. The dark matt-green leaf colour goes well with the blue of the pot.

Low terracotta dish
The bizarre shape of the weeping ponytail plant calls for a plain container such as this terracotta dish. As the roots like to be pot bound, the container is very small for a plant of this size.

Japanese fatsia
Fatsia japonica

Cape leadwort
Plumbago auriculata

Angel wings
Caladium hortulanum
hybrids

Glazed ceramic planter
The bare stems of the bushy angel wings are set off by the attractive shape of the green planter. This unassertive colour allows the patterns in the leaves to stand out well.

Handled rush basket
This vigorous Japanese fatsia with its broad fingered leaves and bushy shape demands a simple but sturdy-looking container.

Hooped rush basket
The hooped handle of this basket forms a support for this small, climbing Cape leadwort. The rough texture of the basket goes well with the rather untidy stems.

Mind-your-own-business
Soleirolia soleirolii

Flat terracotta dish
The flat open shape of this dish suits the creeping habit of mind-your-own-business. The rustic terracotta goes well with the fresh green of the plant's tiny leaves.

Rabbit's ears cactus
Opuntia microdasys

Tip yucca
Yucca elephantipes

Finger aralia
Dizygotheca elegantissima

Square fibreglass planter
The austere form of the upright spiky-leaved yucca is shown off by the extreme simplicity of its white fibreglass container.

Rustic wooden barrel
The arresting shape of this upright cactus requires a container with a simple form. The rough wooden barrel goes well with its vigorous spiny texture.

Large terracotta planter
The success of this combination relies on the contrast between the solidity of the terracotta pot and the filigree effect of this upright plant's bronze-coloured foliage.

Matching plants to containers 2

Groups of containers

One of the ways of adding interest to the layout of a room is by grouping pots and other containers with plants, as incidental points of interest. You can use containers of the same colour to hold a group of plants together and to stabilize the mood of an area within a room. Few groupings of this sort are important enough to become the focal point in a very large room, but can work well in a smaller area.

When choosing your containers, think carefully about how they will match your plants, and about how plants and containers will work together as a group, both in terms of themselves and in terms of their setting.

Counterpoint with colour *right*
These containers were chosen to set up a pleasing interplay of colour between themselves and the plants. The black and red of the containers pick up and complement the leaf colours of both plants.

Painted-leaf begonia
Begonia rex-cultorum

Croton
Codiaeum variegatum pictum

Black aluminium planter

Red plastic container

Mind-your-own-business
Soleirolia soleirolii

Terracotta pots

Terracotta pots *above*
A simple classical grouping of containers that share the same style and colour helps control the random, profligate growth of the plants, and contributes to the effect of a balanced arrangement.

Tall and small *right*
Here, the contrast in shape and scale between the two containers is enhanced by the use of the same plant in each. The monochromatic colour scheme of the pots helps to hold the group together and picks up the silvery-grey leaf variegation in the pothos vine.

Pothos vine
Scindapsus pictus "Argyraeus"

White ceramic pot

Grey ceramic container

Playing with scale *above*
This group works through the repetition of container shape and texture set off by a dramatic contrast in scale of the containers. The use of the same plant in each pot contributes to the satisfying unity of the group.

Repetition *below*
A small plant in a small pot may need reinforcement: this can be achieved by using a larger specimen of the same plant in a larger pot. These pots pick up the very dark-green colour of the polka-dot plants' leaves and contrast well with their pink variegation.

Polka-dot plant
Hypoestes phyllostachya

Black ceramic containers

Unusual containers

Many containers are expensive to buy, particularly if you are thinking of using several of them. It is worth having a look at everyday household objects—wastepaper baskets, preserving pans, galvanized buckets, coal scuttles, kettles, watering cans, china and enamel bowls—which can take on a new look and a new lease of life if used imaginatively. There are no rules for improvisation, it is just a question of what looks right for the plants and for the style of setting they are to inhabit. Experiment with putting potted bulbs in wicker shopping baskets, ivies and other trailing plants in shiny ice coolers, small cacti in colourful pencil holders and any other combinations that suggest themselves. Even an old chimney pot can make an attractive container for a rustic setting (either stand the plant on top of it, in its own planter, or rest the planter on a pile of bricks inside the chimney pot). If you use a container without drainage holes, line it with a layer of gravel or porous clay pellets before planting it up.

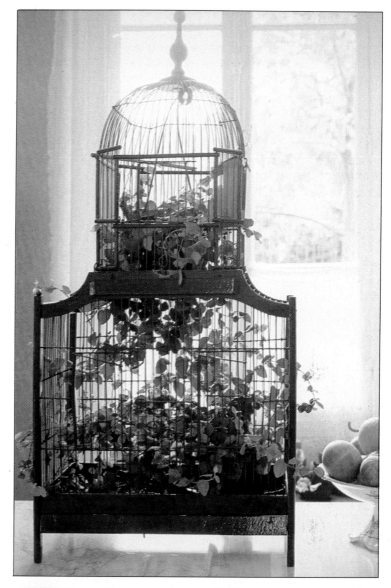

A bird-cage *right*
The delicate bars of the cage provide an elegant framework for the creeping fig (*Ficus pumila*) to ramble over. This plant will climb and trail, as well as creep, and all three habits of growth can be seen here.

An animal container *below*
An out-of-the-ordinary container can attract attention, add an element of humour, and greatly increase the impact of a single plant display—as this rhinoceros pot clearly demonstrates.

A china bust *right*
You can use an object as a container to set up an association and convey a particular mood. Here the combination of fronds of ivy trailing over a classical head recalls overgrown antique statuary.

The principles of arrangement 1

Balancing groups

Making an arrangement of growing plants means both grouping plants together with their containers, as you might on a shelf or table-top for example, as well as placing plants in a room. Special advice for arranging plants in room settings appears in *The Room-By-Room Guide*; but it is easiest to start looking at good groupings of plants together with their planters.

The key to a good arrangement is that it should have visual balance. As a simple rule of thumb, a larger plant has more visual weight than a smaller one. However, certain plants have striking leaf colour, shape or texture which attracts the eye instantly; so a small example of such a plant will have as much visual weight as a large example of a less dramatic plant.

Symmetrical arrangements

Asymmetrical arrangements

Symmetry
Two identical creeping figs (*Ficus pumila*) either side of a Norfolk Island pine (*Araucaria hetero-phylla*) create a perfectly symmetrical arrangement. If a vertical line ran through the middle of the group each side of the line would exactly mirror the other.

PLANT KEY — Creeping fig — Norfolk Island pine

Asymmetry
The pine has more visual weight than a single creeping fig and needs to be balanced by two of the latter. Space can be used to adjust balance: here, merging the two trailing plants together a little gives them more visual weight than when they are separated.

PLANT KEY — Norfolk Island pine — Creeping fig

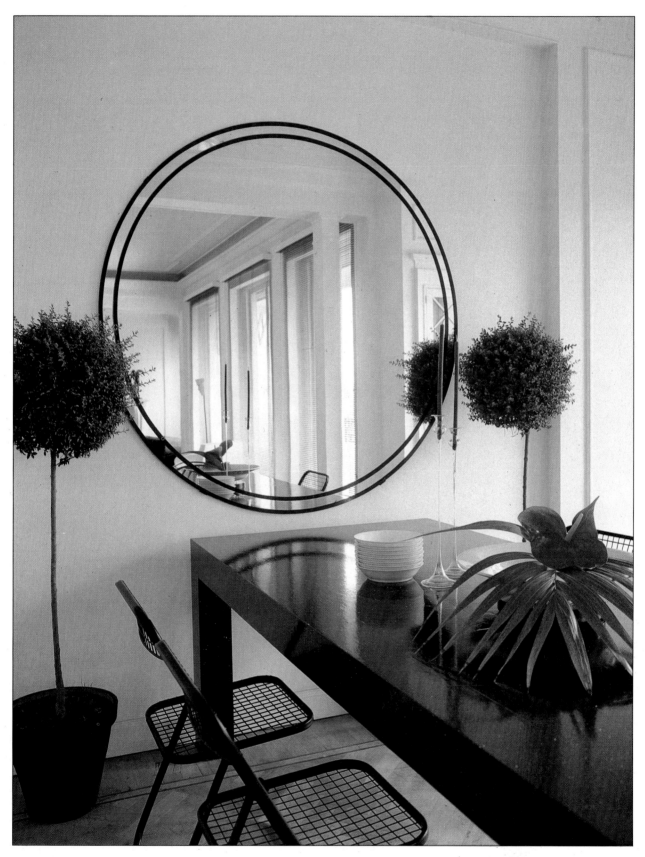

Balancing plants and objects *left*
Two striking bromeliads stand on a console table, either side of a centrally placed urn. To hold this group together, and to highlight the sense of symmetry, ashtrays have been positioned either side of the urn. The success of the arrangement is reinforced by the way the red of the flowers and the green of the urn echo colours in the painting behind them.

Formal balance through symmetry *above*
In general, perfectly symmetrical arrangements suit plants with a very regular shape and rather formal look, such as the common myrtles (*Myrtus communis*) placed either side of this mirror. Bay trees or orange trees would also be appropriate in this context. The simple table arrangement is made of a single flamingo flower (*Anthurium* sp.) and palm frond (*Howea* sp.).

The principles of arrangement 2

Using contrast

If a successful arrangement is one that balances visually, what makes it not merely successful but outstanding? The answer: contrast—the setting off of opposites against one another. You can use bold contrasts of shapes and scale or more subtle contrasts of textures and colours. Compose your groups by experimenting with several different plants—choosing ones which like similar conditions—relying upon your eye to tell you what works and what does not. When planning a group, the best way to use contrast is to restrict it to just one, or at most two, elements. The effect of contrast will always be stronger if it is part of an arrangement that displays some sense of overall order and harmony.

Shape

The upright, spiky-leaved yucca (*Yucca elephantipes*) contrasts with the low, rounded forms of the cacti. The strong form of the yucca gives it a visual weight that needs to be balanced by a number of small cacti. The introduction of the spiky-leaved but low-growing queen agave (*Agave victoriae-reginae*) on the left creates a pleasing link between the two dominant elements in the composition.

PLANT KEY

Queen agave

Tip yucca

Old lady cactus

Mammillaria

Texture *left*

The filigree lightness of the large maidenhair fern (*Adiantum raddianum*) has a similar visual weight to the dense mass of the emerald ripple peperomia leaves (*Peperomia caperata*) because of the different sizes of the plants. The plants balance visually simply by being placed side-by-side.

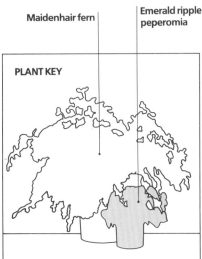

Maidenhair fern

Emerald ripple peperomia

PLANT KEY

Scale

The three plants in this group share the same sort of shape and the same sort of texture—they are all spiky-leaved. Yet they vary enormously in scale. The small queen agave (*Agave victoriae-reginae*) is only a few centimetres high, whereas the large stick yucca (*Yucca elephantipes*) rises to a height of about 1.5 metres. Their similarity in shape and texture, and the fact that they are displayed in all-white containers, serve to emphasize the contrasts in scale. Another way of using contrasts of scale effectively is to group plants in a row—along a mantelpiece or shelf for example—using plants of the same kind but of different heights.

PLANT KEY

Stick yucca

Tip yucca

Queen agave

Colour *right*

Three pink elatior begonias (*Begonia* "Elatior" hybrids) are offset by a single white-flowered variety. By slightly overlapping the three pink plants and setting the white one a small distance away, neither colour predominates but each is strengthened by the element of contrast. Another way of using colour is to juxtapose a plant with variegated leaves with a flowering plant that picks up one of the colours in the leaves.

Elatior begonias

PLANT KEY

Lighting plants

The chances are that your plants are seen as often in the evening, when they are lit by artificial light, as they are during the day. In addition to background lighting, you can use directional lighting to highlight plants and flowers. This type of lighting, where the beam of light is narrow enough to pick out a single object, throws plants into relief, accentuating shape, defining colour and emphasizing texture. Dramatic effects can be achieved through the interplay of light and shade created by directional lights, and the most ordinary of plants can be made into something outstanding.

Another consideration is the quality of light that you want. Incandescent tungsten bulbs, which are the most popular, give out a warm light which emphasizes yellows and reds; while tungsten halogen bulbs give out a more concentrated beam of colder light. To increase the warmth of a light, buy colour-coated bulbs or translucent shades in warm colours. Plants should not be placed right next to the light source, as the heat transmitted by the bulb will damage the leaves. A safe distance is about 60cm away from a 100-watt incandescent bulb.

Natural light

Light acts on the green pigment chlorophyll, which is present in all plants, to start the process called photosynthesis. The violet/blue and red wavelengths are most important for plant growth: the blue stimulates foliage and the red flowering. Incandescent bulbs are low in blue wavelengths and have only a limited effect on plant growth; but there are special lights which can be used as a substitute for daylight (see pp.258-9).

The amount and quality of daylight that a plant needs depends upon its original habitat in the wild. Some plants need full sunlight, some prefer filtered light, which can be given by diffusing daylight with Venetian blinds, lace or muslin, and others good indirect light. The quality of the natural light in your room will dictate the areas in which you can display your plants. At the same time, think about how they will be lit at night, so that their position allows enough natural light for healthy growth and for a directional light to show them off in the evening.

Using a window as a frame *left*
The filtered light received from this tiny window suits the Japanese fatsia (*Fatsia japonica*) and silhouettes its brilliant-green foliage. The scale of the plant and the window are perfectly matched.

Sun on a windowsill *below*
A symmetrical group of a white Cape primrose (*Streptocarpus* sp.) set between two carved birds is arranged on a wide windowsill. The light emphasizes the brilliant white of the flowers, and gives a translucent quality to the leaves which fall directly in its path.

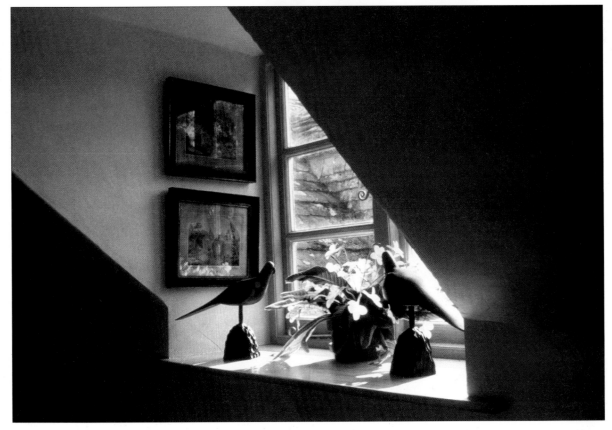

Lighting effects 1

Downlighting

Use a downlight or pendant light over a table to direct light on to a central decoration, such as a flower arrangement, or to hold together a group of small plants.

Using a pendant light *below*
A pendant light suspended a little way above a terracotta bowl of mind-your-own-business (*Soleirolia soleirolii*) picks up the detail of the foliage.

LIGHTING SET-UP   Down light

Using a downlight *right*
A downlight recessed into the ceiling casts an intense beam of light over the plants and objects arranged on this table. It illuminates a bowl of pinks (*Dianthus* sp.), a large bromeliad (*Portea petropolitana extensa*) and a maple tree (*Acer* sp.), which has been brought inside for a temporary display.

Uplighting

Lighting a single plant or a group of plants from below, with an uplighter or floor-mounted spotlight, throws strong shadows on to the wall and ceiling above. The quality of the shadows can be controlled by the position of the lights.

LIGHTING SET-UP   Side view

Back light   Front light

Uplighting from behind
An uplight placed behind the plant creates an abstract pattern of dramatic but distorted shadows, and reduces the plant itself to an attractive silhouette.

Uplighting from in front
Placing the lamp in front of the plant reveals detail and colour in the plant itself, and creates a shadow which echoes the plant's natural shape and form.

Lighting effects 2

Frontlighting and backlighting

By using a spotlight on a table or shelf, you can create a dramatic lighting effect in a small area. Frontlighting will give strong shadows which will enhance the natural shape of plants or flowers, while backlighting produces a softer effect.

LIGHTING SET-UP   Side view

Back
light

Front
light

Backlighting *above*
This light creates an overall warm, translucent quality.

Frontlighting *below*
The shadows enhance the tulips' (*Tulipa* sp.) distinctive shapes.

Sidelighting

Use a wall- or ceiling-mounted spotlight to beam light on to a plant or flower arrangement. With this flexible type of lighting, the angle of beam can easily be adjusted.

Sidelighting from above *below*
This angled light illuminates the soft texture and filigree pattern of the maidenhair fern's (*Adiantum raddianum*) foliage.

LIGHTING SET-UP

Side light

Sidelighting dried flowers

Kitchens are rooms where different types of lighting are needed: bright lights to illuminate working areas and softer, moodier lights for eating areas. Here, two angled spotlights focus beams of light on to dried flowers, revealing their colours and textures. The candles on the table add another warm light.

Styling with plants 1

Few of us have the opportunity of designing a room from scratch—in one go selecting all the materials, furniture, decorative objects and plants needed to create a recognizable style of interior decoration. In spite of practical limitations on the scope of your ideas, it is well worth looking at how plants can be used to evoke and enhance particular decorative styles. Plants and flowers are an integral part of many styles, often being the inspiration for decorative motifs of all kinds. On the following pages you will find an analysis of some of the most popular contemporary styles of interior decoration, combined with advice on what types of plants and flowers to display with them.

Country style

Country style seeks to bring the garden into the house. Flower patterns are everywhere—on wallpaper, curtains, cushions and china—and can be given added freshness by the presence of fresh flowers. Country style can be formal or relaxed, suitable for the town as well as the country. Objects do not have a particular place but rely on number to create a comfortable, lived-in atmosphere. Nostalgia for rural values is an important ingredient of this style which prizes well-crafted wooden furniture, homely designs, natural fabrics and warm colours.

Plants for a country kitchen *right*
Simple glazed pots are filled with an informal array of variegated English ivy (*Hedera helix* hybrids), thyme (*Thymus vulgaris*) and a sickle-thorn asparagus fern (*Asparagus falcatus*).

Elements of formal country style *left*
Colour is more important than shape in country style. Here, foliage and flowering plants with a soft shape complement the patterns found on wallpaper, china and fabric, as do the fresh flowers which are those commonly found in an old-fashioned garden. This type of country style is more formal in feel than that featured opposite. The textures—of bone china and chintz—have more lustre than those of terracotta and unvarnished wood.

PLANT KEY

Peppermint-leaved geranium

Baby's breath

Bedding geranium

Japanese anemone

Old rose

Stocks

Floating flower-head table display *above*
Many types of geranium heads (*Pelargonium* sp.) have been floated in water on two plates to make a colourful display suitable for a centre-piece on a country dining table.

Echoing floral patterns *left*
Flowers are everywhere—on fabric, on china and massed together in dried bunches to create a crowded effect reminiscent of a well-stocked country garden.

Elements of informal country style *right*
Again, the shape of plants or flowers is less important than their colour. Flowers such as these Michaelmas daisies (*Aster nova-belgii*) are fresh and warm in colour, without being vibrant. Dried seed heads have rough textures and monochromatic colours that mix well with the colours and textures of wood, terracotta and basketry. Dried flowers have an immediate association with the countryside, and their soft yellows and blues pick up the colours on the hand-painted ceramics.

PLANT KEY

Tansy
Yarrow
Golden marguerites
Michaelmas daisies
Love-in-a-mist seed heads

Styling with plants 2

Ethnic style

The many manifestations of what can be termed "ethnic" style reflect the traditional cultures of various groups throughout the world. It is based on artefacts made by traditional methods and characterized by the use of lively patterns, which can be abstract or figurative.

Using ethnic textiles *above*
A beautiful kelim is the inspiration for this arrangement; its colours are echoed in the ceramic dish and the ochre-coloured centres of the marguerites (*Chrysanthemum frutescens*).

South-American style *left*
The brilliant flowers and strong form of this Easter cactus (*Rhipsalidopsis gaertneri*) show up well against the rough texture of the stone shelf and stone carving.

Elements of ethnic style *left*
Plants with a strong outline and solid shape are needed to stand up against the abundance of patterns. Cacti are an obvious choice, particularly with objects of South-American origin as shown here. Colours should be warm to harmonize with the colours of natural dyes. Dried flowers, pebbles and bleached driftwood would all fit in to this decorative scheme.

PLANT KEY

Mammillaria

Chilli peppers

Rabbit's ears cactus

Oriental style

The Far East has been a source of inspiration for decoration over several hundred years. As a decorative style it can be interpreted in a number of different ways, since each area—China, Malaya and Japan—has its own recognizable national style influenced in part by the indigenous flora.

Contrasting textures in the Japanese style *left*
The spiky leaves of the bonsai are echoed by the floating chrysanthemum heads and the harsh texture of the rock is offset against the smooth ceramic plate.

Oriental simplicity *above*
Another simple group which relies on strong forms and contrasting textures for its effect. The spiky-leaved iris (*Iris pallida*) and simple fans have an abstract quality very much in an oriental style.

Elements of oriental style *right*
A key element in oriental style is the concentration on a few simple shapes and large areas of neutral colour, offset by focal points of bright colour. Here, the contrast in texture between the coarse-weave bamboo mat and the glistening lacquer table is typically oriental. The feathery umbrella plant (*Cyperus* sp.) suggests bamboo while the vivid basket plant (*Aeschynanthus lobbianus*) adds a more tropical Malaysian feel to the group.

PLANT KEY

Miniature gladioli

Basket plant

Spider chrysanthemums

Umbrella plant

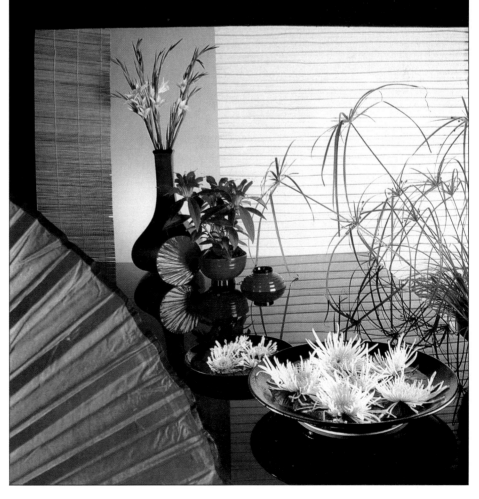

Styling with plants 3
High tech

This is a style based on the utilitarian shapes and materials of industrial products. Decoration is minimal and the overall effect is hard and clinical looking; it is the antithesis of anything organic. Plants need to have a vigorous outline, and flowers must be strong in colour so that they are not swamped by gleaming metallic surfaces and vibrant primary colours.

Using vivid colours *above*
Use flowers with clearly defined shapes and strong colours such as this flamingo flower (*Anthurium andreanum* hybrids). The flowers look almost "unreal" as the texture of the deep-red bracts resembles shiny plastic.

Using strong forms *left*
The aggressive form of a Peruvian apple cactus (*Cereus peruvianus*) emerges in the foreground of this picture. Bright lighting and the reflective white tiling call for large, dominant plants such as the umbrella plant (*Cyperus* sp.) in the background.

Elements of high tech *right*
Suitable plants are those with a great deal of visual weight, such as large agaves, yuccas and cacti. Here, the plants have a well defined shape and foliage whose plain-green colour goes well with the red plastic container and red rubber flooring.

PLANT KEY

Staghorn fern

Cast-iron plant

Art deco

The art deco style of the 1920s and 1930s is still a source of inspiration for interior decoration. It is characterized by the use of strong geometric forms, monochromatic colours and reflective surfaces, such as chrome and lacquered wood.

Informal art deco *above*
Tulips (*Tulipa* hybrids) have a strong shape which suits this style—particularly when they are massed together in a vase of the period.

Formal art deco *right*
This picture shows the geometric shapes, shiny textures and monochromatic colours which are all hallmarks of the style. The regal lilies (*Lilium regale*) in the circular vase, and the ponytail, with its bold shape, hold their own against the strong outlines of the chairs.

Elements of art deco *left*
Plants with a strong outline are needed to complement the hard lines and solid forms of this style. Here, the hard-edged shape of the sculpture is repeated in the form of the lily flowers. The white of the flowers is in keeping with the monochromatic colour scheme. The linear form of the silvery-mauve rosary vine (*Ceropegia woodii*) in the ceramic light fitting is silhouetted against the wall.

PLANT KEY

Regal lilies

Rosary vine

Grouping plants in a single container 1

For a large arrangement, quite dramatic effects can be achieved by grouping several plants together in a single container. Plants grow better when they are grouped together; a micro-climate is established with the moisture given off by one plant becoming available to its neighbour. The individual plants tend to grow into each other and show each other off.

The plants may either be all of the same kind, or they may form a mixed group of several different types with similar growing needs. They can either be knocked out of their pots and planted in a common potting mixture, as shown here, or, if they are for a temporary display, they can be left in their individual pots and stood in moist peat. If you are potting up the plants, select a fairly deep container, so that the potting mixture does not dry out too quickly, and always include a layer of porous material at the base of the container if it is without drainage holes. This method has the advantage that it usually gives the plants a bigger root run, but it does make it more difficult to remove an ailing plant, or to group plants with different watering needs. Sometimes a combination of the two methods is best, allowing you to give a single plant special treatment.

An alternative planting with begonias

A striking and colourful foliage group can be made by planting together a number of painted-leaf begonias (*Begonia rex-cultorum*). These plants have extremely decorative leaves with striking patterns in red, silver, green and black. Choose specimens with different sorts of leaf patterns and textures to create a subtle interplay of colours. Plant them up in peat-based potting mixture and put them in a warm part of the house in indirect light.

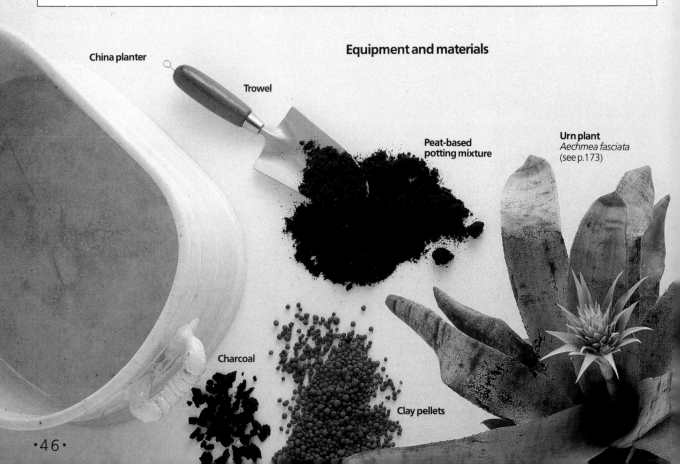

Equipment and materials

China planter

Trowel

Peat-based potting mixture

Urn plant
Aechmea fasciata
(see p.173)

Charcoal

Clay pellets

Planting up a large container

In general, the strongest arrangements of this type are the simplest ones. Often, mixed plantings do not work because they show too much variation in shape and texture; the overall effect is untidy and difficult to place in a room. Here, I have chosen to group together several exotic-looking urn plants. Their vigorous shape called for a simple container and I chose a white china planter whose colour picked up the white sheen on the leaves of the plants.

The finished arrangement
To keep the urn plants in good condition, put them in a warm, sunny place and keep their natural "vase"—formed by the rosette of leaves—filled with water. Small pale-blue flowers will emerge from the pink bracts; these do not last for long but the bracts will remain attractive for up to six months.

Building up the arrangement

1 Line the bottom of the planter with 2cm of porous clay pellets and scatter pieces of charcoal over them. Fill the planter half-full with potting mixture and place one of the plants on the mixture to check that the top of its pot is level with the top of the planter.

2 To remove the urn plant from its pot, first water it well and then, holding the plant between your first and second finger, hit the pot hard against the edge of a table, or strike the base hard with your fist.

3 Build up the potting mixture at the back of the planter, and as you position each plant in the potting mixture tilt it out slightly so that the rosette of leaves and flower heads can be appreciated.

PLANTS
Mini-climate 1
Warm, sunny

An alternative planting with saffron spikes
Grouping saffron spikes (*Aphelandra squarrosa* "Louisae") in the same china planter makes another simple and effective group. Their strong shape and exciting leaf and flower colour are intensified when the plants are massed together.

Grouping plants in a single container 2
Arranging plants in a basket

The choice of a basket as a container will dictate the types of plants which are suitable to be displayed in it. A rush basket calls for unsophisticated plants such as cinerarias (*Senecio cruentus*) and German violets (*Exacum affine*), as well as the examples illustrated here. Potted bulbs can be used in spring and should be massed together in the basket just before they begin to flower.

The plants which you select are for a temporary arrangement as you display them for their flowering period, or when their foliage is at its best. Given that their moment of glory is short there is no need to unpot the plants into a potting medium; and, since they are in separate pots, you can choose to group together plants with different watering needs so long as they like similar amounts of light and heat.

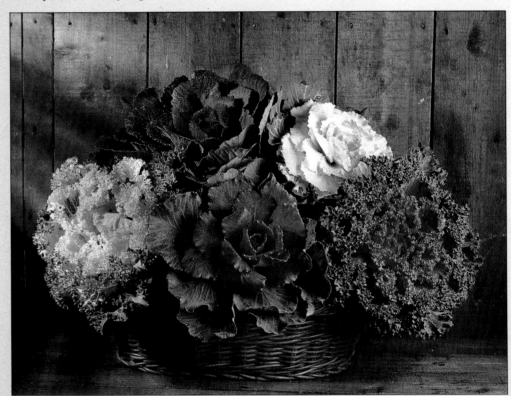

An alternative display with kale
These ornamental kale (*Brassica oleracea acephala*) look like giant flowers when grouped together. Their leaves of rich purple or ivory, both edged with green, can be frilled or plain and are shown off to great effect when several plants are packed together as shown here. Ornamental kale are available in late summer and autumn and, provided that they are given plenty of light and kept in a cool place, they will remain fresh for several weeks.

PLANTS
Mini-climate 5
Cool, filtered sun.

Equipment and materials

Plastic lining

Clay pellets

English ivy
Hedera helix hybrids
(see p.190)

Rush basket

Peat

Scissors

Building up an arrangement with primulas and ivy

1 Place a piece of plastic (a dustbin liner is suitable) inside the basket to form a watertight skin. Cut it to shape allowing a small overhang which will eventually be tucked in. Cover the bottom of the basket with a layer of porous clay pellets about 3cm deep.

2 Fill the basket with 6cm of damp peat. Stand the pots inside and start to build up the composition. Put the three taller, salmon-pink primulas at the back, packing peat around the pots as you go, then let the variegated ivy trail down one side to soften the overall shape.

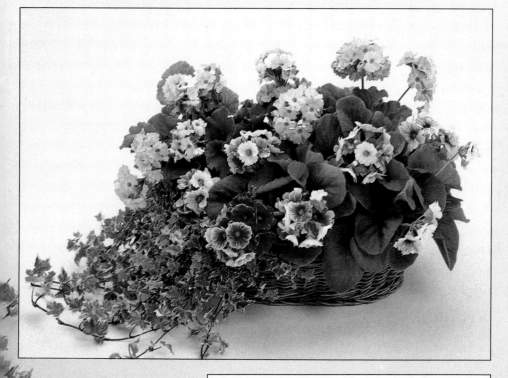

3 Finally, put the remaining primulas at the front of the basket. Make sure that all the pots are standing upright because you will still need to water them—the primulas in particular like plenty of water. To keep the display looking fresh, take off individual flowers as they fade and remove any yellowing leaves. These primulas should last from 6-8 weeks provided they are kept in a cool place.

Primula
Primula obconica
(see p.181)

An alternative display with begonias
Another filling, suitable for a warmer place in the house, would be a collection of small-leaved eyelash begonias (*Begonia* "Tiger Paws"). Their striking green-and-bronze foliage creates a strong enough pattern for them to stand on their own.

Training climbing plants 1
Making a moss-pole

Climbing plants need to be provided with some kind of support in order for them to grow upright. Plants that use aerial roots to climb, such as the philodendrons, Swiss cheese plants (*Monstera deliciosa*) and pothos vines (*Scindapsus pictus* "Argyraeus"), like to grow over a constantly moist medium. A pole made out of wire netting stuffed with sphagnum moss is an excellent, sturdy support, and particularly suitable for climbing plants with thick stems and large leaves. Plants which climb by means of curly leaf tendrils, such as passion flowers (*Passiflora caerulea*) and ivies (*Hedera* sp.), can be trained on canes, wire hoops and trellis work.

Moss-poles can be bought ready-made, but if you make your own with wire netting you can provide far moister moss for the roots of climbing plants. You will need about three or four small plants to grow up a moss pole about 90cm high. Once it is made, remember to keep the moss constantly moist, otherwise the aerial roots will not grow into it.

Equipment and materials

Sphagnum moss

Bamboo sticks

Terracotta half-pot

Drainage dish

Tamping stick

Wire cutters

Roll of corrugated paper

Chicken wire

Sweetheart plant
Philodendron scandens
(see p.188)

Peat-based potting mixture

Trowel

PLANTS
Mini-climate 3
Warm, shady

Wires

Building up the arrangement

1 To form the shape of the moss-pole, take a roll of corrugated paper and wrap chicken wire round it. Cut the wire so that it is 5cm wider than the paper. Join the two cut edges together to form a column shape.

2 Cut two lengths of bamboo, thread them through the netting about 3cm from the bottom. Lash them together where they cross each other, and to the wire column, then wedge them into the pot.

Training plants in the house

Climbing plants can be trained up a blank wall, to make it an attractive feature, and trained round mirrors, doors and windows, to frame them with fresh greenery. To provide support for the plant, string runs of wire or strong nylon cord between nails or screw eyes, and then attach the plant to the support with plant ties, to help maintain the shape that you want.

Training a plant up a wall *right*
The emerald fern (*Asparagus densiflorus* "Sprengeri") is often displayed as a trailing plant, but here its soft, feathery stems have been trained round a picture.

Training a plant round a mirror *above*
A grape ivy (*Cissus rhombifolia*) makes an unusual frame for this large mirror. This attractive vine clings to any support with its wiry tendrils and grows very rapidly—about 60-90cm a year. It is an extremely tolerant plant which thrives in a wide range of conditions.

3 Fill the pot two-thirds full with potting mixture. Start to fill the empty column of chicken wire with sphagnum moss, using a wooden stick to pack it together tightly, and continue until it is full.

4 Pot up the sweetheart plants and attach their stems to the pole with wire, bent to form a hairpin shape.

5 Water the sphagnum moss and the potting mixture well before putting the moss-pole in a warm, shady position. Spray the pole every day to keep the moss thoroughly moist.

Training climbing plants 2
Making a wire support

Many plants suitable for indoor use are rampant climbers in the wild. They are often bought trained round a wire support which is soon outgrown. It is then a good idea to open the plant out and train it round a larger support which will show off foliage and flowers more effectively. Try to match the scale of the plant to the scale of the support: here I trained passion flowers round hoops of wire which suited the delicate tracery of the plants' foliage.

Equipment and materials

Pliers

Wire

Glazed ceramic container

Plant ties

Soil-based potting mixture

Clay pellets

Passion flower
Passiflora caerulea
(see p.185)

**PLANTS
Mini-climate 1**
Warm, sunny

The finished arrangement
Covering one hoop less thickly than the others made the arrangement a more interesting shape. It also gave it a lightness of effect which will make the transitory opening of the curious flowers more visible. You will need to tie in the shoots very regularly in order to maintain the overall shape of the display. If you cut the plants back, as far as the main stems, at the beginning of winter and put them in a cool, frost-free place they should grow back again in the spring.

Building up the arrangement

1 Cut two lengths of wire of the same size to form two hoops. Place them in the container to check that they are in scale with it. Put the hoops to one side; they will be held in place by the potting mixture once you have started planting.

2 If your container has a drainage hole, place a piece of broken shard over it; then line the pot with 2-3cm of porous clay pellets and fill three-quarters full with potting mixture. Unwind a passion flower from its previous support and repot it, firming potting mixture around its roots. Place one hoop in the pot and wind the plant's stems around it.

3 Place the other wire hoop in the container at a 90 degree angle to the other and fix the pair together with plant ties. Remove any dead leaves or unwanted shoots as you go. Plant the last passion flower, training one stem up the remaining bare hoop, and arranging the other stems on the opposite side.

Other ornamental supports

Using bamboo, rattan or wire you can make many different shapes of support. Bamboo stakes can be made into trellis or, for a more unusual effect, into obelisks. Rattan is flexible and can be used to make any sort of rounded form.

Trellis work *below*
Woodland strawberries (*Fragaria vesca* "Alpine") bear small fruit and make an attractive display.

Rattan canes

Bamboo trellis

Bamboo stakes

Creeping fig
Ficus pumila

Rattan hoop

Plastic trellis

Planting hanging baskets 1

Most of us are familiar with hanging baskets displayed on terraces, balconies or porches, but seldom see them used indoors to advantage. When selecting a basket for an indoor display think carefully about its setting: a wire basket is only suitable for a room with a water-resistant floor, such as a conservatory. A practical, but less attractive, alternative is a solid plastic basket with a raised platform inside, a filling tube and water-level indicator, or another type which incorporates a drip-tray. But there is nothing to stop you using a terracotta container or rush basket, if you make your own rope hangings, or using a wall basket in an appropriate material.

It is important to secure the basket properly because it will be very heavy when wet. The chain or rope support should hang from a hook firmly anchored in a ceiling joist, not set into the plaster.

When deciding upon a planting scheme for a basket, remember that you are trying to blend the arrangement with your décor. Limit yourself to one type of plant unless your setting is very plain. For an outdoor planting you can afford to be less restrained with your colours, but it is sensible to choose species which are used to heat and the drying effect of wind.

Planting a wire basket

The attraction of a wire basket is that, once the plants are established, it becomes a spherical mass of flowers or foliage. Here, I set out to create the effect of a large ball of flowers by planting white and blue Italian bellflowers. These should flower continuously from August to November provided they are watered well in warm weather—a good reason for putting this display in a conservatory.

Cross-section of the planted basket

Second layer of plants

First layer of plants

Potting mixture

Basket frame

Sphagnum moss

Plastic lining

Bucket

Plastic lining

Wire basket

A garden room filled with hanging baskets

This light garden room provides an excellent setting for an array of hanging baskets. A dramatic staghorn fern (*Platycerium bifurcatum*) is the focal point of the display. This is flanked on the left by a grape ivy (*Cissus rhombifolia*) in a wicker basket and a busy Lizzie (*Impatiens* sp.), and on the right by several spider plants (*Chlorophytum comosum* "Vittatum"). Notice the wicker wall baskets—one containing dried flowers, the other another grape ivy.

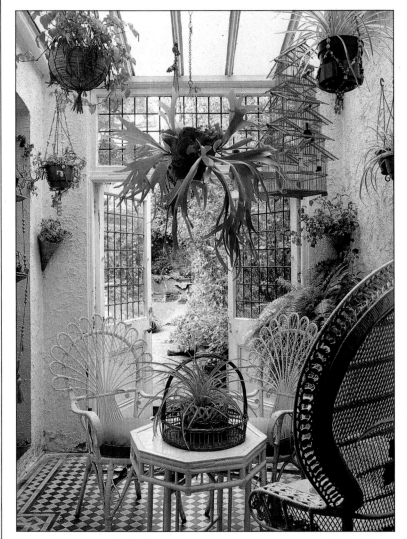

Building up the arrangement

1 Rest the basket on the rim of a flat-bottomed bowl or bucket. Line it with a 5cm layer of damp sphagnum moss. Then, cut a circle of plastic sheeting to fit inside, leaving an overlap of 10cm. Make a circle of holes in the plastic 5cm up from the bottom.

2 You will need to divide some of the larger plants into two to fit them through the holes. First, water the plants before taking them out of their pots; then, holding the plant in both hands, plunge your thumbs into the middle of the potting mixture and pull apart. Insert the divided plants from the outside, pushing the roots through the sphagnum moss and the holes in the plastic.

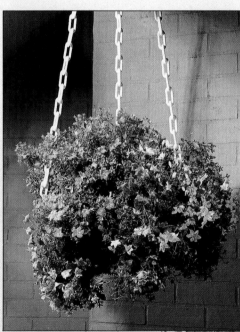

4 Fill the gaps in the top with blue-flowered plants and, when the basket is filled, tuck in the overhanging plastic. Water the basket well before replacing the chains and hanging it in a sunny place.

3 Push one row of plants around the bottom of the basket, cover with a layer of potting mixture, firming it down around them, and then place more plants higher up the sides of the basket to fill the gaps. Plant several large white specimens in the top.

PLANTS
Mini-climate 4
Cool, sunny

Italian bellflower
Campanula isophylla
(see p.191)

Equipment and materials

Scissors

Peat-based potting mixture

Trowel

Sphagnum moss

Planting hanging baskets 2

Planting a wicker basket

Hanging baskets can add freshness and colour to a room, particularly where space at floor level is limited. Think about the place where your basket is to hang and select your plants with an eye to the decorative effect you want, bearing in mind that the plants should like the place you have chosen and be broadly compatible in their requirements. The container you use should not detract from the natural colours of the plants. I felt a wicker basket suited this display where I have chosen to group ferns together, accentuating contrasts of plant form and leaf shape.

Equipment and materials

Wicker basket

Foam matting

Foil

Clay pellets

Trowel

Peat-based potting mixture

Charcoal

PLANTS
Mini-climate 2 Warm, filtered sun
Mini-climate 3 Warm, shady

Asparagus fern
Asparagus setaceus
(see p.183)

Emerald fern
Asparagus densiflorus 'Sprengeri'
(see p.191)

Scarlet star
Guzmania lingulata
(see p.174)

Bird's nest fern
Asplenium nidus
(see p.173)

Boston fern
Nephrolepis exaltata
"Bostoniensis"
(see p.170)

Cretan brake
Pteris cretica
(see p.183)

Maidenhair fern
Adiantum raddianum (see p.183)

Sphagnum moss

The finished arrangement

The final addition of the scarlet stars creates a splash of colour and links the display to its setting by echoing the red of the poppies in the painting. After completing the planting I placed the rope hangings round the basket and hung it from the ceiling by a north-facing window. It is a good idea to use a hook with a universal joint so that the basket can be rotated to ensure plants get an even supply of light.

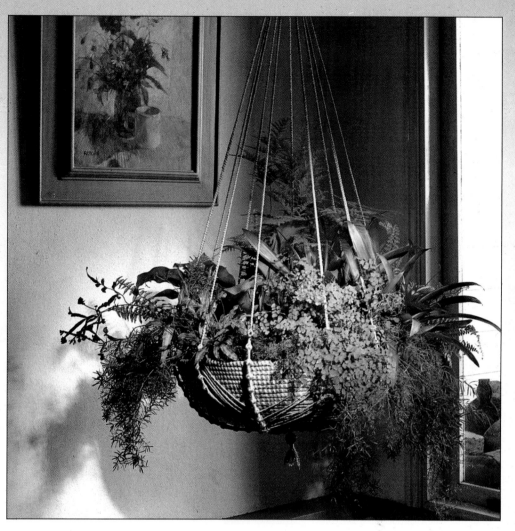

Building up the arrangement

1 Line the basket with foil to stop it rotting, then place foam matting on top and trim to fit. Put some pieces of gravel at the back of the basket to form a higher area for planting. Line the basket with porous clay pellets.

2 Fill the basket with peat-based potting mixture, adding about a handful of charcoal to prevent the mixture turning sour. Allow enough room at the top for watering. Position the first plant where the compost has been built up over the gravel. Use a bushy asparagus fern with delicate feathery fronds to give height to the arrangement.

3 At this stage, it is a good idea to plan the rest of the arrangement by positioning your plants, still in their pots, until you are satisfied with the design. Here I put two trailing emerald ferns either side of the asparagus fern.

continued over

4 To give more substance to the back of the design put two more Boston ferns either side of the asparagus fern. When planting, tilt the ferns out to the side so that their fronds overhang the sides of the basket.

5 To fill the foreground add a maidenhair fern and a Cretan brake. The delicate fronds of the maidenhair fern and the unusual branching fronds of the Cretan brake provide further variation in leaf shape and colour.

6 Placing a bird's nest fern on the left sets up a pleasing contrast between its broad straplike leaves and the surrounding feathery fronds. Finally, add the two scarlet stars, cover any visible potting mixture with damp moss and water well before hanging.

Asparagus fern

Bird's nest fern

Boston fern

Scarlet star

Emerald fern

Cretan brake

Maidenhair fern

Growing bulbs indoors 1

A mass of temporary flowering bulbs can make a beautiful grouping, particularly when there is little other colour around. Most bulbs can be grown in containers without drainage holes, as well as conventional pots. Plant them in soup tureens, vegetable dishes, china pots or glass vases using potting mixture, or grow them hydroponically in pebbles and water.

When garden bulbs are grown in the home they have to experience an artificial "winter" before they will bloom. They will not flower properly unless they are kept cool (6-8°C) and dark for several weeks. You can buy "prepared" bulbs which do not need to be kept in the dark (although they must be kept cool) but these are more expensive. Buy bulbs as soon as you see them on sale—usually in early autumn—and plant them right away. It is a good idea to buy several types so that you can keep replacing fading specimens with fresh ones. Plant bowls of early-flowering crocuses which can be white, yellow, bronze, mauve or purple. Plant hyacinths for their heavy sweet scent as well as their large flowers. Choose daffodils for their fresh and cheerful colours, and lily-flowered and kaufmannia tulips for their strong shapes and colours.

A windowsill of bulbs *above*
Amaryllis (*Hippeastrum* hybrids), narcissi (*Narcissus* hybrids) and hyacinths (*Hyacinthus orientalis* hybrids) line a windowsill. This is a good place to display your bulbs since the cooler the plants are kept, the longer they will last.

Crocuses in a basket *below*
A mass of bulbs and foliage spilling over the edges of a basket can look stunning. Here, brilliant white crocuses (*Crocus* hybrids) have been mingled with the graceful grasslike foliage of the bulrush plant (*Scirpus cernuus*).

Growing bulbs indoors 2

Although bulbs can be bought from retailers, there is such an enormous range of hybrids available that it is worth looking through a specialist catalogue to select bulbs whose colours and shapes particularly appeal to you. For fresh colour and delicate fragrance, narcissi are a good choice. Certain species of narcissi, including *Narcissus* "Cragford" which I have used here, can be grown in gravel or shingle instead of potting mixture or bulb fibre. Plant

them up in glass containers which allow the texture of the gravel to be seen. If you plant your narcissi bulbs in October, and "winter" them as shown below, they should be in flower by Christmas.

Indoor bulbs which flower later in the spring or in the summer include the amaryllis (*Hippeastrum* hybrids), which has huge, trumpet-shaped flowers, and several lilies including the fragrant, white Easter lily (*Lilium longiflorum*).

Equipment and materials

Glass containers

Scissors

Black plastic bag

PLANTS
Mini-climate 5
Cool, filtered sun.

Charcoal

Garden twine

Gravel

Plant ties

Narcissus bulbs
Narcissus "Cragford"
(see p.194)

Thin stakes

Building up the arrangement

1 Mix some gravel with about 20 small pieces of charcoal, having first washed the gravel to remove any dirt which would cloud the water. Fill the container so that it is about three-quarters full of gravel and start planting the first bulbs, making a depression with your finger for each bulb to sit in.

2 Place the bulbs in position with their "noses" coming out of the medium. You should be able to fit about nine bulbs in a container of this size, but make sure that the bulbs do not touch each other. Fill the spaces between the bulbs with more gravel and add water until it is close to, but not touching, the bottom of the bulbs.

3 If you use prepared bulbs, they can grow in the light, but other bulbs must be kept in the dark. Cut a black plastic bag in half, secure it round the container with garden twine or string and stand in a cool, dark place. Look at the bulbs after about four weeks to see if they need more water.

4 After eight to ten weeks, about 1-2cm of growth should be visible and the bulbs can be brought out into the light. Once the narcissi have reached their maximum height, some of their stems and leaves will need support. Attach any untidy leaves or bending stems to thin green stakes with plant ties. Alternatively, use the stakes at an early stage—when about 10cm of top growth has appeared—to support the stems and leaves as they grow.

5 Narcissi do not like very warm rooms. If temperatures are high, their stems become elongated and the leaves soft and sappy. When the flowers have died, remove the dead heads and plant the bulbs outdoors.

Other indoor bulb displays

It is best to plant one colour of a flower per pot because different colours may flower at different times. Hyacinth (*Hyacinthus orientalis* hybrids) bulbs vary so much that it is safest to plant single bulbs in 7cm pots. Once the flower buds are well developed, group together bulbs at the same stages of development.

Hyacinths in full bloom *left*
Hyacinths have large flower heads and, when planted up en masse, make an eye-catching and fragrant display.

Pots of daffodils *above*
A cheerful display of daffodils (*Narcissus* sp.) in clay pots. Grass seeds have been sown on the surface of the potting mixture for decoration.

Planting window-boxes 1

Window-boxes are usually thought of as outdoor containers but there is no reason why they cannot be used indoors, provided you have a window which opens outwards or upwards with a suitable sill. There are many types of boxes: plastic is a light, cheap material suitable for use indoors or out and, if planted with trailers, will hardly be visible through the greenery; fibreglass comes in authentic-looking imitations of lead and stone, and is extremely light but correspondingly expensive; stone is always attractive but is too heavy for most sills and better used on the ground; terracotta suits period houses and formal interior settings; wood is a very useful material for an outdoor box as it can be made to measure and, if fitted with a waterproof zinc liner which can be lifted out, is easy to replant with the new season's flowers.

Your window-box should have holes at the bottom to prevent the lower layers collecting sour water and causing roots to rot. Wooden, stone and terracotta boxes have holes drilled and plastic ones have indentations which you can tap out with a screwdriver. Always fit a drip-tray underneath the box to prevent any surplus water over-flowing. Whether your box is to go indoors or out, select one that is as deep as is practical; this will prevent the potting mixture from drying out too quickly, although you will find that any box will need very frequent watering in warm weather. If your box is placed high-up where it could fall and cause damage below, secure it in place with a brace on either side attached to the window surround, or within an angled bracket fixed to the wall or window. Never use window-boxes on weak or rotten sills.

Types of window-boxes

The material of your window-box should be in keeping with the style of your house—if it is to go outside—and the style of your room—if it is to go inside. In either case, it is best to choose a box which is as low-key as possible to show off the plants. If you use a purpose-made wooden box it can be painted to match the colour of your walls. Your choice of plants will depend on the season in which you are planting, and on the orientation of your window.

A cedarwood box *left*
This deep, wooden window-box sits snugly on its sill. Its simple planting of scarlet gera-niums (*Pelargonium hortorum* hybrids) will flower for almost all the year and makes an eye-catching display set against the deep-yellow wall.

A painted wooden box *below*
This box of painted wood is almost completely obscured by the purple lobelia (*Lobelia erinus pendula*) trailing over it. Deep-pink primulas (*Primula obconica*) and marguerite daisies (*Chry-santhemum frutescens*) complete a colourful summer planting attrac-tively framed by the wrought-iron sill-surround.

A brass box *above*
The glistening brass of this indoor window-box is set off by the austere, white-leaded window. It is planted with blue German violets (*Exacum affine*) whose golden stamens pick up the colour of the brass. Other alternatives suitable for a brass box would be a bronze-leaved wax begonia (*Begonia semperflorens-cultorum*) or busy Lizzie (*Impatiens wallerana* hybrids), rust-coloured florist's chrysan-themums (*Chrysan-themum morifolium* hybrids) or a collection of richly coloured painted nettles (*Coleus blumei*).

Planting an indoor window-box

Begin by thinking about what types of plants will like the quality of light offered by your window and make sure that those you choose have similar growing needs. For this summer group I used a plain white plastic window-box and chose pink and purple Cupid's bowers and a tradescantia with pink stripes to pick up the colour of the flowers. Alternative plantings for a spring box would be bulbs or herbs and for a winter box you could use jonquils.

Building up the arrangement

1 Line the box with a layer of shards making sure that the pieces face downwards so that water will drain off them (if you do not have any broken terracotta pots, most garden centres will supply shards free of charge). Add a 5cm layer of potting mixture, putting more at the back to give height to the back of the arrangement.

2 Set the plants out in the box and experiment with the design until you are satisfied that it looks balanced. Begin by planting six purple Cupid's bowers along the length of the box, leaving room between them for the pink-flowered kinds and the trailing foliage of the tradescantia.

3 Place a tradescantia in the centre of the box, letting some stems trail down in front and threading the others through the Cupid's bowers. Finally, fill the remaining spaces with pink Cupid's bowers and another tradescantia.

The finished arrangement
Both plants like a sunny position and will be happy on a south-facing windowsill. The Cupid's bowers will flower from June until October and, as they grow, will trail attractively over the edge of the box.

Equipment and materials

PLANTS
Mini-climate 1
Warm, sunny

Shards

Tradescantia
Tradescantia fluminensis
"Variegata"
(see p.189)

**Soil-based
potting mixture**

Cupid's bower
*Achimenes
grandiflora*
(see p.181)

**Window-box
and drip-tray**

Trowel

Secateurs

Planting window-boxes 2

Planting an outdoor window-box

Winter is the season when you long to see greenery and colourful flowers. One way of improving the view from your windows, particularly if you live in the city, is to plant a window-box using plants with colourful berries and evergreens with attractive foliage. The window-box I have planted below will need protection from the frost, since the Christmas cherries and florist's chrysanthemums are not hardy; put it at a window where it can easily be brought inside in cold weather or, alternatively, use it as an indoor window-box for a cool place.

Building up the arrangement

1 Line the window-box with 3cm of clay pellets (you can also use shards or gravel) to provide drainage. Place a layer of potting mixture over the pellets to a depth of about 6cm.

2 With the plants still in their pots, experiment with the design, putting the Christmas cherries in the middle and the chrysanthemums at the edge. Place the ivies in the box to see where their trailing fronds will look best.

3 Take the plants out of their pots and shake off excess potting mixture. Put two Christmas cherries in the centre of the box and plant the florist's chrysanthemums on either side. Let the four small ivies trail down at the sides and in the front of the box. Firm potting mixture around the plants and water well before putting in position.

Florist's chrysanthemum
Chrysanthemum morifolium hybrids (see p.181)

Equipment and materials

Clay pellets

Trowel

Peat-based potting mixture

English ivy
Hedera helix hybrids (see p.190)

Terracotta window-box

PLANTS
Mini-climate 4
Cool, sunny
Mini-climate 5
Cool, filtered sun

Christmas cherry
Solanum capsicastrum
(see p.180)

Other ideas for window gardens

There are other ways to decorate windows besides using window-boxes. You can set potted plants on tiers of glass or perspex shelves across a window, or use wooden shelves lined with metal to protect them from water. Your choice of plants will depend upon the orientation of your window. Place sun-loving desert cacti and succulents and tropical species at a south-facing window, flowering plants at west- and east-facing windows, and plants which like indirect light at north-facing windows. Alternatively, it is possible to build a special window for plants, similar to a miniature conservatory.

Tiers of plants *right*
Rows of plants ranged on glass shelves obscure the view but make an attractive display in themselves. Placing all the plants in the same type of container introduces a sense of order into a crowded arrangement. Most of the plants shown here are desert cacti and succulents which are used to bright sunlight in the wild. Plants with variegated leaves, such as the polka-dot plant (*Hypoestes phyllostachya*) on the bottom shelf, will also thrive in good light, which will intensify the colour of their foliage.

A miniature conservatory *below*
Plants benefit from being grouped together and, if they are also given good light, they will grow fast. In a glass box, such as the one shown here, it is necessary to provide some form of shade from the summer sun, to ensure good ventilation, and to increase the humidity, particularly when it is hot. To do this, stand plants on trays filled with moist pebbles.

Planting bottle gardens

Bottle gardens provide optimum growing conditions for plants which like a humid atmosphere, so it makes sense to plant particularly slow-growing specimens if you want your garden to look attractive for a year or more. Tempting as it may be to plant African violets (*Saintpaulia* hybrids), it is not a good idea since, once the flowers fade, they can look very dull. It is best to create a colourful effect by using plants with variegated leaves and to build an interesting group with contrasts of shape and texture. Any sort of bottle is suitable, provided plants can be passed through the neck. If the bottle is made of coloured glass it will block out some light and, to compensate for this, you should move the garden into brighter light than would be normal for the plants inside.

Circle of paper

Funnel

Glass bottle

Maidenhair fern
Adiantum raddianum microphyllum
(see p.183)

Sphagnum moss

Peat-based potting mixture

Clay pellets

Charcoal

Miniature trowel

Equipment and materials

Sponge

Spool

Fork

Spoon

Little snakeskin plant
Fittonia verschaffeltii argyroneura "Nana"
(see p.193)

Snakeskin plant
Fittonia verschaffeltii
(see p.193)

Building up an arrangement

Australian maidenhair fern
Adiantum hispidulum
(see p.183)

PLANTS
Mini-climate 3
Warm, shady

1 Cut a circle of paper the same size as the planting area of the bottle and experiment with the design—placing the taller plants at the back and the low-growing ones in the foreground.

2 Pour a 3cm layer of clay pellets into the bottle through a funnel made of stiff paper. Add a handful of charcoal, and fill the bottle with 5-7cm of damp peat-based potting mixture.

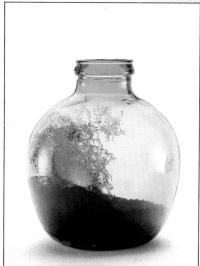

3 Build up the potting mixture at the back of the bottle to give more height to the group. Use the spoon to smooth out the surface of the mixture and make a hole at the back for the roots of the first plant.

4 Remove a maidenhair fern from its pot and shake off excess potting mixture. Stick the fork into the root ball and lower the plant into the hole made for it. Release the plant, cover the roots and gently firm down the potting mixture around it.

5 Put another maidenhair fern at the back of the group and then add an Australian maidenhair to vary the outline. Make sure that the plants are not too close together—leave about 3cm between them to allow room for growth.

PLANT KEY

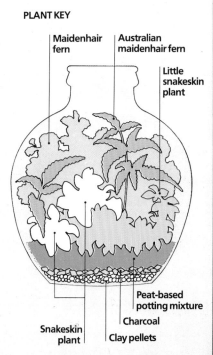

Maidenhair fern

Australian maidenhair fern

Little snakeskin plant

Peat-based potting mixture

Charcoal

Snakeskin plant

Clay pellets

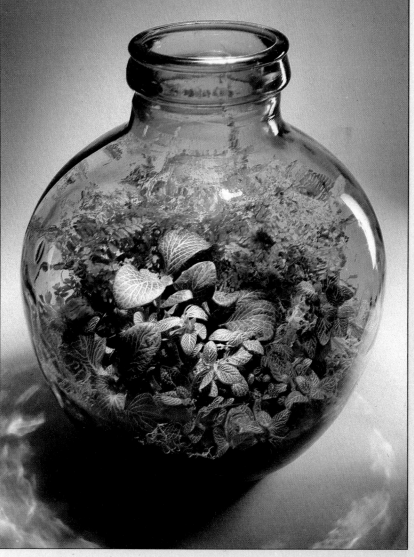

6 Place the little snakeskin plants in the foreground. Their solid silver-veined leaves provide a pleasing contrast to the mass of delicate fronds above them. Then, to give the arrangement a focal point and to add colour, plant a snakeskin plant with red leaf veins in the centre. Finally, decorate any bare area of potting mixture with sphagnum moss, and pour a cup of water into the bottle by directing it against the glass. You can put a cork in the top to make the atmosphere more humid, but it will make the glass mist up more quickly.

Planting terraria

Terraria are glass cases which offer the same humid environment as bottle gardens, since the moisture given off by the leaves of the plants inside condenses and runs back into the soil. As it is easier to prune and remove plants from a terrarium than from a bottle garden, you can use suitable fast-growing kinds such as the mosses and polka-dot plants planted in the terrarium opposite. For the same reason, small flowering plants such as miniature gloxinias (*Sinningia pusilla*) can be planted, and replaced when they have faded. Here, I used a leaded-glass terrarium resembling a tiny conservatory which suggested the choice of palms to form the background of the group.

Equipment and materials

Terrarium

Gravel

Spreading club moss
Selaginella kraussiana
(see p.192)

Charcoal

Miniature trowel

Peat-based potting mixture

Sponge

Club moss
Selaginella martensii
(see p.192)

Parlour palm
Chamaedorea elegans "Bella"
(see p.171)

Eyelash begonia
Begonia "Tiger Paws"
(see p.183)

Polka-dot plant
Hypoestes phyllostachya
(see p.179)

**PLANTS
Mini-climate 2**
Warm, filtered sun

Other types of terraria

Terraria originate from the 19th-century vogue for glass cases planted with ferns. Today, they can be bought in many different shapes and sizes. It is best to avoid those embellished with stained glass and choose one made of clear, plain glass or plastic with an attractive shape that will show off the plants you plan to use.

A pagoda *above*
One species of plant massed together looks very effective in a small terrarium.
A miniature greenhouse *left*
Moss-covered rocks make an interesting addition to this group.

Building up the arrangement

1 Line the terrarium with 2cm of gravel, spread lumps of charcoal over it and then fill with 5cm of damp potting mixture. Place some of the plants you have chosen inside the terrarium and plan your group.

2 Make a depression and plant the tallest parlour palm, spreading the roots out horizontally and gently packing potting mixture around them. This will not harm the plant and will slow down its growth.

3 Plant another parlour palm at the back of the terrarium on the left. Then, beneath it place an eyelash begonia next to a club moss which matches the brilliant green in the begonia's leaves.

PLANT KEY

Parlour palm

Spreading club moss

Polka-dot plant

Club moss

Eyelash begonia

4 Put another club moss in the front of the terrarium and a spreading club moss behind the larger parlour palm to give it more bulk. Then, fill the remaining spaces around the palm with polka-dot plants, and decorate any bare potting mixture with gravel. Mist-spray plants and potting mixture and close any aperture.

Cleaning the terrarium
Use a small sponge attached to a bamboo stake to remove condensation or algae from the inside surface of the glass.

Cacti and succulent gardens

Cacti and succulents with similar growing needs can be planted up together to make a miniature desert landscape. As they do not have deep root systems, they can be planted in shallow containers. If your container does not have drainage holes, line it with porous material to prevent the roots from rotting, and water the plants more sparingly than is recommended in *The Plant Finder's Guide*.

Queen agave
Agave victoriae-reginae
(see p.200)

Equipment and materials

Coarse sand

Trowel

Gravel

Soil-based potting mixture

**PLANTS
Mini-climate 4**
Cool, sunny

Bishop's cap
Astrophytum myriostigma
(see p.198)

Powder-puff cactus
Mammillaria bocasana
(see p.199)

Terracotta dish

Building up the arrangement:

1 Line the container with 3cm of gravel. Mix coarse sand and soil-based potting mixture together in measures of one part of sand to two of soil. Spread a 3cm layer of this mixture over the gravel.

2 With the plants still in their pots, experiment with the design. Consider any decorative pebbles which can be used on the surface of the potting mixture.

Mammillaria
Mammillaria sp.
(see p.199)

3 Fold up a piece of brown paper, wrap it round the spines of the cactus and lift the plant out with one hand, pulling the pot away with the other.

4 Lift the queen agave out of its pot and place it at the back of the dish. Plant the two bishop's caps and mammillarias, trickling the potting mixture gently around their roots.

Brown paper

Decorative finishes

Most nurseries and garden centres stock a wide variety of stone chippings, pebbles and gravel that can be used to decorate the surface of the potting mixture. Marble chips can be obtained from stone masons, and aquarium dealers often have a good selection of coloured pebbles. Coverings of pebbles and gravel tend to look best with cacti and succulents, since they are in keeping with the plants' arid or semi-arid natural habitat, but try out other finishes as well.

Pebbles

Shells

Coarse-grade blue glass

Limestone chips

Fine-grade green glass

Shells

Marble chippings

Shingle

Decorating a cactus garden
A large area of potting mixture between plants looks dull. Cover it with stone chippings and interestingly shaped pebbles, which resemble rocks, and you have a suitably rugged and arid-looking miniature landscape for these desert plants.

Patterns and textures *above*
Building up a series of decorative concentric rings made out of contrasting colours or materials is simple and effective. The sharp conical shells are arranged to mimic the spines of the cactus.

Adding a decorative finish *right*
Using a small scoop or spoon, add a thin layer of decorative material to the top of the potting mixture.

Making water gardens

Hydroculture is a relatively new name for an old practice of growing plants in containers filled with water and aggregate to which soluble plant foods are added. In place of soil, plants are held in position by the aggregate. Special containers are available (see pp.260-1) but you can make a simple and attractive planting in a glass vase.

It is best to use plants that have already made roots in water before putting them into the new medium, since the roots made in water are quite different from those made in soil. "Prepared" plants can be bought, or you can use cuttings of soft-stemmed plants that have been rooted in water. If you do transfer a plant from soil to water you must wait for the old roots to be replaced by new succulent ones. This process takes between 8-12 weeks and, during this time, the plant will need to be encased in a plastic bag to keep it in a warm and humid atmosphere.

Equipment and materials

Glass containers

Pothos vine
Scindapsus pictus
"Argyraeus"
(see p.188)

PLANTS
Mini-climate 1
Warm, sunny

Tradescantia
Tradescantia albiflora
"Albovittata"
(see p.187)

Pebbles

Charcoal

Aggregate

Miniature trowel

Building up the arrangement

1 Line the container with 2-3cm of aggregate which has previously been soaked to wash away impurities. Place a layer of pebbles over it and add some charcoal to keep the water sweet.

2 Fill the container two-thirds full with aggregate. Pour in enough water to fill the container one-third full and let the aggregate absorb the water.

3 Place the plant inside the container and trickle aggregate around its roots. If you are moving a plant grown in potting mixture carefully wash all traces of it away before planting.

The finished arrangement
A pothos vine and a trades-cantia have been planted in aggregate decorated with pebbles to create layers of different textures in the transparent containers. Plants are fed by adding food in the form of a powder or a sachet which releases nutrients into the water when they are needed (see p.260).

Alternative arrangements

Almost any plant can be successfully grown by hydroculture. It is a technique that has several advantages over conventional methods: it is convenient for flat dwellers since potting mixture does not have to be stored; it is less messy; watering and feeding are simpler; growth is more vigorous; and plants are not subject to soil-borne pests and diseases.

A vegetable garden *above*
The sweet potato (*Ipomoea batatas*) is usually grown for its tuberous edible roots; here the root is growing in water and decorative heart-shaped leaves rise from it.

An oriental garden *left*
This umbrella plant (*Cyperus* sp.) likes boggy conditions in the wild and is therefore a natural candidate for hydrocul-ture. Here, I built up a layer of white pebbles at the front of the container and filled the rest of it with the aggregate.

Caring for bonsai

The word bonsai means literally "plant in a tray". It is a technique by which any tree or shrub can be turned into a dwarf specimen by restricting its growth, and by pruning its roots and branches. As developed by the Japanese and Chinese, the technique was applied mainly to hardy trees of all kinds, such as maple, silver birch, beech, larch and pine. Today, these are referred to as "outdoor" bonsai since they need to spend most of the year outdoors. They should not be brought into a heated room for more than a few days in winter, but in summer, when the temperatures inside are similar to those outside, they can be brought in more frequently. A new development is the "indoor" bonsai: these are tropical or semi-tropical species which are happy to be kept indoors all the year round.

All bonsai need a great deal of light and, as their roots are restricted in a very small container, they must be watered frequently, particularly in warm weather.

Equipment and materials

Stoneware bonsai pots

Green wire

Perlite and flint chippings

Bonsai wire

Root teaser

Garden twine

Branch clipper

Bonsai potting mixture

Root clipper

Leaf pruner

Indoor and outdoor trees

Bonsai can be grown from seed or cuttings, or bought as young and mature plants. If properly cared for, these trees can live for many years; their price depends on age and the complexity of the shape of the tree.

Bonsai should be grown in shallow frost-proof pots with large drainage holes. Imported from Japan, these pots come in a variety of shapes and in plain, subtle colours which do not detract attention from the trees.

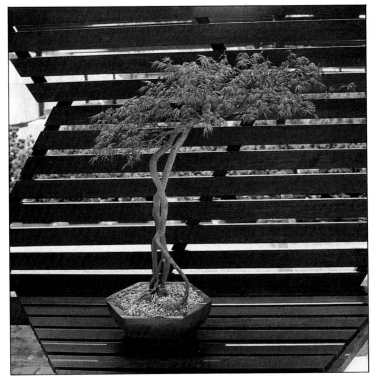

An outdoor bonsai
This Japanese maple (*Acer palmatum* "Dissectum") has a double twisted trunk and graceful upright shape. The leaves turn this beautiful, coppery-pink colour in autumn.

An indoor bonsai
This fig (*Ficus retusa*) is 15 years old and its trunk has splayed roots with an interesting shape. Display at an east- or west-facing window, but provide shade for it from the late afternoon sun.

Training and pruning

The Japanese have many different styles of bonsai, named according to their shape and the angle of the trunk in the pot. You can train your tree to grow in unusual shapes with wires, and by pruning the branches and leaves. To wire branches, it is best to use specially imported bonsai wire, which is very stiff, to hold branches rigid in the position you want to train them to follow. Training and pruning should be done in the very early spring, just before the new growth appears. Leaf pruning can be done all through the growing season and will encourage the growth of smaller leaves, which are in scale with the tree.

Complementary shapes *left*
Before you start to train and prune your tree, decide what shape you want it to have. If you want to display it with another tree, put the two together. Here, the smaller tree is to be trained to a fan shape with a flat top to complement the taller specimen behind it.

1 Loop the bonsai wire round the trunk of the tree and push it into the shape you want the branch to follow. Secure the branch to it with thinner garden wire.

2 Prune the stem back almost to the point at which it is wired. Cut just above the leaf axil as this is where new growth will develop.

3 Continue to prune the tree, cutting out all unwanted branches and shortening any long branches by half. Shorten all stems, and where there are multiple shoots crowded together leave just one.

Root pruning and repotting

Established bonsai need repotting every two or three years in spring in order to replenish the potting mixture, and to restrict their roots. They should not be moved into a larger pot because this will encourage them to grow bigger. Use a special soil-based potting mixture which is well-aerated and rich enough to sustain active growth. If you plan to prune your tree as well as repot it, leave three weeks between each operation so that the plant can recover its strength.

1 Take the plant out of its pot. Remove excess potting mixture by gently teasing it from the roots with a special tool or kitchen fork.

2 Prune the roots with a pair of root clippers, cutting away about half the growth and any damaged roots.

3 Line the pot with perlite and flint chippings. Tie the roots up with garden twine and thread the ends through the drainage holes to hold the plant rigid until new roots appear.

·3·
CUT-FLOWER ARRANGING

There is a special joy in using cut flowers in the home; they have an immediate freshness which house plants seldom achieve. Many books have been written about the techniques of flower arranging but, apart from the Japanese *ikebana* arrangements, where different combinations of flowers have symbolic meanings, it cannot be learnt by following a set of rules.

The beauty of an arrangement is in the flowers themselves, and the way they are arranged should enhance their inherent qualities rather than impose a formal structure at odds with their natural habit of growth. My personal preference is for simple, informal arrangements which allow the natural shapes, colours and textures of the flowers to be appreciated.

While flower arranging cannot be learnt systematically, you will find that, through practice and experiment, you will discover the qualities of different flowers and foliage and acquire an instinctive feeling for how to arrange them. The design of a flower arrangement depends on an appreciation of shape, colour and texture and an ability to orchestrate these qualities to produce a harmonious group.

Always think about the setting for your arrangement before you choose the flowers and, at the same time, decide whether it is to be a dramatic display for a special occasion or an informal day-to-day display. These considerations will dictate the size, shape and overall colour scheme and help you to create a display which complements its surroundings.

A simple arrangement of orchids
The vibrant colour of these orchids
(*Phalaenopsis* hybrids) is set off by the black
vase. The simple lines of the container
allow the intricate shape of the
flowers to stand out.

Using the colour wheel

Successful flower arranging depends upon an appreciation of colour. The ability to mix colours together comes with experience, and, by experimenting with colours yourself, you will soon develop an instinctive feeling for how to use them. It is also useful to know a little about colour theory. Here, a selection of cut flowers and foliage has been arranged in a circle with the colours following the same order as the spectrum—this is known as the colour wheel.

Triadic colour schemes
Orange, violet and green are secondary colours produced from an equal mixture of the two primary colours either side of them on the wheel. Used together they form a triadic colour scheme, as they are equidistant from each other on the colour wheel. You can put red, blue and yellow together for a strong triadic combination or, for a more subtle effect, use shades of orange, violet and green.

BLUE
Primary

GREEN
Secondary

YELLOW
Primary

The colour wheel
The wheel is composed of primary and secondary colours and each segment of colour represents a whole family of tints (the colour plus white), shades (the colour plus black) and tones (the colour plus grey).

·USING THE COLOUR WHEEL·

VIOLET
Secondary

RED
Primary

ORANGE
Secondary

Complementary colour schemes

Each secondary colour is the complementary colour of the one primary not used in its make up. For instance, violet, which is formed from red and blue, is the complementary of yellow. Use two complementary colours, in a variety of shades and tones, as the theme of an arrangement.

Analagous colour schemes

Analagous, or related, colours are harmonizing colours from adjacent sections of the wheel. Strong reds, oranges and yellows may look harsh together, so use shades of each colour for a more subtle scheme. Monochromatic colour schemes use various shades of the same colour, and very beautiful and sophisticated displays can be made by using a variety of plant material in just green or grey.

PLANT KEY

Carnation | Rose | Transvaal daisy | Lily | Chrysanthemum | Chrysanthemum | Rose | Daffodil | Cypress | Fern | Iris | Brodiaea | Hyacinth | Statice | Anemone

Cutting and preparing flowers

It is important to realize when you cut a flower that it is still alive and growing. The best time to cut flowers is in the morning, when they contain most fluid. Failing this, cut your flowers in the evening, when the plant will have been producing food all day, giving it a reservoir of nutrients to help it survive in the container. Once picked, slit the stems and put them straight into deep water, then leave them in a cool place for several hours.

When choosing flowers at the florist, make sure that petals are firm and colours are strong, and that foliage is green and not beginning to wilt. A good way of telling how fresh flowers are is to look at their stamens. If they are hard, this indicates that the flower has only recently opened. Never buy flowers that have been left outside in hot sun.

Cutting soft stems

When a freshly cut flower is left out of water, the water-transporting tubes start to close up. To help a soft stem take up water, cut the stem as cleanly as possible by using a sharp knife or florist's scissors. If you have only a few flowers to arrange, cut the stems in water so that water, not air, is drawn up immediately.

1 Cut the stem at a 45 degree angle to increase the surface area for water intake. It will also stop the stem resting flush against the bottom of the vase, thus cutting off its water supply.

2 Make a vertical slit about 5cm long to further increase the area capable of taking up water. Put the cut stems in deep water for a long drink before arranging. This ensures that they become full of water (turgid), and will therefore last longer.

Cutting woody stems

Cut woody stemmed flowers and foliage at a 45 degree angle using secateurs. If the stem is very hard, remove the bark from the base of the stem as well. Do not hammer the stems, since this reduces their capacity to take up water. Strip off all the leaves that will be underwater in your vase, as they will rot and foul the water.

1 With stems which are particularly woody, such as roses (*Rosa* sp.), lilac (*Syringa* sp.) and foliage sprays, scrape off 5cm of bark with a sharp knife.

2 Make a 5cm slit with secateurs or a sharp knife to increase the surface area for water intake.

Sealing bleeding stems

Narcissi, euphorbias, poppies (*Papaver* sp.) and many other plants bleed when cut, exuding either a sticky or milky juice. (The milky juice of euphorbias can cause skin irritation.) This sap flow results in a loss of nutrients to the flower head and, if lost into the flower water, will block up the water-conducting tubes of the stem and encourage bacteria; so spend a little extra time conditioning flowers which bleed, before using them in an arrangement.

1 Seal bleeding stems by first cutting them at an angle and then either dipping them in boiling water or placing them in a flame for 30 seconds. This will not prevent them from taking up water.

2 Place the treated stems, by themselves, in warm water until they have finished bleeding. They can then be arranged with other flowers.

Useful tips

● To prolong the life of flowers with hollow stems, such as delphiniums (*Delphinium* sp.) and Cape lilies (*Crinum* sp.), fill each stem with water and plug the end with cotton wool.

● Harden weak stems by putting them in water containing a special florist's conditioning solution. Leave in a dark place where water loss by transpiration will be reduced.

● Condition young foliage by immersing it completely in water for two hours before arranging.

● To remove thorns from roses, rub the stems very hard with the back of a pair of scissors. Roses are much easier to arrange once the thorns have been removed.

● Add one or two drops of household bleach to your arrangement water, as this will help prevent the growth of bacteria. Dissolve a teaspoonful of sugar in warm water to provide flowers with valuable glucose.

● Add water to your arrangement daily. You will find that certain flowers, such as dahlias (*Dahlia* hybrids), asters (*Aster novi-belgii*) and stocks (*Matthiola incana*), foul their water very quickly, so it is worth changing their water completely once a day.

● Remove any dying heads immediately, as they emit an ethylene gas which will cause wilting in other flowers.

● Position your arrangements away from bright sunlight, heat and draughts. These will all shorten the life of your flowers, since they increase transpiration.

● Mist-spray your flowers daily with a fine spray of luke-warm water. This will make them last longer.

Removing an airlock

If your flowers have been out of water for some time, it is possible that air may be trapped in the stems. Air-bubbles prevent water from being taken up into the stem and lack of water will cause the flowers to wilt prematurely.

Preparing tulips

Forced tulips (*Tulipa* sp.) have weak stems which droop in an awkward way, making them difficult to arrange. They can be straightened by wrapping them in paper and putting them in warm water containing a conditioning solution.

Pricking a tulip to remove an airlock
To release trapped air, sterilize a needle in a flame, then prick the stem just below the flower head.

1 Having cut and slit the stems, and removed some of the leaves, wrap the flowers in brown paper, newspaper or waxed florist's tissue which will retain its rigidity in water.

2 Stand the tulips in warm water for several hours. To assist the process and strengthen the stems, add special florist's conditioning solution to the water; this contains sugar for food and a bactericide.

Supports for flower arrangements

Using wire netting

Crumpled chicken wire is an effective stem holder, particularly for woody stems or heavy flowers. It can be used on its own—and is the best anchor for flowers which will only last if arranged in deep water—or it can be used with plastic foam for extra support. You can buy chicken wire by the metre in various gauges: use the fine gauge for slender stems and the wider gauges for more robust flowers and foliage. If you need to support one, or several, very heavy stems, secure them on a pinholder attached to the bottom of the container with adhesive clay, using wire netting as well if necessary.

1 Cut a piece of wire netting with wire cutters to make a square several times larger than the aperture of the container. You can use ordinary household objects, such as this mixing bowl, as a water-tight container inside a more decorative outer container, such as a wicker basket.

2 Crumple the wire in your hands, moulding it so that it will fit into the bowl and have an uneven surface. Be careful to avoid scratching yourself against the raw edges of the metal.

3 Place the crumpled wire in your container. For larger arrangements it may be necessary to secure the netting in place by passing wires, or pieces of colourless adhesive tape, over it, and securing them beneath the container.

4 Place the mixing bowl filled with crumpled wire inside the basket, and insert the first stems through the layers of netting which will secure them.

Using plastic foam

Water-absorbent plastic foam is another useful stem holder which will support flowers in place at any angle. It is available in several shapes and sizes: in large bricks for large arrangements and in cylinders and squares for smaller displays. The foam can be used whole, or cut to fit any shape of container. Plastic foam should be soaked in water for half an hour before use, since it will otherwise suck water out of the flowers as they are being arranged. If you are arranging long- or heavy-stemmed flowers, you may need to secure the foam in position with clear adhesive tape. A block of plastic foam can be re-used several times.

1 Place the plastic foam in the container. For a low arrangement (shown made up on p.85), trim down the plastic foam so that it is flush with the side of the container. If you want to insert stems at an angle, so that they will point downwards, allow several centimetres of plastic foam to extend above the rim of the container.

2 Having soaked the plastic foam in water, insert the stems by pushing them carefully into the foam. Top up the container with water once all the flowers are in position.

The principles of arrangement 1

Where do you begin with a flower arrangement if you are starting from scratch? First of all, think about where the arrangement is to go, and plan it with the setting in mind. Consider how it will be lit and the angle from which it will be seen. Then think about a suitable container for the place you have chosen. Containers range from kitchen bowls, jugs and baskets to purpose-made vases in all sorts of shapes and materials. Before you start to arrange your flowers, look at their shapes, textures and colours and work out a design based on a simple shape. Prepare and condition the flowers as described on pp.80-1, and select the first stems to establish the basic outline for the arrangement. Then fill out the shape, placing the largest foliage and flowers at the bottom and the most slender at the top. Position the most striking material in the centre of the arrangement.

Making a large informal arrangement *right*
For a large arrangement, avoid following a shape too rigidly; allow the natural outlines of the flowers to show. Here, I have established the outline with foliage, white lilac (*Syringa* sp.) and baby's breath (*Gypsophila paniculata*), and added red flowers for focal interest.

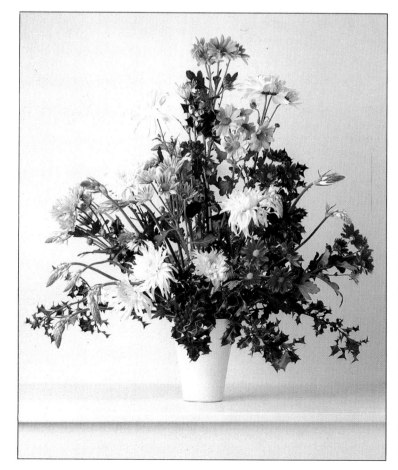

A triangular arrangement

Fill the vase with plastic foam or wire netting. First, establish the apex of the triangle and the outline of the two sides with chrysanthemum (*Chrysanthemum* hybrids) sprays. Then strengthen the shape with holly (*Ilex aquifolium*), choosing branches with a suitable outline and good berries. Add the corn-shaped heads of chincherinchee (*Ornithogalum thyrsoides*) for outline, and use some large chrysanthemum heads for focal point.

FLOWER KEY

Chrysanthemum

Chrysanthemum

Chincherinchee

Common holly

The principles of arrangement 2

A circular arrangement

This shape of arrangement suits all types of cottage flowers. Put plastic foam inside the vase so that it is flush with the top. Establish the shape with baby's breath (*Gypsophila paniculata*) and then strengthen it with white lilac (*Syringa* sp.). Then add sprays of white daisy-shaped chrysanthemums (*Chrysanthemum* hybrids), orange lilies and pink-and-green Peruvian lilies (*Alstroemeria* sp.).

FLOWER KEY

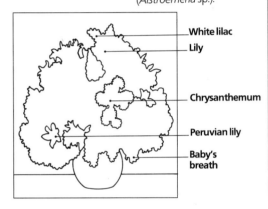

- White lilac
- Lily
- Chrysanthemum
- Peruvian lily
- Baby's breath

A semi-circular arrangement

This thin, lozenge-shaped container and the bare twigs suggested a stark, modern arrangement. Insert wire netting into the top of the container and let it extend a little way over the edge, so that stems can be inserted at an angle. Establish a semi-circular shape with the twigs, letting one trail down in front. Insert the orchid stems so that they follow the lines of the twigs.

FLOWER KEY

Dogwood | Orchid

A vertical arrangement

FLOWER KEY

White Iris

Iris leaves

The stiff, linear form of the iris (*Iris* sp.) and vertical container suggested this oriental-style arrangement; sword lilies (*Gladiolus* hybrids) would also be suitable. Fill the vase with plastic foam so that it extends about 3cm above the edge. Insert one stem to establish the height and arrange the others at different heights.

A low triangular arrangement

I have used irises again to make this low horizontal arrangement. Establish the outline on both sides with blue flowers, then add iris leaves for outline. Cut the stems of the white irises short and insert them in the middle at varying heights for focal interest.

FLOWER KEY

Blue iris

Iris leaves

White iris

A spring flower arrangement

Narcissi are simple, unsophisticated flowers which need to be arranged informally; they do not mix well with other flowers in a more formal display. I like to arrange them so that their stems curve outwards, mimicking the way they grow in clumps in the wild. Mass the flowers together in a simple wicker basket and include some of their own foliage to increase the natural look of the display. Put the arrangement on a side table, or use it as a centrepiece for a country kitchen table. If you place the arrangement in a cool spot, the flowers will last much longer.

Building up the arrangement

1 Place a glass mixing bowl inside a circular reed basket and cut a block of plastic foam to fit inside so that it is flush with the top. Cut a large piece of wire netting, mould it into peaks, and secure it around the edge of the basket.

Equipment and materials

Wire netting

Wicker basket

Mixing bowl

Plastic foam

Florist's scissors

Wire cutters

Daffodil
Narcissus
"Golden Harvest"

Jonquil
Narcissus
medioluteus
hybrids

Large-cupped narcissus
Narcissus "Fermoy"

Small-cupped narcissus
Narcissus
"Soleil d'Or"

Jonquil
Narcissus
"Barrii"

Large-cupped narcissus
Narcissus
"Armada"

Large-cupped narcissus
Narcissus
"Ice Follies"

2 Narcissi have stems which exude a sticky juice, so seal them before arranging (see p.80). Begin by outlining a semi-circular shape, arranging the flowers with their leaves.

3 Continue to fill in the basic shape, using the larger daffodils and leaves, cutting the stems to the height you want. Rotate the arrangement as you work, for, if used as a centrepiece, the display will be seen from all angles.

4 Use the small, delicate jonquils to fill in any obvious spaces. Add more large flowers and leaves to emphasize the outline and give body to the arrangement; bend down some of the lower stems below the line of the basket to give a slightly more rounded shape. Other flowers can be cut down and positioned to give body to the middle of the arrangement. Cut a few of the smaller ones very short and insert them around the edges of the basket so that they disguise the wire netting.

A summer flower arrangement

There is such a profusion of flowers in the summer that you should think carefully about the setting for your arrangement, and the effect you wish to create, before picking or buying the flowers. Here I wanted to create a display with a light and airy feel suitable for a side table or an alcove.

I chose to contrast strong shades of blue and golden yellow against a subtle background of grey and white flowers and green foliage. Taking an asymmetrical triangle as my basic shape, I selected a white oval casserole dish as a container since it will be obscured by the flowers.

Building up the arrangement

1 Cut a block of foam to extend above the rim of the container and secure in position with adhesive clay. Form the outline with the strongest shapes—the cylindrical globe thistles and the dried sea holly.

2 Fill the shape out laterally with eucalyptus and, at the front of the arrangement, push sprigs of foliage into the foam so that they hang down over the edge of the container. Add the deep yellow flowers of St John's wort to create focal points of colour.

Equipment and materials

Golden marguerite
Anthemis tinctoria "E.C. Buxton"

Florist's scissors

Secateurs

Stub wires

Eucalyptus
Eucalyptus gunnii

St John's wort
Hypericum androsaemum "Tutsan"

Marguerite daisy
Anthemis cupaniana

Casserole dish

Sea holly
Eryngium giganteum

Yellow yarrow
Achillea filipendulina "Coronation Gold"

African lily
Agapanthus "Headbourne Hybrids"

White yarrow
Achillea sp.

Plastic foam

Globe thistle
Echinops ritro

Butterfly bush
Buddleia davidii "White Cloud"

3 Now strengthen the yellow areas by adding several golden yarrow heads to create yellow focal points in the middle of the design. As you position each flower, you will need to cut the stem to an appropriate length to maintain the overall shape. Place the most dominant yarrow head right into the centre of the group, cutting its stem short so that your eye is led into the design. Add a couple of sprigs of white yarrow to fill out the base of the arrangement.

4 The largest flowers should be positioned at the base of the arrangement. Use the long and heavy heads of the sweetly scented butterfly bush at the front, and at the sides, to give them more bulk. As the arrangement fills out in all directions, the foam and the casserole dish become obscured by the delicate mass of flowers and foliage.

5 Since a full African lily head would be out of scale with the other flowers, pull off the individual florets and wire them by pushing a fine-gauge stub wire up the length of each stem.

6 Lighten the design with touches of golden and white marguerite daisies. Finally add the wired African lily florets, concentrating them on the right-hand side of the design to balance the daisies on the left.

An autumn flower arrangement

The colours of autumn are much darker than those of spring and summer. Here I chose to contrast russet- and gold-coloured flowers and berries with deep-purple foliage, highlighted with scarlet dahlias and rose hips. I decided to make a horizontal arrangement designed to be seen from above—either on a low table or as a table centrepiece—

where the addition of fruit would enhance the autumnal feel of the display. Since the arrangement may be put on a table where people eat, it should be low enough to allow conversation across it. I chose a wooden basket, whose natural colour harmonized with the flowers, and fitted a glass pie dish inside the basket to act as a watertight container.

Equipment and materials

Wooden basket

Glass dish

Plastic foam

Stub wires

Secateurs

Florist's scissors

Cotoneaster
Cotoneaster sp.

Elder
Sambucus nigra
"Aurea"

Iceplant
Sedum spectabile
"Atropurpureum"

Crab apples
Malus
"Golden Hornet"

Guelder rose berries
Viburnum opulus
"Fructo-Luteo"

Dahlia
Dahlia hybrids

Rose hips
Rosa sp.

Barberry
Berberis thunbergii
"Rose Glow"

Rose hips
Rosa moyesii

Ragwort
Ligularia dentatum
"Desdemona"

Coneflower
Rudbeckia fulgida deami

Building up the arrangement

1 Cut a piece of foam to fit the glass container, allowing it to extend above the rim so that stems can be pushed in horizontally. Lay two purple elder branches and two circular ragwort leaves over the foam to establish the overall shape which will relate, of course, to where you plan to put the arrangement.

2 Once you are satisfied with the outline, decide whether you are going to look down on your arrangement or whether it will be seen from the side, and plan the design accordingly. Slide the foliage into the foam, then, to give bulk to the arrangement, add the purple iceplant flowers.

3 Add the golden coneflowers for focal interest and open out the arrangement by adding a couple of stems of barberry, following the lines established by the elder. Put a sprig of cotoneaster berries at the front to fill an empty space. The flowers and branchlets which you are using should have been cut at an angle, and the stems split, to provide a greater area for water intake. Be careful not to push the cut stems flush with the side or bottom of the container as this will reduce the amount of water available to them.

4 Wire several stems of crab apples together and add the bunch to the arrangement. Add dahlias to create bold points of colour and echo their scarlet tones with stems of rose hips placed at one end of the display. At this stage, fill the bowl with cool water and move it to its setting. You will need to top up the water after a day or so as the plastic foam absorbs a considerable amount.

5 Guelder rose berries are sparsely distributed on their stems, so wire two sprigs together. Hold the stems tightly and wrap a fine-gauge stub wire around them. The wired bunch can easily be pushed into the foam.

6 Add several bunches of wired guelder rose berries to fill the hole at the front of the display and reinforce the red area on the right by adding another stem of rose hips. Place a bunch of grapes and a few crab apples beside the arrangement.

A winter flower arrangement

Flowers are at a premium in winter, but in the garden you will find a surprising amount of material suitable for arrangements. Some of the autumn berries remain, much of the variegated foliage is in good condition, small buds are beginning to open on shrubs and trees, and the early flowering hellebores appear after Christmas. Here, I have made a predominantly green arrangement, exploiting the different shapes of the foliage and adding white and yellow flowers and orange berries for colour. An old pottery jug makes a suitable container for this unsophisticated display.

Building up the arrangement

1 Shave the sides off a block of plastic foam so that it will fit inside the jug, and push it in so that it is flush with the top. Begin the arrangement by inserting branches of witch hazel and cypress.

Equipment and materials

Plastic foam

Secateurs

Pottery jug

Winter-flowering cherry
Prunus subhirtella
"Autumnalis"

Hellebore
Helleborus corsicus lividus

Laurustinus
Viburnum tinus

Stinking iris
Iris foetidissima

Persian ivy
Hedera colchica
"Paddy's Pride"

Mahonia
Mahonia sp.

Black calla
Arum italicum
"Pictum"

Silk tassel bush
Garrya elliptica

True cypress
Cupressus glabra

Witch hazel
Hamamelis mollis

2 Position a large branch of mahonia in the centre of the arrangement and a tall spray of the silk-tassel bush, covered with some early catkins, behind; this establishes the height and basic triangular shape of the display.

3 Insert a large flower head of hellebore in the centre as a focal point, after trimming off all the lower leaves and some of the upper ones. Place a spray of laurustinus to fill out the space at the back of the arrangement.

4 Now position the yellow-and-green ivy leaves and place the bright-orange iris berries at the top of the arrangement. Add the narrow, spiky iris leaves to contrast with the heavier forms of the other foliage, and place a branch of winter-flowering cherry behind the cypress on the left. Finally, include the highly patterned black calla leaves to provide interest at the base of the container. This arrangement should remain attractive for about a fortnight, providing you put it in a cool place and top up the water level every day.

·4·
DRIED-FLOWER ARRANGING

Living plants require regular care and a particular environment in order to thrive, and the beauty and freshness of cut flowers lasts for a few weeks at most. But dried flowers need neither water nor light and, once arranged, they do not flop or drop their petals. Dried arrangements can be put anywhere and, through the winter, when fresh material is hard to come by, will evoke the abundance of the summer season. As with fresh flowers, the principles of proportion and use of colour, texture and shape apply to each display. Containers are important: baskets—plain or painted— terracotta pots and glass vases all help show dried flowers to their best advantage. Do not restrict yourself to flower arrangements—garlands and wreaths are simple to build up with dried material. Make a dried-flower tree, or mix up a fragrant pot-pourri whose heady scent may be reminiscent of a late spring meadow or warm summer night. Drying herbs and bunches of flowers in your kitchen will also bring back the smells of summer.

If dried displays catch your imagination, enjoy discovering all the different forms they can take. As well as flowers, you can include leaves, grasses, berries, cereals, fruits and seed heads, to give countless variations of colour and texture. You will soon develop a "collector's eye"—scanning every garden, bank and hedgerow for suitable materials to be dried and incorporated in your arrangements.

An informal arrangement of dried flowers
A collection of dried flowers, grasses and seed heads have been massed together in a simple terracotta container. The arrangement is held together by its autumnal colour scheme and complemented by the orange pumpkin placed beside it.

How to dry flowers 1

Drying flowers requires neither time-consuming techniques nor expensive equipment. Many plants need only to be collected at the right time, tied in bunches and hung up to dry. Others, depending on their shape, can be dried upright or laid flat. The more delicate garden flowers, or those likely to lose their colour if air-dried, may be put in an airtight box and covered with a suitable desiccant.

Although the techniques by which plants are dried are not difficult to follow, you will find that, however careful you are, your results will vary from year to year as the process is affected by the weather conditions. Pick flowers only when the weather is dry, and begin the drying process as soon as possible after you have picked them. Avoid putting them in direct sunlight, as this causes colours to fade.

Air-drying

This technique is suitable for most flowers, grasses and seed heads. Arrange them in small bunches, hanging large flowers, such as hydrangeas (*Hydrangea* sp.), separately so that they do not touch each other. Check after a day or two and if those with fleshy stems, such as delphiniums (*Delphinium* sp.), are not drying, apply moderate heat.

Drying in bunches

1 Strip the leaves off the stem as far as the flower head, unless they form a natural rosette around the flower, as those of straw flowers (*Helichrysum bracteatum*) do, in which case leave them so the stems do not look so naked.

2 Tie up the flowers with an elastic band so that the bunch stays together as the stems contract. Do not make your bunches too large, otherwise the flowers in the middle will fail to dry and will become mouldy.

Baby's breath

Statice

Rose

Straw flower

Larkspur

Tansy

3 Hang your bunches in a well-ventilated, warm, dry place such as an attic, cellar, linen cupboard or spare room. Leave them until they feel dry and crisp before bringing them into a more humid atmosphere.

Drying upright

Most flowers which can be air-dried can also be dried upright. Use this method for flowers or grasses with particularly delicate heads, as it will preserve them better. Leave the flowers standing in a little water until they have absorbed it all and become crisp to the touch.

Drying flat

Most seed heads, grasses and seed pods can be dried in open boxes or laid flat on newspaper or brown paper.

Preserving in desiccants

This is a slightly more complicated process, but it is worth using on more delicate flowers and on roses, which lose some of their colour when air-dried. You need an airtight container, such as a biscuit tin or plastic food box. It need only be large enough to dry the flower heads; as wire stems are attached once they are dry.

1 Line your container with a 3cm layer of equal parts of borax and alum. Alternatively, use silver sand and silica gel crystals, and heat the mixture to eradicate moisture.

2 Cut a piece of wire netting to fit the container and lay it on top of the desiccant mixture. This will keep the flower heads upright.

3 Take a flower, such as a Transvaal daisy (*Gerbera* sp.) and cut about 2cm below the head, leaving enough stem to insert the wire into, when the flower has dried.

4 Place the flower heads in the netting, making sure that they do not touch. Dry flowers of one type together so that they will be ready at the same time.

5 Add more of the desiccant powder, sieving it over the flower heads to avoid damaging them. Continue until they are covered by about 2cm of powder.

6 Seal the container and leave undisturbed in a warm, dry place for four to fourteen days, depending on the density of the flowers.

How to dry flowers 2

Preserving in glycerine

This is a preserving, rather than a drying, method which can be used for whole branches of foliage, berries and large leaves. It is also suitable for preserving long flower spikes, such as foxgloves (*Digitalis* sp.). The stems are placed in a mixture of glycerine and near-boiling water and left until they have absorbed enough of the solution. This takes about a week for light foliage, and from six to eight weeks for heavy foliage. The leaves gradually become deeper and richer in colour, and when

drops of glycerine appear on them they will have absorbed enough of the solution. Remove them, as excessive absorption will cause wilting, and wipe them clean. Immerse single leaves and very tall branches, when the top stems might not take up the mixture, in a bath of glycerine and water solution.

1 Remove the lower leaves from the stems with secateurs. Cut them at a 45 degree angle, pare away any bark from woody stems, and make a 5cm slit to increase the area for glycerine intake.

2 Mix one part of glycerine with two parts of near-boiling water in a narrow container and stir the solution vigorously.

3 Pour the glycerine and water solution into a heatproof container. Fill to a depth of 10cm, so that it will cover the prepared part of the stems.

4 Stand the stems in the solution and place the container with the foliage in a cool, dark room until the leaves have absorbed sufficient glycerine.

Pressing

Most leaves—including ferns, grey-tinted shrubs and maples (*Acer* sp.)—can be dried by pressing. Only a little pressure is needed for large leaves and ferns, otherwise they become too brittle to arrange. Once covered in blotting paper or newspaper, they can be put under a carpet or mattress and left to dry for about a week. Smaller leaves, bracts and the delicate heads of wild flowers can be put in a bought press and left for a fortnight.

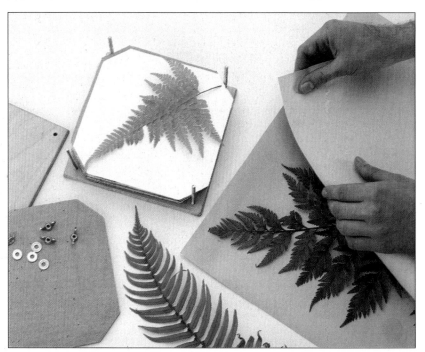

Two methods of pressing leaves
Place large leaves between pages of blotting paper, and small leaves and flowers between the absorbent sheets of a bought flower press.

Making pot-pourri

Pot-pourri means "rotten pot"—the original method was to mix dried petals with salt so that they fermented, giving off a strong scent. Although its smell is more fugitive, the dry pot-pourri is much easier to make.

Rose petals
Rosa sp.

Larkspur
Delphinium consolida

Hop-clover
Trifolium agrarium

Juniper berries

Rose petals for decoration

Pot-pourri essence

Bay leaves
Laurus nobilis

Dried lemon peel

Orris root powder

Sea holly
Eryngium maritimum

Lemon-scented geranium leaves
Pelargonium crispum

Larkspur
Delphinium consolida

Lavender
Lavandula sp.

1 Dry petals, leaves and the lemon peel on a surface that allows plenty of air to circulate round them. It will take up to ten days for them to become crisp.

2 Mix all the petals and leaves together. Crush the lemon peel into small pieces and add it to the mixture with the spices and a few drops of essence.

3 Add dried flower heads and rose petals dried in borax for decoration. Seal the container and leave it for six weeks to mature, shaking it occasionally.

Ingredients for pot-pourri
Sachets have been filled with dried flowers and leaves from the terracotta bowls. These bowls contain some of the most popular ingredients for making pot-pourri. Lavender has a strong scent and is an ingredient of many pot-pourris. Sweet-scented roses are often used as the base of a pot-pourri and the whole heads, as seen here, can be added for decoration. The small grape hyacinth florets (*Muscari* sp.) are intensely blue and help to give colour to a pot-pourri.

Arranging flowers in a basket

The place where you decide to put an arrangement will help to suggest an appropriate size and shape. I selected a windowsill where the flowers would be attractively framed by the window. For a display such as this, which will not be seen in the round, I chose a flat-backed asymmetrical triangle as my basic shape.

I decided to use blues, whites, creams and yellows, adding cereals and seed heads to give substance and texture to the design. Let an arrangement reflect the natural growth of the flowers themselves. Here, the graceful curve of the barley lent itself to trailing over the sill, contrasting with the stiffer wheat used to outline the shape.

Equipment and materials

Basket

Plastic foam

Knife

Florist's scissors

Stub wires

Dried moss

Wheat
Triticum vulgare

Larkspur
Delphinium consolida

White statice
Limonium sinuatum

Barley
Hordeum vulgare

Helipterum
Helipterum roseum

Sea lavender
Limonium latifolium

Blue statice
Limonium sinuatum

Baby's breath
Gypsophila paniculata

Poppy seed heads
Papaver sp.

Lady's mantle
Alchemilla mollis

Holly mahonia
Mahonia aquifolium

Sea holly
Eryngium maritimum

Oats
Avena sp.

Rose
Rosa sp.

Heather
Erica sp.

Straw flower
Helichrysum bracteatum

Love-in-a-mist seed heads
Nigella damascena

Dyed baby's breath
Gypsophila paniculata

The finished arrangement
This light and delicate arrangement suits the small window with its pretty lace pelmet and neutral-coloured curtains. Think carefully about the décor of your room before selecting flowers and a container so that the colours and style of your display will be in keeping with its surroundings.

Building up the arrangement

1 Cut one block of foam—using the stiffer variety made for dried flowers—for the centre of the basket and two smaller ones to fit either side. Press the foam down firmly and shear off all edges with a knife. Cut some wires into thirds and bend to form a hairpin shape. Cover the foam with dried moss secured with the wire pins. Position the wheat to establish the shape of the design.

2 Having established the height using the basket as a guide—it should be a third of the overall height—start to establish the shape of the arrangement with the sea lavender. When you cut the foam, make sure that it extends above the rim of the basket so that flowers can be inserted downwards.

continued over

3 Introduce colour and tone with larkspur and blue statice to the left and white statice to the right. Take a few blue flowers over to the right to help link the two sides of the design.

4 Elongate the design with barley and helipterum wired into small bunches (see p.110). Add lady's mantle and baby's breath and position the poppy seed heads and the sea holly in the centre for focal interest.

5 Cross the design with love-in-a-mist seed heads and infill with oats to give bulk to the paler side of the group. Fill the spaces with the darkest elements in the design—holly mahonia, dyed gypsophila and heather. Add the roses and the straw flowers which should be wired to give them extra length. Then, having put the display in its setting, stand back and adjust the outline as necessary.

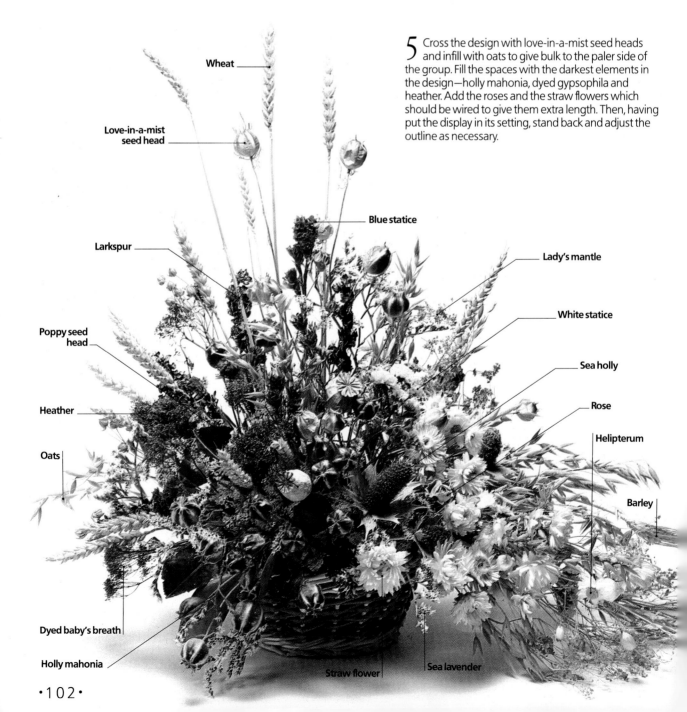

Wheat

Love-in-a-mist seed head

Blue statice

Larkspur

Lady's mantle

White statice

Poppy seed head

Sea holly

Rose

Heather

Helipterum

Oats

Barley

Dyed baby's breath

Holly mahonia

Straw flower

Sea lavender

Further ideas for arrangements

There are an enormous number of ways in which dried flowers can be arranged. For informal displays use baskets of any kind, or earthenware pots, as containers. Try filling a large basket with grasses, seed heads and cereals in creams, beiges and very pale greens, inserting stems at an angle so that the flowers appear to radiate from the centre. Alternatively, fill an earthenware pot with bunches of flowers.

Neutral tones *below*
A tall container can set off a rounded mass of flowers, and frosted glass will disguise stems and wires. Here the neutral colours of the vases do not overshadow the delicate flowers of sea lavender (*Limonium latifolium*) on the right and wild garlic (*Allium* sp.) on the left.

Still life *above*
Arrange dried hydrangeas (*Hydrangea macrophylla*) in a simple vase and the subtlety of their colour and texture is enough to make an attractive display. The figs, grapes and pomegranates complete a still life group which looks good enough to paint.

Informal groups *left*
Bunches of flowers placed in baskets can look very effective in the right kind of setting. Here, the neutral tones and rough textures of the love-in-a-mist (*Nigella damascena*) and poppy (*Papaver* sp.) seed heads suit the coarse-weaved basket. A sheaf of ribbed seed pods in the foreground picks up the textures of the baskets.

Making dried-flower trees

Dried-flower trees are much easier to make than you might imagine and, once you have mastered the basic techniques, you can experiment with different types of flowers and different shapes of tree. Here, I have used pink, blue and white flowers and parchment-coloured seed heads to make a light and delicate tree.

Blue larkspur
Delphinium consolida

Bells-of-Ireland
Moluccella laevis

Blue statice
Limonium sinuatum

Poppy seed heads
Papaver sp.

Equipment and materials

Sea lavender
Limonium latifolium

Winged everlasting
Ammobium sp.

Helipterum
Helipterum roseum

Straw flower
Helichrysum bracteatum

Pink larkspur
Delphinium consolida

Wire cutters

Ribbon

Baby's breath
Gypsophila paniculata

Plastic pot

Ball of plastic foam

Stub wires

Pink statice
Limonium sinuatum

Sea holly
Eryngium maritimum

Stones

Fresh moss

Interior wall filler

Bamboo stick

Building up the arrangement

1 Take a plastic plant pot 12cm in diameter, line it with foil and fill with stones in order to secure a bamboo stick about 35cm high. Spoon a mix of wall filler into the pot until it reaches the surface.

2 Push the ball of plastic foam on to the bamboo stick. Make sure that the stick only goes half-way through the foam. Pack moss around the outside of the ball.

3 Attach the moss to the foam with pins, made by cutting stub wires into thirds and bending the pieces over. As you work, be careful not to push down too hard on the foam ball.

4 Start to outline the shape with the blue larkspur and blue statice. You will find that you need to break small branches of flowers off the main stems to achieve the right scale for this size of tree.

5 Break off some small segments of sea lavender, and place them where they will be seen. Wire together some winged everlastings to form small bunches, and add to cover the surface of the tree. Infill with pink statice and pink larkspur.

6 Add the round heads of straw flowers and pink helipterum to fill some of the gaps. Place poppy seed heads, sea holly and small pieces of bells-of-Ireland to give texture, and finally add small sprigs of baby's breath to soften the outline.

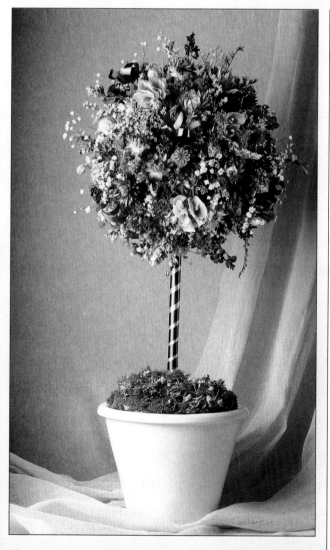

Other types of dried-flower tree

For a strong and simple country-style tree, use the flat heads of golden yarrow (*Achillea filipendulina*) to form the tree itself and use a plain terracotta pot for the base. To create a different type of tree, take a branch with an interesting outline and decorate it with rough-textured flowers, cereals and seed heads in creams, browns and greens.

7 Place the completed tree in a white pot and put some moss and a few flower heads over the stone base. You can leave the bamboo stick plain, or decorate it with ribbon to create a maypole effect. Take two strips of ribbon, glue them to the top of the stick and twine them round it, securing at the bottom with sticky tape.

A tree for Christmas
The basic form of this tree is the same as the one featured above. Instead of flowers, I have covered the foam base with wired pine cones, and added a few artificial fruits to add colour and give it a more festive look.

Decorating a basket of pot-pourri

The art of making pot-pourri is experiencing something of a revival. Consequently, there are many bought varieties to choose from or it is possible to make your own by following the recipe on p.99. Pot-pourri is valued not only for its subtle smell but also for the attractive colours and textures of the dried petals from which it is made. Put it in a pretty basket decorated with dried flowers and you will have a delicate and sweet-smelling display with many decorative uses. If you wish to add a spicy quality to the fragrance of the pot-pourri, place a pomander in the middle of the basket. Alternatively, these can be decorated with ribbon and hung around the house or put in drawers.

Equipment and materials

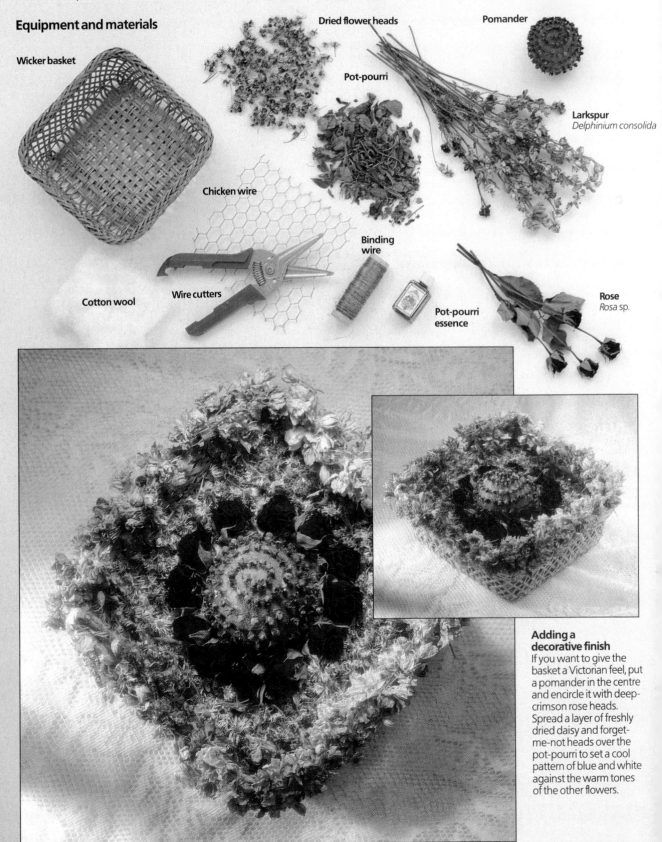

Wicker basket

Dried flower heads

Pomander

Pot-pourri

Larkspur
Delphinium consolida

Chicken wire

Binding wire

Cotton wool

Wire cutters

Pot-pourri essence

Rose
Rosa sp.

Adding a decorative finish

If you want to give the basket a Victorian feel, put a pomander in the centre and encircle it with deep-crimson rose heads. Spread a layer of freshly dried daisy and forget-me-not heads over the pot-pourri to set a cool pattern of blue and white against the warm tones of the other flowers.

Building up the arrangement

1 Line the basket with a thin layer of cotton wool. Cut a piece of fine chicken wire to fit inside the basket resting on the cotton wool. This will keep the pot-pourri dry and stop it becoming "fusty" by allowing air to circulate underneath it.

2 Sprinkle a few drops of bought pot-pourri essence (or use your own essential oils distilled from fresh flowers) to enhance the existing natural fragrances. Fill the basket two-thirds full with pot-pourri made from rose petals, lavender, scented-leaved geraniums, dried lemon peel and orris root (see p.99).

3 To make the garland, take three stems of larkspur and bind them together using fine binding wire. Arrange the stems so that the flowers are equally distributed along the garland and wrap the wire around the stems being careful not to damage the flowers.

4 Continue to make the garland until it is long enough to fit right round the basket. As an alternative to the pink larkspur you could use blue larkspur mixed with deep red straw flowers or xeranthemum flowers.

5 As the garland is flexible, adjust it to the shape of your basket and secure it in position with wire. The illustration opposite shows how to add a decorative finish using blue and white dried flower heads and a pomander centrepiece.

Making a pomander

Take an orange—preferably a Seville orange—and, if you are planning to hang up your pomander, place masking tape on the orange where the ribbons will go. Stick the cloves into the orange and then roll it in the orris root and cinnamon. Put it in a dark, well-ventilated place for several weeks.

Masking tape

Orange

Cinnamon powder

Ribbon

Cloves

Orris root powder

Inserting the cloves *above*
Stick the cloves into the orange leaving the width of one head between them.

Making wreaths

Wreaths made out of dried materials can be used in a number of ways. They can be hung on a door, on a wall, or from the ceiling, or used flat to make a table decoration. Here, I have made a rough-textured wreath with brown nuts and neutral-coloured grasses, highlighted with the warm tones of yellow, orange and red flowers.

Equipment and materials

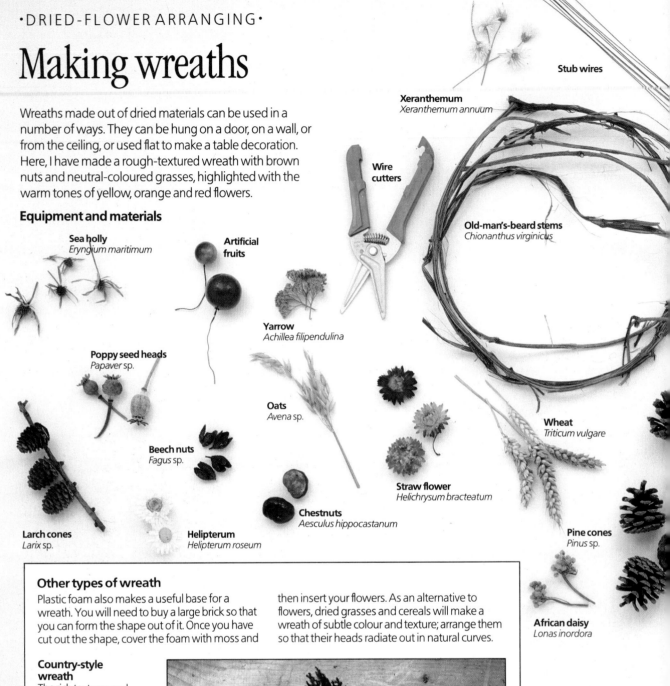

Stub wires

Xeranthemum
Xeranthemum annuum

Wire cutters

Old-man's-beard stems
Chionanthus virginicus

Sea holly
Eryngium maritimum

Artificial fruits

Yarrow
Achillea filipendulina

Poppy seed heads
Papaver sp.

Oats
Avena sp.

Wheat
Triticum vulgare

Beech nuts
Fagus sp.

Straw flower
Helichrysum bracteatum

Larch cones
Larix sp.

Helipterum
Helipterum roseum

Chestnuts
Aesculus hippocastanum

Pine cones
Pinus sp.

African daisy
Lonas inordora

Other types of wreath

Plastic foam also makes a useful base for a wreath. You will need to buy a large brick so that you can form the shape out of it. Once you have cut out the shape, cover the foam with moss and then insert your flowers. As an alternative to flowers, dried grasses and cereals will make a wreath of subtle colour and texture; arrange them so that their heads radiate out in natural curves.

Country-style wreath

The rich textures and colours of this wreath suit a background of natural wood. Radiating lines of pink helipterum (*Helipterum roseum*) are interspersed with the deep-red tones of love-lies-bleeding (*Amaranthus caudatus*) and sea lavender (*Limonium latifolium*) dyed pink. The striped seed heads of love-in-a-mist (*Nigella damascena*) add further texture to this tightly packed wreath.

Building up the arrangement

1 Make the circular base of the wreath with old-man's-beard stems. Wrap the thickest stems around each other about four times, forming a circle, then wrap the thinner parts of the stems over this. Vine prunings can also be used as the base.

2 Beech nuts, chestnuts, pine cones, and straw flowers need to be wired. To wire a pine cone, insert a wire between the scales of the cone and twine the shorter side of the wire around the longer.

3 Encircle the wreath with wired pine cones. Wire the chestnuts by pushing a stout needle through the centre to make a hole (see step 2). Wire the beech nuts in the same way as the pine cones.

4 Add groups of wired chestnuts to the wreath. Insert larch cones on their short stems, wired beech nuts, poppy seed heads, sea holly, wheat and oats to create the main body of the wreath.

5 Add helipterum, yellow, orange and red straw flowers, xeranthemum, yarrow and African daisies wherever there are holes which need filling.

6 You can leave the wreath as it is or, if you want to decorate it for Christmas, add some red artificial fruits and a large red ribbon to attach it to a door knocker.

Pine cone

Larch cone

Chestnut

Wheat

Xeranthemum

Beech nut

Poppy seed head

Yarrow

Sea holly

Straw flower

African daisy

Oats

Helipterum

Making decorations

Dried flowers can be used to make decorations for festive occasions. Floral balls, corn stars and "snowy" pine cones make unusual tree decorations and a brightly coloured chain of straw flowers can be hung on a tree or chimneypiece.

Floral balls

Straw flowers
Helichrysum bracteatum

Wire cutters

Stub wires

1 Push a wire through the centre of each flower, bending it over at the top and pulling it back through the flower head.

2 Wire five flowers, then arrange them so that they form a ball. Twist one of the wires around the others to secure them.

Corn stars

Wire cutters

Helipterum
Helipterum roseum

Wheat
Triticum vulgare

Ribbon

1 Cut the corn stalk between the nodes to make 10cm lengths, and strip off the outer sheath. Make a slit in one stalk and slip another through it at 90 degrees.

2 Continue until you have a star with as many points as you require. Take the ribbon and twist it under and over each prong of the corn to make a central disc.

Snow-covered pine cones

Pine cones
Pinus sp.

Washing powder

Stub wires

Wallpaper paste

1 Wire the pine cones as shown on p.109; dip each one into a solution of wallpaper paste until half of the cone is covered in paste. Take it out and shake well to remove the excess paste.

2 When the paste feels tacky, dip the cones in the washing powder, making sure that they receive an even covering of white. Shake off any excess and leave them to dry before hanging on the tree.

A chain of dried flowers

Crochet thread

Darning needle

Straw flowers
Helichrysum bracteatum

Cut a piece of thread to the length that you require. Thread the darning needle and push it through the centre of each straw flower. As you thread each flower, make sure that its front faces the back of the one it is next to on the chain; this will ensure a more even effect.

·5·

THE ROOM-BY-ROOM GUIDE

Pot plants and flowers have been used to decorate rooms since as early as the seventeenth century, but it was the start of the nineteenth century that saw a vast influx of exciting new plants into Europe. This was when the first painted-leaved begonias, paper flowers and a large array of tropical foliage plants arrived, and those who could afford them began to display them in their homes and conservatories. However, it is only recently that an enormous range of plants have become available to everyone.

The following pages feature the different rooms in the home and show how plants can be actively incorporated into the decorative scheme of a room, rather than featuring merely as added extras. Each room in the home has a different function and its practical use will determine the sort of environment, or *mini-climate*, it can offer to plants. Each room also has a specific mood and plants can be used to enhance this particular atmosphere.

The period of your house and the style of your room will determine the way in which you display your plants. A traditional interior calls for plants to complement an existing setting and, for instance, co-ordinate with fabrics or a collection of objects. A modern interior may call for plants to be used in an architectural way, as an integral part of the landscaping of the room.

Using plants and flowers in a room
These two milkbush plants (*Euphorbia tirucalli*) are used as a counterbalance to the large bookcase, and are of a scale to match it. They like the warm conditions of a living room and are easy to keep provided they are not overwatered. The vase of flowers on the table is part of an incidental coffee table grouping.

Mini-climates in the home

Throughout this book I have used a system of mini-climates to identify the different environments offered by the average home. Each plant featured in *The Plant Finder's Guide* has a mini-climate reference indicating its optimum levels of heat and light. This need not be interpreted too rigidly; a great attribute of many of our most popular house plants is their tolerance of a wide range of growing conditions.

Mini-climate advice may need to be adjusted in some cases. For instance, plants grown in the middle of a large industrial city receive a lower quality of light than that found in the country, so plants that thrive in the country in filtered sun may need direct sunlight to do well in the town. Day length varies with latitude, as does the outside air temperature.

Winter sunshine will not harm any plant grown in northern latitudes, and one that ideally needs filtered sun when the sun is high may need direct sunlight in winter, when the sun is weaker and days shorter.

Very few plants will suffer if placed in a slightly higher temperature than that recommended—as long as higher levels of humidity, and probably a little more water, are provided. Water plants less if you grow them cooler than the given mini-climate, and remember that it is much better to underwater than to overwater.

Very high summer temperatures often cannot be brought down without the aid of air conditioning units, which dry the air. A high level of humidity, adequate watering and frequent mist-spraying will all help to counteract this but, in any case, do not keep plants near an air conditioning unit.

When choosing plants to group together in the home, it is not enough merely to consider their decorative qualities; if the display is to remain attractive, you must also ensure that the mini-climate requirements of the plants are compatible. A plant which likes direct sunlight can be put quite happily with a plant that likes filtered light, but it is not sensible to group a tropical shade-lover with a temperate flowering plant.

Mini-climate 1
Warm, sunny

A *warm* room is one kept at a temperature of 15°-21°C—the range preferred by many popular house plants—but all plants can tolerate a slightly higher, or lower, level for a short time. A normal heating system prevents temperatures falling below 15°C.

A *sunny* position is one that gets direct, unobstructed sunlight for part of the day. A plant standing in or very near to a south-facing window is in a sunny position; those in east- or west-facing windows receive less sun each day.

White walls contribute to brightness of the room by reflecting light.

Hanging basket receiving direct light, but away from heat rising from cooker.

Two large windows provide plenty of direct sunlight for plants and flowers.

Steam rising from kettle increases humidity in the kitchen.

Timber ceiling absorbs heat, preventing sudden temperature changes.

Hot air rises, creating warm conditions for these tropical plants.

Bare brick wall catches light and has heat-retaining qualities.

Full-length windows provide the amount of light needed for this large, plant-filled room.

Mini-climate 2
Warm, filtered sun

A *warm* room is one kept at a temperature of 15°-21°C—the range preferred by many popular house plants—but all plants can tolerate a slightly higher, or lower, level for a short time. A normal heating system prevents temperatures falling below 15°C.

A room receiving *filtered sun* may face south, east or west (or south-east or south-west) but direct sunlight is baffled by translucent blinds or curtains, a tall building or leafy tree outside a window.

Sub-tropical plants thrive in these conditions.

Fine net curtain serves as filter for sunlight.

White fittings and large mirror over bath reflect light, greatly increasing room brightness.

Steam rising from bath provides high levels of relative humidity.

Leafy tree outside window serves to baffle sunlight.

Venetian blind needed to filter direct light by the coast or in lower latitudes.

Wall-mounted mirror reflects sunlight and increases brightness of the room.

Umbrella plant benefits from filtered sun and humidity of the bathroom.

Mini-climate 3
Warm, shady

A *warm* room is one kept at a temperature of 15°-21°C—the range preferred by many popular house plants—but all plants can tolerate a slightly higher, or lower, level for a short time. A normal heating system prevents temperatures falling below 15°C.

A *shady* position, in our definition, receives no direct or filtered sunlight, but does not have "poor" light (which is too low for healthy plant growth). Plants that like some shade can be grown away from the window in a room that is well-lit, or in the window of a room that is not well-lit.

Conditions are ideal for this thriving Swiss cheese plant.

Light filtered by trees outside and curtains.

There is not enough light in this corner of the room for healthy plant growth.

Dark floor absorbs light, reducing brightness in the room.

Curtain serves to reduce light entering large window.

Staghorn fern thrives when suspended out of direct light.

Dark furnishings absorb light reflected by pale floor and walls.

Large pot catches the drips from watering.

Mini-climate 4
Cool, sunny

A *cool* room is one kept at a temperature of 10°-15°C. This is the range preferred by many temperate zone plants, although plants from warmer climates may also be able to thrive—and temporary flowering house plants often live longer—at these temperature levels.

A *sunny* position is one that gets direct, unobstructed sunlight for part of the day. A plant standing in or very near to a south-facing window is in a sunny position; those in east- or west-facing windows receive less sun each day.

The large leaves of this banana plant require strong direct sunlight, but this plant can tolerate temperatures as low as 10°C.

Cool, airy landing with high ceiling is ideal environment for large-scale feature plants.

Spacious, open-plan staircase forms part of very large, unenclosed area of cool air.

Very large, unshaded window provides plenty of light for this assortment of plants.

Mini-climate 5
Cool, filtered sun

A *cool* room is one kept at a temperature of 10°-15°C. This is the range preferred by many temperate zone plants, although plants from warmer climates may also be able to thrive—and temporary flowering house plants often live longer—at these temperature levels.

A room receiving *filtered sun* may face south, east or west (or south-east or south-west) but direct sunlight is baffled by translucent blinds or curtains, or a tall building or leafy tree outside a window.

Creeper outside window prevents strong light being reflected from white wall.

Heavy draped curtains may be partially drawn to keep room temperature down.

This thriving ivy is shielded from the window by the mass of the arrangement.

Suitable plants for these conditions include Japanese fatsia.

This plant can be given the amount of shade it requires by the Venetian blind.

White walls and bed linen contribute to the cool environment by reflecting heat.

Full-length blinds filter the sunlight entering the room.

Living rooms 1

For most people, the living room is the show-piece of the home and the room in which most entertaining takes place. A considerable amount of money may be spent on furnishings, fabric and general decoration. Broadly speaking, living rooms may be traditional or modern, with elements of one style being adapted and combined with those of others. Plants provide a restful background and fresh colours, and should enhance the layout of the room without dominating it. Living rooms usually contain large items of furniture, and plants should be of an appropriate size to counterbalance them: one or two large ones usually look much better than a clutter of smaller ones. Arrangements

of cut or dried flowers and small-scale plants can be used for incidental groupings on coffee tables, side tables and shelves.

Position your plants away from radiators or open fires, in a place which provides adequate light for their specific needs, and where you can water them easily. It is very important that plants should not be in the way of people moving about, both for the convenience of the human inhabitants and the protection of the plants themselves. So, once you have decided on the type of plant and the scale you need, work its positioning into your basic plan making sure that plant and container are an integral part of your design concept.

Linear forms *below*
A classic modern interior of oriental simplicity, composed of linear forms —the table, sofas and pictures—and muted colours without patterns. The focal point of the room is the arrangement of dried twigs on the table, which is counter-balanced by the ornament and bonsai. The large rainbow plants (*Dracaena marginata*) soften what might otherwise be too spartan a room.

Black and white
The placement of the furniture in this severe, modern interior is governed by the position of the chimney breast and the view of the terrace. The plants used inside are very low-key, but nonetheless link the two spaces effectively. It is interesting that the designer felt that this uncompromisingly robust interior should be softened by a trailing tradescantia (*Tradescantia* sp.). The all-white flower arrangement is in keeping with the overall colour scheme, and picks up the white of the floor and walls in an area where black predominates.

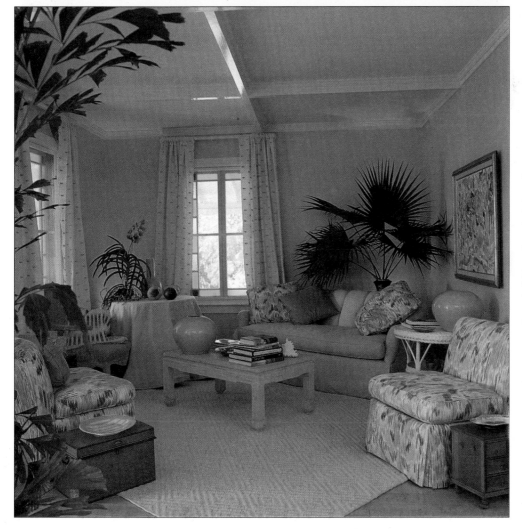

Pattern and colour
A softer decorative look permeates this room with much use of fabric in the full drop of the curtains and the table covering. Bright colours and patterns call for large plant forms that will accompany, but not dominate, decoration. Behind the sofa stands a European fan palm (*Chamaerops humilis*) and part of a fishtail palm (*Caryota mitis*) can be seen in the foreground. The central feature is the low coffee table with its clutter of books and the large bowl, whose shape is cleverly echoed by the smaller bowls on the corner table, and contrasted with the curving leaves of an impressive orchid (*Cymbidium* sp.) in flower.

Living rooms 2

Rustic style
In this cottage living room the overall effect is cluttered and without a single dominant feature. Spectacular tropical species would be out of character, but small-leaved temperate plants are used to good effect, as are the bowl of pot-pourri and a bird's nest in the foreground. Rustic wooden furniture, botanical prints and floral patterns are all in keeping with the gentle mood of this type of decoration.

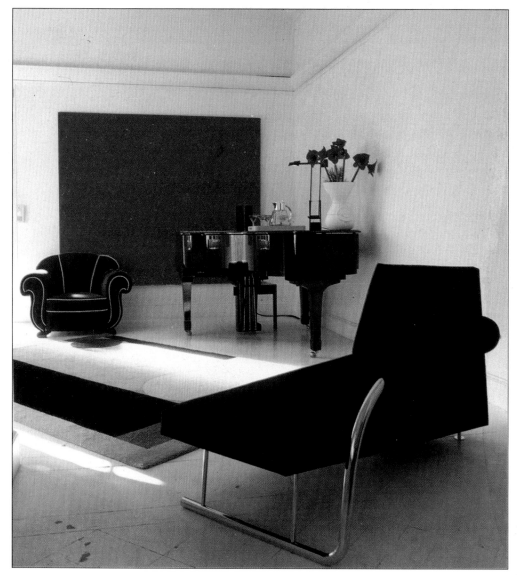

Bold colour contrast *left*
Compared to the room above, the overall impression here is one of severity, although all the furniture is, in fact, highly decorative. The strong colour contrast of black, red and white is brought together in the patterned carpet, and given a final flamboyant touch with the addition of the vase of huge cut amaryllis (*Hippeastrum* sp.) which echo the red of the canvas.

Low-key *right*
The blinds in this room give it a soft lighting effect which creates a tranquil mood not disturbed by heavy patterns or assertive colours. The gentle green foliage of the bamboo (*Arundinaria* sp.) is in keeping with the relaxed atmosphere. The cut flowers and small house plant are additional features which serve as minor points of interest.

Size, shape and colour co-ordination *right*
The large leaves of the African hemp (*Sparmannia africana*) are in accord with the geometric wall patterning behind the plant. The foliage of the foreground Kentia palm (*Howea belmoreana*) is similar to the leaf shape in the painting, and the soft colours of the room are repeated in the table arrangement of cut flowers.

Horizontal lines *below*
Downlighters pick out the colours of the simple furniture and patterned fabric, echoed by the flowers, plants and objects. The bold horizontal patterning of blinds and floor unify the diverse points of interest.

Living rooms 3

Part of creating a comfortable, inviting living space is building up one or more attractive seating areas which draw the visitor into the room. Whether these are in the corners of the room, at one end, or in alcoves, window bays and recesses, house plants can play a large part in making the most of them. Plants can highlight a fabric, either by forming a total contrast or by echoing colours and patterns in the curtains or soft furnishings. Alternatively, the shape and form of plants can enhance and soften these settings—gracefully overhanging a sofa or armchair perhaps, complementing a picture, or providing a solid background for a group of cane or wicker chairs in a corner.

Making a feature of the ceiling *right*
Distinctive roof supports are something of a feature in this room, and the shiny spotlights are certainly there to be noticed. So two trailing plants set up high enhance the effect and save space in the room.

Sofa in a window bay
above
A tall golden-feather palm (*Chrysalidocarpus lutescens*), arching its delicate fronds over the sofa, makes the whole area more inviting. Light filtered from the window gives the plant a strong silhouette. The two other house plants are a small parlour palm (*Chamaedorea elegans* "Bella") and white arum lily (*Zantedeschia aethiopica*).

Modern sofa setting
right
This cushion seating is backed by a window in a modern living room. The effect is clean and sharp but, at the same time, softened by the arrangement of creamy-white hydrangeas (*Hydrangea* sp.) on the left.

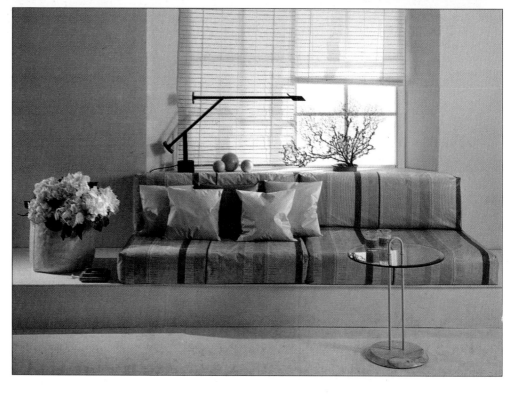

Making a plant grouping for a corner of a room

Here, I have set out to compose a little period piece to accompany the easy chair and draped curtain. The site is a corner of a living room decorated in neutral shades, next to an east-facing window. Since the room is not in constant use, and therefore not always heated, I needed plants suited to a cool room. When you are aiming to create a particular atmosphere like this, you may find that certain of your possessions suggest themselves as "props".

The setting and overall styling
below and right

This is an attractive corner, but the décor shades are muted and monotone, and something bright and colourful is needed to guide the eye towards the large window. An arrangement of plants or flowers will look well on the graceful occasional table. As the room is not used very often, an arrangement of potted plants will enhance the corner for longer than an arrangement of cut flowers. The arrangement needs to be large, without dominating the corner. To continue the period feel, I added a pair of Victorian dolls and a small footstool. The red of the footstool and the velvet cushion picks up the exact red of the cyclamen.

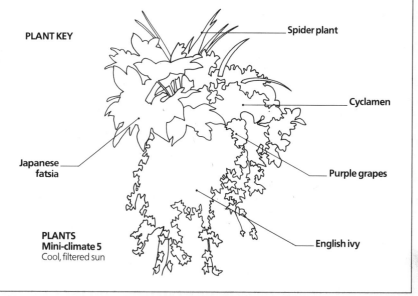

Making up the arrangement

I used a plastic tray in which to stand the various pots, so that the plants can be watered according to their individual needs. I planned the arrangement around the two cyclamen (*Cyclamen persicum* hybrids), making sure they were offset by the solid greenery of the Japanese fatsia (*Fatsia japonica*). Then I added a spiky green spider plant (*Chlorophytum comosum*) to provide outline interest, and lightened the whole effect with trailing stems of variegated ivy (*Hedera helix* hybrids) to mask the edge of the table. Finally, just for fun, I included a bunch of grapes, and these actually have the effect of "lifting" the green/red/beige scheme.

PLANT KEY

Spider plant

Cyclamen

Japanese fatsia

Purple grapes

English ivy

PLANTS
Mini-climate 5
Cool, filtered sun

Living rooms 4
Focal point

Sometimes, plants are allowed to become the dominant feature of a room. Whereas strong patterning and bold colours tend to obscure vegetation by competing with it visually, simple fabrics, plain coloured walls and the long, low lines of modern furniture all serve to draw attention to house plants or flower arrangements.

Bold leaves *below*
A plant with small leaves would look weak in this airy setting, but the massive fiddle leaf fig (*Ficus lyrata*) looks superb and automatically becomes the focal point of the room. Such a sizeable plant easily draws attention from the large studio windows.

Small-scale setting *right*
This ponytail (*Beaucarnea recurvata*) is a fairly dominant plant which has been used here with a table and a lamp to make an interesting group. The pebbles on the table and floor help to link the treelike plant to its setting.

On a grand scale *right*
The imposing banquette is surmounted by an arching Kentia palm (*Howea belmoreana*), providing a magnificent central feature. The palm's graceful lines are echoed by the pair of white sails (*Spathiphyllum* "Clevelandii") on the console table, and combine with the panelled door and ornate coving to make this room evocative of past grandeur.

Splash of colour *left*
Almost minimalist in style, this dark-coloured furniture makes a restrained setting for an arrangement of larkspur (*Delphinium consolida*) in a glass vase. Thus the simple, colourful display immediately becomes a focal point.

Contrasting textures *right*
Here, the arrangement is one of scale, line and textural contrast. The hard geometry of the dark-coloured beams is emphasized by the soft hanging English ivy (*Hedera helix* hybrids) and the graceful clumps of the umbrella plant (*Cyperus alternifolius*).

Living rooms 5
Table-top ideas

In any style of living room there will usually be side tables and coffee tables which can be made into smaller focal points of interest. Plants and flowers should relate to other objects, such as ornaments, books or lamps, which may in themselves suggest the choice of a plant or group of flowers.

A question of scale *right*
A small plant would be swamped by this bold interior, but the magnificent painted nettle (*Coleus blumei*) is large enough to demand attention. The red markings of the foliage pick up the colour of the sofa.

Mellow tones *above*
A basket of dried flowers and grasses blends in with the warm colours of leather-bound books and polished wood, bringing a touch of summer to a library setting.

Graceful lines *above*
The graceful curved neck of this decoy swan is echoed in the lines of the tulip stems and the shape of the central pot. The soft colours match those of the sofa.

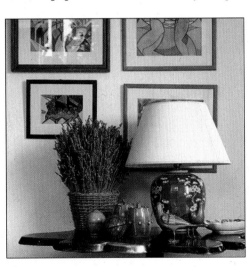

Contrasting forms *above*
The basket of dried lavender and the cluster of spherical wooden objects combine with the dominant, oriental lamp base to form a pleasing group.

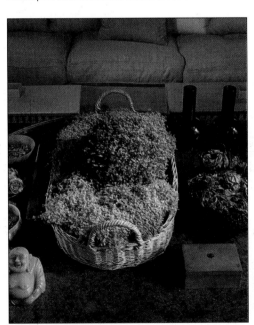

A dominant feature *above*
Mind-your-own-business plants (*Soleirolia soleirolii*) arranged in a basket make a dominant central display that needs to be surrounded by low-key furnishings that do not vie for attention.

Imposing order *left*
In this eclectic mixture of furnishings, an eye-catching arrangement of Swiss cheese plant leaves (*Monstera deliciosa*) and foxtail lilies (*Eremurus* sp.) serves to unify the diverse features.

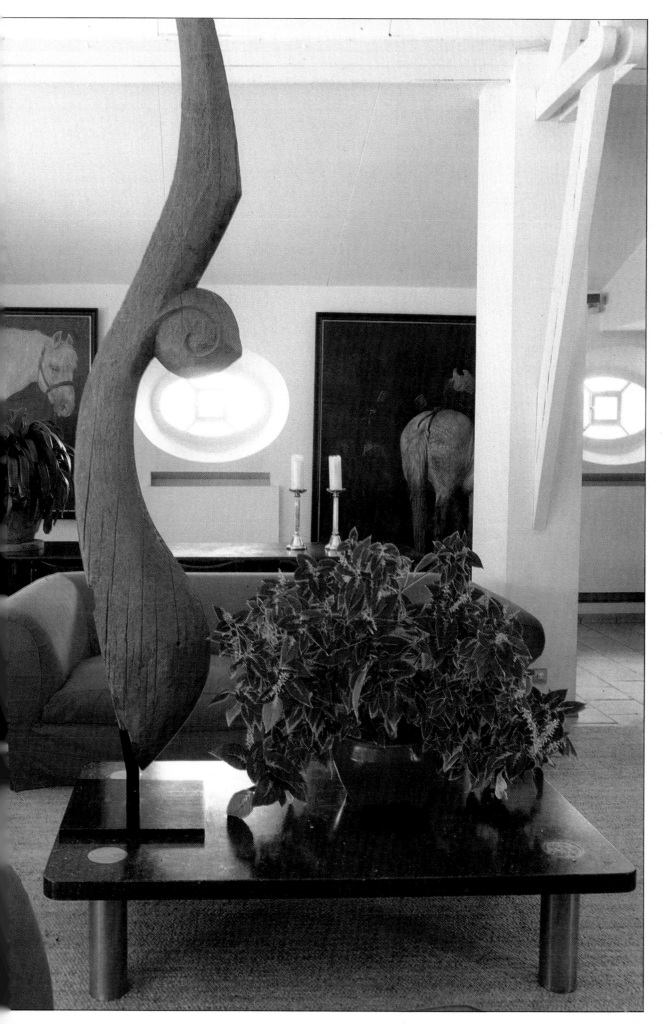

Living rooms 6

Although designed expressly for putting things on, shelves and mantelpieces do not usually promote the long-term well-being of plants. Lack of space and light means that arrangements of cut or dried flowers are usually the best choice, or, perhaps, flowering annual plants or bulbs.

Shelves of cacti *left*
Because of their simple, compact shapes, cacti look good ranged on shelves. Moreover, a set-up like this alcove—with an overhead light source, backing mirror and glass shelves—will help to maximize the impact of the group. The overhead lighting has the effect of highlighting any fluffy down or dramatic spikes on the cacti. Notice how glass shelves look green in cross section (due to refraction), which enhances the plant display—try for a similar effect with a collection of tumbling greenhouse plants, or a collection of ferns, making sure there is sufficient light.

Using dried flowers
above
Five bunches of dried flowers provide a lower-edge "frame" for this large over-mantel mirror. They form part of the "ordered clutter" of objects and ornaments around and on the marble mantelpiece. When displaying dried flowers for any length of time, blow the dust off them occasionally.

Using wild flowers *right*
Wild flowers are easy on the eye and, in general, have softer-hued flower heads than garden varieties. Too strong an arrangement of plants in this gothic setting would have been out of character, but two light, feathery bunches of wild flowers do not detract from the delicate tracery of the wall decoration. Beneath this shelf is a radiator, which should be turned off when any fresh flowers are displayed on the shelf. Wild flowers, especially, wilt very quickly if not kept in cool conditions. (Grow your own rather than picking from the wild.)

Making wreath decorations for mantelpieces

An open fireplace easily becomes the focal point of a room. But when there is no fire lit, a mantel decoration can counteract the empty void below.

The setting *right*
This dried wreath succeeds in echoing the style and natural colours of the fireplace and the remainder of the décor—the books, wooden decoy ducks and an old straw hat. The wreath is positioned off-centre and is balanced by the objects on the left.

PLANT KEY

Old-man's beard stems
Bracken
Straw flower
Oats
Bells-of-Ireland
Lady's mantle
Wheat
Baby's breath
Yellow statice

Decoration for a special occasion *right*
This idea for a festive occasion includes fresh flowers, so do not light the fire, unless the blooms only need to last a few hours for a party. The two swags are made of white-painted magnolia (*Magnolia* sp.) leaves, pampas grass (*Cortaderia* sp.) and lemons, wired to a base of crumpled netting, which is filled with damp moss into which yellow chrysanthemums (*Chrysanthemum* sp.) have been pushed.

Living rooms 7
Plants and pictures

Various styles of painting will suggest different types of display; by using plants or flowers in conjunction with a picture, you can recreate a still life with fresh material or pick up the patterns, textures or colours in a painting. Each composition may be a little set piece on its own or, if you are working with a large painting, it may dominate the whole room.

Old and new *above*
Lilies (*Lilium auratum*) and Transvaal daisies (*Gerbera jamesonii*) in a modern vase make a humorous contrast with a traditional still life.

Linking textures *above*
There is a textural harmony between the painting, the table inlay and the mottled leaves of the leopard plant (*Ligularia* sp.).

Picking up a colour *above*
It is colour that unifies this triangular mantelpiece display—the yellow of the painted sun is echoed by that of the lilies (*Lilium* hybrids).

Using a dominant colour *right*
Colour again provides the association here, between the flowers in the painting and those in the vase. The vibrant yellow stands out in a monochromatic setting.

Dining rooms 1

It is not easy to be specific about current styles of interior decoration for any room, as there are so many styles about and the dividing lines between them are often not exact.

Styles for dining rooms show the same range as living rooms. One of the most popular current styles is based on fabrics inspired by eighteenth- and nineteenth-century prototypes and casual country furniture. Temperate plants, fresh garden flowers and dried flowers will all enhance this type of room. Offshoots of this style are the informal American colonial look and an eclectic ethnic style based on imports from the Far East and India. Another style of interior decoration has its origins in industrial high-tech, which first appeared in the late 1970s. It still has a utilitarian look, but one which has been adapted by popular chain stores to furnish a sophisticated urban market. Large, architectural plants used with this décor continue the austere effect. Another style currently in vogue is a softer look, full of pastel colours and the use of drapery, which recalls the mood of the 1920s.

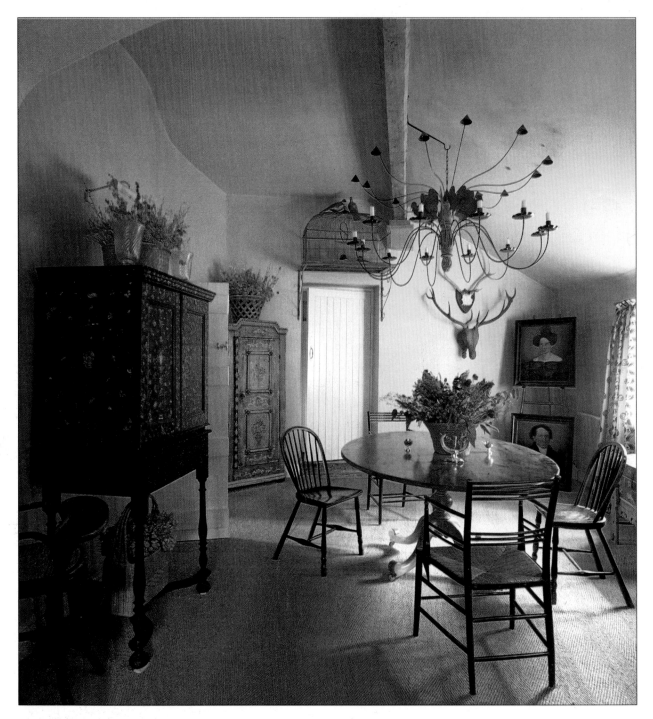

Country style *above*
This dining room epitomises country style in its furniture, floor covering and small-print curtain fabric. Large baskets of dried flowers are in keeping with the rustic mood and their subdued colours harmonize with the rich, dark colours of the antique furniture.

Softening sharp angles *right*
The wiry, angular shapes of the lamp and chairs in this eating area are reminiscent of popular furniture in the 1950s. Their harshness is softened by the large leaves of the avocado pear plant (*Persea americana*).

Hard-edged sophistication *above*
This glass table increases the impact of a flower arrangement, and the shape of the dining chairs is repeated in the curved glass bowls. Red tulips (*Tulipa* sp.) contrast spectacularly with the black furniture.

Using a mantelpiece *above*
A softer, period look with a froth of baby's breath (*Gypsophila paniculata*) as a central feature on the polished table. Mind-your-own-business plants (*Soleirolia soleiroleii*) line the mantelpiece.

Dining rooms 2

Opulence on a small scale
right
This attic dining room, although small, has a baronial feel. The tapestry-covered dining chairs and gleaming silver table accessories are complemented by two large, bushy crotons (*Codiaeum variegatum pictum*). The predominant colours of the decoration —red and green—are repeated in the leaves of the plants.

Large-scale dining space
below
This interesting, airy setting is overhung by a footbridge on the upper level. At one end of the dining table, a luxuriant mass of the cut-leaved finger plant (*Philodendron bipinnatifidum*) and ferns is a fittingly dramatic backdrop. The plants look equally attractive viewed from above.

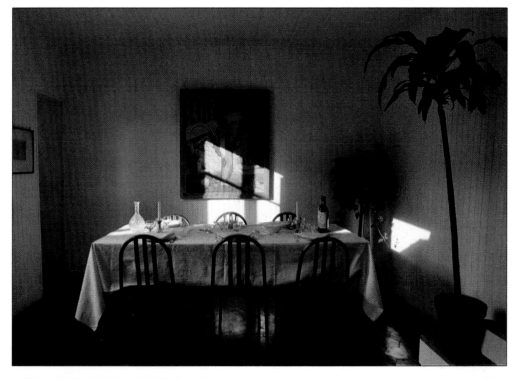

Successful decoration with two plants *left*
The spectacular palm dominating one corner of this dining room catches your eye immediately. But the smaller bushy foliage plant, cleverly placed on a lower level, has the effect of drawing the eye down and towards the table which, after all, is the focal point of the room.

Thematic table setting *below*
For a special occasion, display cut flowers or flowering house plants which match your china. Here, yellow and white flowers echo the colours of the table mats and plates, while a huge African hemp (*Sparmannia africana*) brings fresh greenery into the room.

Dining rooms 3

The focal point of a dining room must be its table. Floral centrepieces should be in the mood of the table setting but should not impede conversation across the table. Just a few flower heads floating in water will make an attractive display, particularly if they complement the colours of the food. Other arrangements in the room should not distract attention from the centrepiece.

An elegant still life *left*

A charmingly simple still life composition on a dining room side table which is not too demanding on the eye. The arrangement is enlivened by the addition of a regal lily (*Lilium regale*) in a narrow vase.

Echoing floral motifs *right*

Even without its centrepiece, this dining room setting conjures up a mood of summer with its vibrant colours and abundance of greenery. An ivy patterned wallpaper, a floral tablecloth and two weeping figs (*Ficus benjamina*) on either side of a fireplace set the scene for a stunning central arrangement of red trumpet honeysuckle (*Lonicera brownii*) mixed with English ivy (*Hedera helix* hybrids) in a basket.

Co-ordinating colours *right*

In certain situations artificial flowers are perfectly acceptable, and perhaps the dining table is one of them. The chance to recreate a summer arrangement in midwinter is always welcome. Here, the bright colours provide a strong contrast to the predominantly white table setting and furniture. The mixture of orange, white and purple flowers and green foliage picks up the colours in the floral pattern of the china perfectly.

Kitchens 1

Kitchens can be of two types: working galley kitchens and kitchens to live in. By definition, the worktop surfaces are practical and do not lend themselves to too much decoration—add to this the hazards of steam and constantly changing temperatures and you may not have ideal growing conditions. However, some plants will prefer the added humidity and warmth of the kitchen environment. Arrangements of dried flowers, and bowls of gourds, fruit and vegetables, can be most attractive as long as they do not impede the cook. Window-ledges can be utilized, but plants must be protected from the fall in temperatures at night if there is no double glazing. Plants can be displayed in hanging baskets, but only in places where it is easy to water them frequently.

Period feel *below*
Something of a period mood has been created here with copper pans, wooden spoons and basketware—all visually strong in themselves. However, the white tulips (*Tulipa* sp.) are the focal point.

Strong primaries *left*
Cut chrysanthemums (*Chrysanthemum* hybrids) make a bright addition to the edible strawberries, lemons, peppers and tomatoes which complement the strong primary colour scheme of this streamlined kitchen unit. The location of the display makes imaginative use of the concealed, split-level lighting.

Practical and decorative *left*
The typical type of clutter one might expect to find on the wide sill of a country kitchen. Drying herbs hang in a swathe above the window, their presence serving both a practical and a decorative use. The bowl of fruit and the cyclamen (*Cyclamen persicum* hybrids) on the sill itself contribute to the overall impression of a warm, welcoming room and a place of work.

Casual and homely *left*
This breakfast area is enlivened by an informal arrangement of garden flowers, foliage and grasses in a jug, and a sweetheart plant (*Philodendron scandens*) trails attractively over the shelves which house a collection of American blue-and-white spatterware. These plants like a warm and humid atmosphere, as their natural habitat is the tropical rain forest.

Square patterns *right*
A high-tech kitchen which has ingeniously utilized squared wire mesh for hanging utensils above the sink, and repeated the motif as a support for a mosaic of climbers against the window. These are positioned in such a way as to benefit from the light of the window whilst not interfering with the work of the cook. The square pattern is repeated in the wall and floor coverings, but the angular style of the kitchen is softened by the presence of the plants.

Utilizing a high ceiling *right*
The ceiling of a large kitchen which does not get too steamy makes an ideal place to hang and dry summer flowers and herbs. When the ceiling is high, bunches of flowers can make the room seem less bare and are in no danger of getting in the way of the cook. In this country kitchen, baskets, rattan blinds and a bird cage complement the simple pine furniture and complete the styling.

Kitchens 2

In a compact kitchen, the chances are that you will not want any plants cluttering up your valuable worktops. Yet it seems a pity to do without greenery, and there are several ways of solving the problem practically and safely, while keeping plants off surfaces and away from kitchen appliances.

Making a feature of a plain wall *right*
People hang pans and utensils in the kitchen, and there is no reason why you cannot hang up plants. A plastic-coated grid attached to the wall makes an attractive base to which you can fix a selection of small potted herbs so that they are to hand when you are cooking.

Decorating an eating area
above
This kitchen eating area is en-livened by an Algerian ivy (*Hedera canariensis* hybrids). The simple white décor focuses attention on the green foliage.

A kitchen corner *below*
Several house plants enliven this kitchen, but none of them occu-pies a working surface. The luxuriant Boston fern (*Nephrolepis exaltata* "Bostoniensis") is sus-pended by a chain from the ceiling.

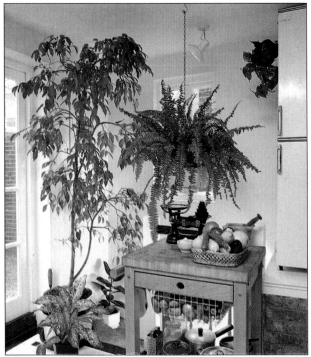

Decorating a kitchen dresser

A collection of blue-and-white china looks very appealing ranged on the dresser of a traditional country kitchen. But perhaps the scene is a little stark. Dresser shelves are quite narrow and normally used for display, rather than as functional shelves for much-used kitchen items. So a dresser is an ideal "showcase" for plants, provided you observe the rules of lighting and watering, and change the plants when necessary.

The setting *below*
The areas of white wall behind the dresser look rather austere and would benefit from some "filling in". But introducing a random collection of plants would interrupt the subtle styling of the kitchen.

PLANT KEY

PLANTS   Christmas cherry
Mini-climate 4
Cool, sunny

Making up the arrangement
As a solution, I selected five plants of the same variety—the Christmas cherry (*Solanum capsicastrum*). Its orange berries provide a colour contrast, without being too distracting to the eye, and complement the china collection.

The overall styling *above*
Within the country-style setting of this kitchen interior, the Christmas cherries, with their bright berries and small, pretty leaves, warm and soften what could easily be too severe a room-scheme.

Looking after the plants *left*
This useful little winter berrying plant, which has insignificant flowers earlier in the year, lasts up to two months. Given a coolish interior, it appreciates a degree of humidity and should be misted every day or so. Since the dresser does not offer the direct light these plants prefer, move them to a sunny position for several hours a day.

Bedrooms 1

Your bedroom is a highly personal part of your house and one where you can indulge your most imaginative ideas about decoration. An arrangement of fresh or dried flowers in a guest room is a thoughtful touch, too. Yet displays must still be practically planned. If space is a problem, consider fixing up a hanging arrangement in the form of a wreath or garland, or using a pedestal to support a plant or flower arrangement in one corner.

Balancing vibrant colours *below*
This unusual bedroom is decorated in bright colours and excitingly lit. A stylish combination of artificial white tulips in two large, yellow vases and a tall euphorbia (*Euphorbia pseudocactus*) help reinforce the whole effect.

Art-deco style bedroom *right*
A large house plant sits on a beautiful ceramic jardiniere, totally in keeping with the collection of art-deco paraphernalia and the floral design of the window blind. Place pedestals like this where they will not be knocked over.

Creating a romantic mood *left*
A nostalgic bedroom is reflected in this floor-length mirror decorated with garlands of dried flowers. The bed's brass corner poles are adorned with ribbons and bunches of artificial rosebuds.

Maintaining a spacious feel *below*
A magnificent weeping fig (*Ficus benjamina*) stands in a sunny corner of this airy bedroom. Although large, the plant is positioned well out of the way and adds to, rather than detracts from, the feeling of lightness and space.

Bedrooms 2

Complementing a picture *above*
The chest of drawers provides a solid support for a single cineraria (*Senecio cruentus* hybrids) which subtly reinforces the subject of the picture hanging directly above it.

A conservatory corner *above*
Sunlight flooding through a bedroom window illuminates this collection of plants. A large fuchsia (*Fuchsia* sp.) contributes to the "conservatory" feel.

A place for artificial flowers *left*
Occasionally, people may be physically averse to plants or fresh flowers in the room where they sleep. Instead, try an artificial, but informal, decoration such as this enchanting basket filled with artificial forget-me-nots. Country-style bedrooms can be enhanced by using painted or stencilled baskets as containers for flower arrangements.

A romantic bedroom *right*
A vase of cut lilac (*Syringa* sp.) glimpsed through a mirror fills a softly pretty bedroom with fragrance. The lilac complements the lace-covered pillows and delicate pink-and-white wallpaper. Always place bedroom vases somewhere safe, where they will not be knocked over while you dress or make the bed. Use other fragrant flowers and plants as they come into season.

Co-ordinating colour scheme *right*
In a carefully put-together period room, a tall vase of dried Chinese lanterns (*Physalis franchetii* "Gigantea") stands on the mantelpiece, helping to make a focal point of the fireplace area and the cosy coal fire. The green and orange lanterns co-ordinate perfectly with the colour scheme of the bold designs on the wardrobe, fabric and wallcovering.

Bathrooms 1

The relaxing surroundings of a bathroom can form a stylish setting for some of your more striking plants, and matching containers to the bathroom fittings ensures a successful display.

Provided that they have good light, bathrooms come nearest to providing the ideal growing conditions for a number of the most popular house plants. They are generally warm places and, two or three times a day, the air becomes saturated with moisture. Quite a high level of humidity can continue for some time after someone has taken a bath, while damp towels dry out and moisture on surfaces and fabrics gradually evaporates. Even if obscured glass is fitted to windows, there is little light loss; direct sunlight becomes bright, filtered light.

A "jungle-look" corner *above*
In this Victorian-style bathroom, an empty corner provides a good home for a large Swiss cheese plant (*Monstera deliciosa*), which offsets the white, antique bath. This plant loves warmth and humidity, so it is an ideal bathroom plant.

Oriental-style bathroom *left*
There is a Japanese feel about this bathroom, with its clean black and white surfaces. The fine, filigree foliage of an umbrella plant (*Cyperus alternifolius*), which needs to be grown in a constantly wet medium, is shown to perfect advantage on the windowsill.

A fragrant bathroom *right*
An elegant bathroom with potted gardenias (*Gardenia* sp.) standing on the bath surround. Their perfume will dominate the bathroom and they thrive in a moist atmosphere.

A temporary display *below*
Although you will need to change a plant such as this African lily (*Agapanthus campanulatus*) every three weeks or so (there being no natural light), it makes a beautiful addition to the bathroom.

Cut flowers in the bathroom *left*
The fresh pink, green and white colour scheme of this bathroom is picked up by the cut flowers at the window and on the edge of the bath.

The small bathroom *right*
Mirrors are a superb device for increasing the apparent size of a small bathroom. Green plants used as decoration will have double the effect. Here, a pair of stick yuccas (*Yucca elephantipes*) add the final touch to a smart, masculine bathroom.

Bathrooms 2

Although space may be at a premium in the bathroom, different styles of plant decoration are possible. There is a "cluttered" look, with various small plants appearing among the soap and toothpaste; or, for a more dramatic effect, just one or two large plants can be used.

Using shelves *right*
Ferns like the warm and humid conditions of a bathroom, and small shelves above a basin surround make a suitable home for various potted specimens including a bird's nest fern (*Asplenium nidus*).

Country-style simplicity *above*
In this traditional, stencilled bathroom, a wall shelf-unit is balanced by a plant arrangement either side of the head of the bath. The rather bare, bleached feel of the room lends itself to plant decoration.

Real and painted *left*
Two exquisite viridiflora tulips (*Tulipa* sp.) stand in an elegant vase against a mural which continues the floral theme of this bathroom.

A flower-filled bathroom *above*
The design of the blind fabric has been continued on the walls with hand-painted primulas and rose sprigs. Fresh flowers and potted plants add to the effect.

Displaying airplants in a bathroom window recess

Airplants make a fascinating display in a bathroom. Most bromeliads are native to the tropical regions of the Americas, where they cling to rocks or trees. Their roots are used merely for support—the plants survive on moisture in the air, so spray them regularly with rain water or distilled water.

Making up the arrangement *right*
Single airplants are difficult to display well; the best approach is to mass them together. A collection of shells and coral provides decorative support for the plants and gives them an underwater look suitable for the bathroom.

The setting *below*
Airplants like the moist air in a bathroom and, despite their delicate appearance, are very tolerant. This well-lit window recess with glass shelves makes an ideal setting.

PLANT KEY

Tillandsia butzii

Tillandsia bulbosa
Tillandsia ionantha

Tillandsia ionantha
Tillandsia argentea

Tillandsia bulbosa

Tillandsia juncea

PLANTS
Mini-climate1
Warm, sunny

Details of the airplant arrangement *above left and right*
Mounted on coral, shells, pieces of wood, cork or minerals, airplants have a magical feel. Here, the delicate grey-green leaves contrast with the strong shapes of the shells and coral. The glass shelves allow light to filter between the plants and reflect the pearly sheen of the shells. Tuck or gently tie the plants into the shells, or use a special airplant fixative; in time they will probably attach their roots to the support.

Halls and entrances 1

Front doors and entrance halls are the first areas you see on entering the house. Decorated attractively, they can be warm and welcoming, drawing the visitor into the heart of the house. So first impressions are important, yet halls and lobbies often have poor light and fluctuating temperatures. You will need to plan displays for the hall using the most tolerant house plants. Cast-iron plants (*Aspidistra elatior*) and mother-in-law's-tongues (*Sansevieria trifasciata*) are good choices. Dried flowers and foliage are particularly useful for displaying in any hall or entrance with a lighting problem. People pass through the hall at standing height, so scale up plants accordingly and avoid using trailing plants in awkward places. Any plant which is constantly brushed against will inevitably become damaged.

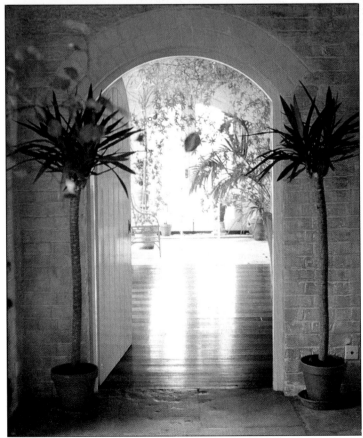

Decorations for a large entrance hall *above*
The plain brick walls of this hall are softened by a mass of dried beech leaves (*Fagus sylvatica*) whose warm tones harmonize with the mellow brick. Two stick yuccas (*Yucca elephantipes*) stand either side of the door, and a bowl of gourds relieves the expanse of bare table-top.

Framing a doorway *left*
Two sturdy yuccas frame the doorway leading into the conservatory beyond. Tumbling light-green foliage makes an inviting transition between the two rooms.

An impressive focal point *right*
A magnificent staghorn fern (*Platycerium bifurcatum*) dominates the centre of an entrance hall. A large pot standing underneath catches drips from watering and prevents people from walking too close to the plant and damaging it.

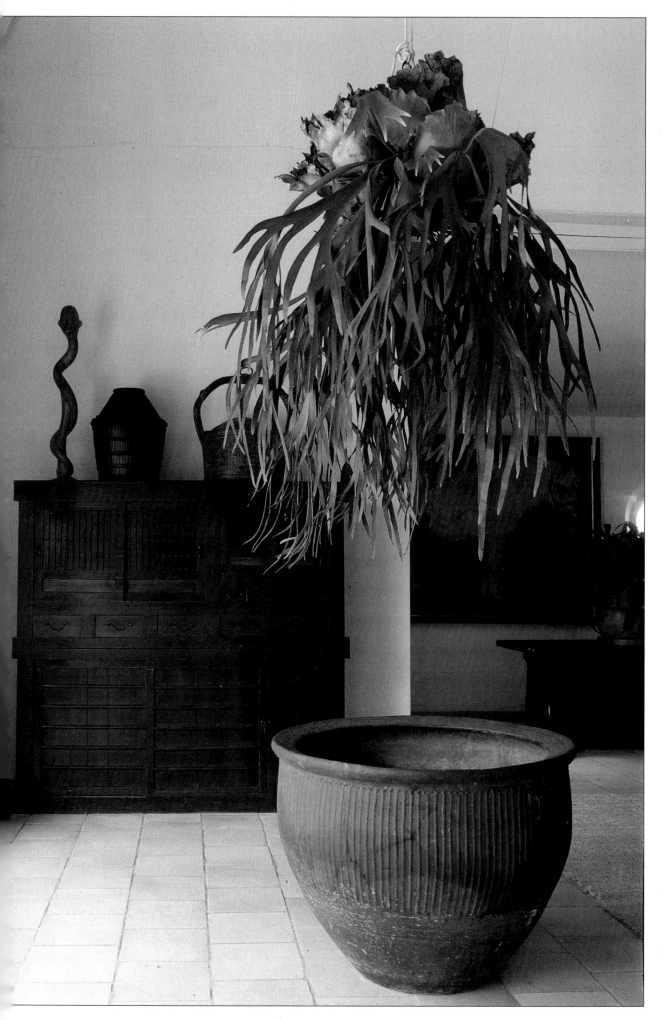

Halls and entrances 2

If you have a hall large enough to furnish, you will have the opportunity to go for maximum effect in your plant and floral arrangements. However, even in a hall which is little more than a passageway, there are several devices you can use to make sure your decorations do not go unnoticed by people passing through.

If space is a real problem, make up a swag using wire netting with dried flower heads entwined in it. Wreaths are also pretty and festive, especially at Christmas.

Using a mirror *above*
A huge mirror placed behind the side table doubles the effect of the two plants—a dragon tree (*Dracaena marginata*) and a glossy grape ivy (*Cissus rhombifolia*). Also, the mirror enlarges the apparent size of the hall and reflects light on to the plants.

Using a shelf *right*
A pretty marble shelf bracketed to the wall provides the perfect surface for an arrangement of dried roses and grasses. Two small vases containing more roses stand on either side of the central glass vase, and a tall mirror makes the most of the arrangement.

Scaling up to fill a space
left
Because it is likely to be cooler than a living room, the hall is often a good place to site an arrangement of fresh-cut flowers to help them last longer. Here, a large, informal arrangement of day lilies (*Hemerocallis* sp.) and fennel (*Foeniculum* sp.) helps to fill an area of bare whitewashed wall in a country cottage hall. The flowers, which stand on a beautiful black inlaid chest, pick up the warm colours in the furnishing fabric, helping to make the hall cosy and welcoming.

Making a winter arrangement for a hall

In a rather dull corner of this hall, in front of some pine doors opening to a seldom-used cupboard, I sited a winter arrangement of red and yellow cut flowers, including berries, early flowering blossom and evergreen foliage to soften the effect. I used a mixing bowl and a large block of plastic foam 15cm higher than the container.

The setting *above*
This corner of the hall is well lit from the side and gives easy access for replacement of water. The honey-coloured stripped pine makes a pleasing background for the arrangement whose triangular outline helps to soften the vertical lines of the area. As the pedestal is turned slightly to one side, emphasis is drawn towards the light source.

Making up the arrangement

A triangular arrangement
To outline the shape, I used bold mahonia sprays, and then I added the large chrysanthemums—yellow at the outer edge, deepening to bronze-red at the core. More sprays of jasmine, freesias and evergreen foliage added dimension.

FLOWER KEY

Crab apple

Chrysanthemum

Winter jasmine

Mahonia

Freesia

Spider chrysanthemum

Cotoneaster

Narcissus

Japanese fatsia leaves

Persian ivy

Stairs and stairwells

The staircase may not be the first place you think of for displaying plants but, if you follow the principles outlined for halls and entrances, the results can be effective. Stairs and stairwells can be cold and draughty, so select the hardier house plants.

The stairs themselves should normally be kept free of obstructions, but there may be space on a wide turn of the stairs for a large specimen plant or a collection of smaller ones. If the staircase turns round a central well, and receives some daylight, try placing a tall, upright plant or a climber in the otherwise redundant space.

Landing windowsills and skylights at the top of the stairs are two possible light sources which can help plants thrive. Large hanging baskets filled with easy-care plants such as tradescantias (*Tradescantia* sp.), spider plants (*Chlorophytum* sp.) and Swedish ivies (*Plectranthus australis*), can be secured to the framework of a skylight. The plants will soon cascade impressively, several metres down the stairwell.

Making a feature of a landing *left*
This landing halfway up a flight of stairs is well lit and deep enough for a large display of plants. Furniture, pictures and ornaments are all of the period and the twin vases of tall pampas grasses (*Cortaderia* sp.) enhance the Victorian flavour, as does trailing greenery framing the lower portion of the window.

A landing on the grand scale *right*
This imposing period staircase leading on to a wide, sunny landing is a fine enough setting for the massive foliage of a banana plant (*Musa* sp.). The huge bay window means a selection of large plants can be housed on the landing, and the backlighting from the sun shining through the different leaf shapes creates a dramatic effect.

Making use of a skylight
Suspended plants dominate this small Edwardian landing, which is toplit from the large skylight. The arrangement of green plants, which include spider plants (*Chlorophytum* sp.) and ferns (*Nephrolepis* sp.), is reflected in a wall mirror, increasing the "cluttered" effect which is in keeping with the style of the period.

A cascade of greenery
This cool, wide stone staircase is filled with hanging plants, but has an open, spacious feel. A magnificent ladder fern (*Nephrolepis cordifolia*) dominates the foot of the stairs, while great swathes of grape ivy (*Cissus rhombifolia*) hang from the upper balcony and are silhouetted by the toplighting.

Flowers on a landing
A peaceful corner of the stairs is brought into focus by an informal arrangement of garden flowers, illuminated by sidelighting from the landing window. The flowers balance the picture above, while still maintaining the neutral tones of the rest of the interior.

Sunrooms and conservatories 1

Traditionally, the conservatory was a place in which to display plants that had been raised in the greenhouse, where they were returned when the display started to deteriorate. The modern sunroom is more a place in which people relax and enjoy the warmth, but it is also one that suits plants. Real fanatics may transform the room into something resembling a jungle, where greenery takes over, but fewer plants, well displayed, can be just as effective.

Rooms like these provide light and airy conditions, a moist atmosphere and space for plants to spread. With careful watering in winter, a wide range of plants can be grown in a room heated to only 10°C. Some form of shading is usually needed where there is a large amount of sun in summer.

Furnishing a dining area with plants *right*
This conservatory-like house extension has a tall, airy feel. This has been maintained by using a relatively small number of plants to furnish it, and soften the architectural lines. The majority of these sit on waist-level shelves fitted all round the outer edge of the room. A large rubber plant (*Ficus elastica*) stands in one corner. The conservatory is one place where large-leaved plants like this can be given their head and allowed to fill as much space as they want.

A warm sunroom *below*
This spectacular room needs to maintain a considerable temperature in winter to sustain the tropical plants growing here. Windows must be double-glazed to prevent heat loss through the large areas of glass. Huge plants are placed in pots, baskets and specially constructed brick troughs. The hanging platform which provides extra space for a suspended "island of greenery" is a most unusual, and practical, feature, since it can be lowered for watering and maintenance.

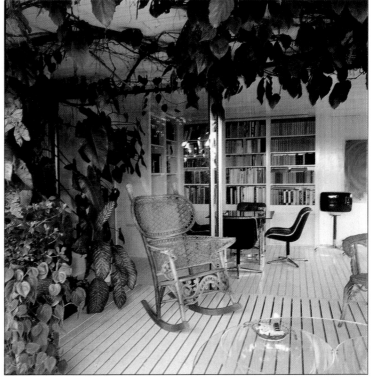

An elegant conservatory *below*
This pretty room with its distinctive glazing bars contains a selection of flowering plants, as well as a citrus tree. Colour accents are provided by a poinsettia (*Euphorbia pulcherrima*) and a Christmas cactus (*Schlumbergera* sp.).

Plant-filled sunroom *above*
Here, the living space extends through sliding glass on to a sunroom floored with white decking. The large plants include a dumb cane (*Dieffenbachia* sp.) and a thriving chestnut vine (*Tetrastigma voinieranum*).

Sunrooms and conservatories 2

The sunroom windowsill *left*
This windowsill is flooded with light all day, and four attractively shaped fans are used to shade the cyclamen (*Cyclamen persicum* hybrids) and Kafir lily (*Clivia miniata*) from bright light. The small cacti (*Mammillaria* sp.) are happy in full sun.

Variety for a rustic-style sunroom *below*
At least ten different varieties of green plants decorate this sunroom. The green of their leaves contrasts vividly with the warm apricot wash on the walls. A bunch of dried flowers hangs upside-down above the riot of foliage.

Conservatory shelves *above*
An idea for making the most of a group of busy Lizzie plants (*Impatiens* sp.) is to combine the plants with a collection of glass or china such as these coloured glass vases.

Decorating a corner *right*
An array of plants and cut flowers establishes the conservatory theme in this well-lit corner. On the table stand lilies (*Lilium* hybrids), white sails (*Spathiphyllum* "Clevelandii") and English ivy (*Hedera helix* hybrids). A huge stone vase of cut wild garlic (*Allium giganteum*) and a basket of white chrysanthemums (*Chrysanthemum morifolium* hybrids) complete the arrangement.

A place for herbs indoors *left*
A well-lit, cool conservatory can be a home
for potted herbs. There is attractive colour
variation in this studied arrangement of
fennel (*Foeniculum vulgare*), chives (*Allium
schoenoprasum*), feverfew (*Chrysanthemum
parthenium*), parsley (*Petroselinum crispum*)
and lady's mantle (*Alchemilla vulgaris*).

A green oasis *right*
Consider what your conservatory looks like
from inside the house. This one, glimpsed
through an arch, has a hanging curtain of
greenery which makes a charming transition
from the interior.

·6·
THE PLANT FINDER'S GUIDE

The first function of *The Plant Finder's Guide* is to provide a catalogue of the various forms of plant material that can be used in the home. There are sections dealing with cut flowers and foliage and all kinds of dried matter, as well as nearly 150 of the most popular house plants. Colour photographs provide a visual guide, and advice is given on how to display your material. Additionally, the guide gives special care advice, by way of readily recognizable symbols.

In the case of house plants, the symbols indicate the preferred light, temperature, watering and humidity levels of each plant, plus the relative ease of its cultivation. The entries are classified according to the basic shape of each plant—a prime factor in determining its decorative use in the home—and information is given regarding the probable dimensions of mature specimens. Similarly shaped plants of the same genus are listed, where appropriate, and briefly described. The amount of light and heat needed by each plant is described in terms of its *mini-climate:* a system which enables you to see, at a glance, which plants are compatible. Using this, it is possible to determine which upright plants, for example, would be suitable for a warm and sunny position, or for a warm and shady one—thus allowing you to choose easily between different plants that are suitable for a given position.

Choosing plants and flowers
Plants come in such an overwhelming variety of shapes, sizes and colours and, depending on their origins, need a variety of different conditions: in order to choose the right ones for your home, you need to be aware of both their decorative qualities and growing needs.

How to use The Plant Finder's Guide

For easy reference, *The Plant Finder's Guide* is divided into three separate guides: one for house plants, one for cut flowers and one for dried flowers.

The guide to house plants contains almost 150 colour photographs of the most widely used indoor plants, each with a detailed entry. Most of the entries are arranged in eight different shape categories: upright, arching, weeping, rosette-shaped, bushy, climbing, trailing and creeping. Of course, plants change shape as they grow and these categories are generalizations only. Each category is then sub-divided according to the shape and size of the leaves: large-leaved plants are those with leaves over 15cm in length; small-leaved plants have leaves less than 15cm in length; and compound-leaved plants have leaves divided into two or more leaf segments. There are separate sections in the guide for flowering bulbs, and for cacti and succulents, which are arranged according to their own shape categories. At the end of the house plant section there is a photographic colour guide to a selection of flowering house plants, running through the spectrum from white to violet, and there is also a seasonal guide, in the form of a chart, to indicate their flowering or fruiting periods.

Within *The guide to cut flowers*, the flower entries are arranged according to season and the foliage entries are organized according to colour. Each entry describes how to use and prepare the material and, of the 100 entries, 85 have a colour photograph.

The guide to dried flowers is separated into flowers themselves, arranged according to colour, and into other dried material, arranged according to type. A total of 65 species have been photographed and each has an entry giving advice on how to use it and on the best method of drying.

Symbols give additional information in all three guides.

SAMPLE PAGES

The guide to house plants

The plants are classified by their pattern of growth and foliage characteristics. An introduction to each group describes the main characteristics of the plants contained within it. Every plant has a colour photograph. A key to the symbols used in the guide is given.

Common name in bold type. Scientific name (genus and species) in italics, followed by hybrid/cultivar name where applicable

A general description of each plant, mentioning its main decorative qualities and how to use it

Size entry gives the maximum dimensions of the plant and tells you in what form it is offered for sale

Feeding entry gives advice on the most suitable fertilizer and how often to use it

Potting entry gives comprehensive advice on when and how to pot the plant, and the type of potting mixture to use

Plant care symbols give a pictorial summary of each plant's needs: temperature, light, humidity, watering and ease of care

Mini-climate categorization enables you to see at a glance which plants are compatible and can be displayed together

Special points (where applicable) for keeping a plant in a healthy state

Similar-shaped species entry (where applicable) lists similar plants of the same genus and describes how they differ from the featured plant

---

How to use the symbols

The guide to house plants

Temperature

Cool with winter rest Plants should be kept at 10°-15°C from spring to autumn, and 7°-10°C in winter.

Cool The plants which thrive in a cool climate should be kept at a temperature of between 10° and 15°C all year, if possible.

Warm The plants which thrive in a warm climate should be kept at a temperature of between 15° and 21°C all year, but endure higher or lower ranges for reasonable periods.

Light

Sunny A sunny position is one near a south-, east- or west-facing window which receives unobstructed direct sunlight.

Filtered sun This is indirect sunlight, which shines through a translucent curtain or blind, or is baffled by a leafy tree outside a window.

Shady A shady position is one close to a north-facing window, or to the side of an east- or west-facing one which receives no direct or indirect sun.

Humidity

Low humidity The air surrounding the plant should be approximately 30-40 per cent saturated with water. Few plants tolerate low humidity.

Moderate humidity The air surrounding the plant should be approximately 60 per cent saturated with water.

High humidity The air surrounding the plant should be approximately 80 per cent saturated with water.

Watering

Water sparingly This involves barely moistening the whole mixture, and allowing it to dry out almost completely each time.

Water moderately This refers to moistening the entire mixture, but allowing the top 2cm or so to dry out before watering again.

The guide to cut flowers

Cut flowers, blossoms and berries are classified according to their seasonal availability, and foliage is classified according to its colour. An introduction to each section describes the variety of material available. A key to the symbols used in the guide is given.

The guide to dried flowers

Dried material is classified according to colour or type. An introduction to each section describes the variety of material available and gives general suggestions on how to use it. Colour photographs show examples. A key to the symbols used in the guide is given.

Common name in bold type. Scientific name (genus and species) in italics followed by hybrid/cultivar name of flower or foliage where applicable

Symbols show whether the flowers are fragrant, long-lasting, have useful foliage or are suitable for drying

Description of how to use the flowers/ foliage and what to mix them with

Colours available (flowers only)

Advice on how to prepare and condition the flowers/foliage

Common name in bold type. Scientific name (genus and species) in italics followed by hybrid/cultivar name where applicable

Advice on decorative uses, and details of any other colours which are available

Symbols give the most suitable method of drying the material

ANEMONE
Anemone coronaria

These delicate flowers are available in a wide variety of shapes and sizes, although the ones pictured here are the most familiar. Their fragile flowers are made up not of petals but of sepals (these are usually green and are the leaf like structures which surround the flower), and these form a cup shape round a deep-blue central disc. In the garden, anemones of different species can be found in spring, summer and autumn but, in florists' shops, they are available throughout the year. Although they can be mixed with other flowers, they look best massed in a glass vase. Pack them in tightly, as their stems have a tendency to bend and this can make a vase look untidy.

Colours available Red, blue, mauve, pink, white, yellow, magenta and scarlet. Many have a central disc ringed with another colour.

Preparation Cut the stems on a slant and make a 5cm slit with a sharp knife. Dip the cut ends in boiling water for a few seconds. Give a long, cool drink before arranging.

CELOSIA
Celosia argentea "Cristata"
The purple or pink blooms have a mossy texture and provide dramatic focal point for a large arrangement.

Water plentifully This means keeping all of the potting mixture moist at all times, not letting even the surface dry out.

Care

Easy Plants which are termed "easy" to care for are those which can be grown successfully with only the minimum of attention.

Fairly easy Plants in this category require the basic care plus some attention to their individual growing needs.

Challenging These plants must be provided with their very specific growing needs or they will not thrive.

The guide to cut flowers

Long lasting Flowers or leaves which remain attractive for a particularly long time when cut.

Useful foliage Flowers whose own leaves are suitable for using in any arrangement, with or without that particular flower.

Fragrant Flowers which have a pleasant scent.

Suitable for drying Flowers, or their seed heads, or foliage which can be successfully preserved and used in dried displays.

The guide to dried flowers

Air-dried This refers to plant material dried naturally, without the use of chemicals, and usually involves hanging material upside-down in bunches.

Glycerine method This method involves standing foliage stems, or immersing leaves, in a solution of glycerine which, when absorbed by plant cells, preserves them.

Silica/borax This process uses desiccants which absorb moisture from the plant material, retaining its lifelike appearance when dried.

Pressing This is a mechanical method which preserves leaves or flowers by means of compression but does not retain the original shape.

Upright plants 1

These are plants with a distinctly vertical habit of growth. They vary in size from the treelike crotons and large-leaved rubber plants to relatively low-growing species such as the pileas and calatheas. Some of the treelike plants in this category, such as the yucca, have a central unbranched stem with leaves at the top only. Others, such as the Norfolk Island pine and the finger aralia, have a central, upright stem with branches at intervals along it. Not all upright plants have both stems and leaves. The mother-in-law's tongue is stemless, with the leaves rising directly out of the potting mixture. Many upright plants, which otherwise grow too tall for a domestic setting, can be made into shorter, rounder shrubs by pinching out the main growing shoot or tip and allowing side-stem growth to develop; the rubber plant is a good example of this. Leaf shape differs widely within the group and leaf size varies from under 15cm to over 60cm. Leaf colour is also well represented; from the green-and-cream leaves of the spotted dumb cane to the red leaf markings of the croton. There are some beautiful flowering upright plants including the spectacular bird-of-paradise flower and the delicate flowering maple. With this range of form and size you can find plants for very different situations: imposing specimen plants, such as the Norfolk Island pine, which look best displayed on their own; plants of more modest size which contrast well with low-growing, creeping or trailing plants, and spiky-leaved plants which mix well with the rounded shapes of some cacti.

SMALL-LEAVED UPRIGHT PLANTS

CALAMONDIN ORANGE
Citrus mitis

These ornamental orange trees bear fragrant flowers, unripe green fruits and ripe orange fruits all at the same time. The oranges produced are small and bitter but are excellent for making marmalade. The plants will fruit when still quite young and are best as specimen plants or arranged in formal groups.

Mini-climate 4 Cool, sunny.
Size Orange trees take several years to reach a maximum height of 1.2m with a similar spread. Small specimens bearing fruit are offered for sale.
Feeding Feed every two weeks with a tomato-type fertilizer all year except in winter.
Potting Repot in spring using soil-based potting mixture but only if the roots have completely filled the existing pot. If you don't want to move an older plant into a larger pot topdress instead.
Special points Destroy any scale insects you may find. Water more sparingly in winter.

Similar-shaped species
Citrus limon will produce lemons of up to 7cm in diameter.
Citrus sinensis is the only species which produces sweet fruit. Its stems have sharp spines.

ALUMINIUM PLANT
Pilea cadierei

The raised, silver leaf markings give the foliage of these attractive plants a quilted look. This effect is caused by pockets of air under the upper surface of the leaf. Group them with other attractively marked plants, or mass dwarf varieties together in a shallow bowl or in a bottle garden or terrarium.

Mini-climate 2 Warm, filtered sun.
Size Aluminium plants will reach a height of about 30cm in one year. A dwarf variety is available, which reaches a maximum height of about 15cm.
Feeding Feed with standard liquid fertilizer every two weeks in spring and summer.
Potting Repot every spring using a mixture of two-thirds peat moss and one-third coarse sand or perlite. Once plants are in 7cm pots topdress instead.

Similar-shaped species
Pilea spruceana has triangular, quilted, bronze-green leaves with a silver stripe down the middle.

FLOWERING MAPLE
Abutilon hybridum "Canary Bird"

Flowering maples are pretty, woody plants which can be trained when young. They have maplelike leaves from whose leaf-joints come the bell-shaped flowers. The flowers of the hybrids are red, pink, yellow or white. Flowering maples are long-lasting, making them suitable for use as feature plants, especially in front of a window.

Mini-climate 1 Warm, sunny.
Size Flowering maples may reach a height and spread of 1m in three years. Pinch out growing tips to maintain bushy growth.
Feeding Feed with standard liquid fertilizer every two weeks in summer.
Potting Repot every spring using soil-based potting mixture. Once plants are in 24cm pots topdress instead.
Special points Water more sparingly in winter and cut back any untidy stems in spring.

Similar-shaped species
Abutilon pictum "Thompsonii" has green and yellow variegated leaves and flowers which may be composed of one colour, two colours or two shades of the same colour.

LARGE-LEAVED UPRIGHT PLANTS

TI PLANT
Cordyline terminalis

These plants have large leaves patterned in red or green. The patterns of leaf colouring vary from plant to plant and ti plants look impressive when massed together to form a tapestry of colour in a warm room containing richly coloured fabrics.

Mini-climate 2 Warm, filtered sun.
Size Ti plants can grow to a height of 1.2m with a spread of 45cm. Small plants are offered for sale.
Feeding Feed with standard liquid fertilizer every two weeks from April to September.
Potting Repot every two years in spring using soil-based potting mixture. If you don't want to move an older plant into a larger pot topdress instead.
Special points Water more sparingly in winter. Clean leaves with a damp sponge.

RUBBER PLANT
Ficus elastica

The shiny, dark-green leaves are oval in shape with a pronounced point at their tip. The growth point is covered in a pink sheath for protection. Rubber plants have a strong shape and look best displayed as specimen plants in a modern setting.

Mini-climate 3 Warm, shady.
Size Rubber plants can grow up to 2m in height. Plants of all sizes are offered for sale.
Feeding Feed with standard liquid fertilizer every two weeks in spring and summer.
Potting Repot in spring using soil-based potting mixture but only if the roots have completely filled the existing pot. If you don't want to move an older plant into a larger pot topdress instead.
Special points Clean older leaves regularly with a damp sponge. Do not clean young leaves.

Similar-shaped species
Ficus lyrata has huge puckered leaves which are shaped like a violin.

BELGIAN EVERGREEN
Dracaena sanderana

Also known as "ribbon plants", these are the most dainty of the dracaenas. They are slender, upright plants with narrow, cream-striped leaves. Because they rarely branch, three or four specimens should be planted together in a pot to create an interesting spiky mass of leaves.

Mini-climate 2 Warm, filtered sun.
Size Belgian evergreens are slow-growing but will reach a maximum height of 90cm. Small plants, usually three to a pot, are offered for sale.
Feeding Feed with standard liquid fertilizer every two weeks from mid-spring to early autumn.
Potting Repot every two or three years in spring using soil-based potting mixture. Once plants are in 12cm pots topdress instead.
Special points Water more sparingly in winter.

SPOTTED DUMB CANE
Dieffenbachia exotica

Spotted dumb canes are bold feature plants with handsome, variegated leaves. Older plants tend to lose their lower leaves giving a solitary plant a bizarre look; but several plants grouped together make a dramatic display in a modern setting.

Mini-climate 3 Warm, shady.
Size Spotted dumb canes will grow to a height of 1.5m and a spread of 60cm. Plants of all sizes are offered for sale.
Feeding Feed with standard liquid fertilizer every two weeks from early spring to mid-autumn.
Potting Repot every spring using soil-based potting mixture in clay pots. Once plants are in 20cm pots topdress instead.
Special points The sap is poisonous and can cause severe inflammation of the mouth.

Similar-shaped species
Dieffenbachia amoena has 45cm long, pointed leaves which are dark green with herringbone markings in cream.
Dieffenbachia maculata has 25cm long dark-green leaves marked with white and pale green.

Upright plants 2

LARGE-LEAVED UPRIGHT PLANTS continued

CROTON
Codiaeum variegatum pictum

Crotons are striking, highly coloured, tropical shrubs with many variations in leaf shape, size and colour. Young leaves have a green colour; reds, oranges and purples develop with age. Crotons naturally drop their lower leaves with age but will retain them longer in a humid atmosphere. Mass together plants with different coloured leaves for a vivid display.

Mini-climate 1 Warm, sunny.
Size Crotons rarely grow larger than 90cm tall, with a similar spread. Small and medium-sized plants are offered for sale.
Feeding Feed with standard liquid fertilizer every two weeks from spring to autumn.
Potting Repot every spring using soil-based potting mixture. When plants are in 20-25cm pots topdress instead.
Special points Stand plants on trays filled with moist pebbles to increase humidity.

AFRICAN HEMP
Sparmannia africana

Also known as "indoor limes", these plants have large, apple-green leaves, covered in fine, white hairs. A plant blooming in a cool room can produce clusters of small, white flowers nearly all year round. African hemp plants look best displayed on their own as feature plants in both modern and traditional settings.

Mini-climate 4 Cool, sunny.
Size African hemps grow to about 1.5m in height with a spread of 1m wide in two years. Small plants are offered for sale.
Feeding Feed with standard liquid fertilizer every two weeks.
Potting Repot in spring using soil-based potting mixture but only if the roots have completely filled the existing pot. Once plants are in 30cm pots topdress instead.
Special points Water more sparingly in winter.

SILVERED SPEAR
Aglaonema crispum "Silver Queen"

The beautiful foliage of these plants is green only at the margins and main veins; the rest of the leaf is silvery-white and cream. As plants age they lose some of their lower leaves and develop a short, trunklike stem. They are excellent as part of a bold, leafy arrangement, particularly if contrasted with dark-green foliage plants.

Mini-climate 2 Warm, filtered sun.
Size Silvered spears reach a maximum height of 1m with a spread of about 60cm.
Feeding Feed with standard liquid fertilizer once a month from spring to autumn.
Potting Repot every spring using soil-based potting mixture. Once plants are in 15cm pots topdress instead.

BIRD-OF-PARADISE
Strelitzia reginae

These plants have spectacular orange-and-blue crested flowers which emerge in succession over a period of several weeks from a beak-shaped bud. Birds-of-paradise are unusual specimen plants for a modern interior; a large-scale setting is best as leaves and flowers become very big.

Mini-climate 1 Warm, sunny.
Size Birds-of-paradise will grow to 1m in height with a spread of 60cm. Young plants are offered for sale but will not flower until they are five years old.
Feeding Feed with standard liquid fertilizer every two weeks in spring and summer and once a month in autumn and winter.
Potting Repot every spring using soil-based potting mixture. Once plants are in 30cm pots topdress instead.
Special points Clean leaves with a damp sponge.

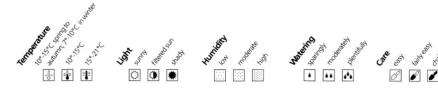

Temperature 10°-15°C spring to autumn; 7°-10°C in winter   10°-15°C   15°-21°C   Light sunny filtered sun shady   Humidity low moderate high   Watering sparingly moderately plentifully   Care easy fairly easy challenging

CAST-IRON PLANT
Aspidistra elatior

As their name suggests, cast-iron plants will tolerate a certain amount of neglect. They were much used by the Victorians as specimen plants, but despite these associations, cast-iron plants can be used to great effect, either massed together or grouped with other, smaller plants. They are ideal plants for filling difficult, darker spaces.

Mini-climate 5 Cool, filtered sun.
Size Cast-iron plants have a maximum height and spread of 1m. Small plants are offered for sale.
Feeding Feed with standard liquid fertilizer every two weeks in spring and summer.
Potting Repot every three years using soil-based potting mixture but only if the roots have completely filled the existing pot. If you don't want to move an older plant into a larger pot topdress instead.

TREE IVY
Fatshedera lizei

Also known as "fat-headed Lizzies", these plants have palmate, glossy-green leaves and can be displayed as upright feature plants, either alone or to give height to a group of smaller plants. They will also climb and can be trained, if tied to supports, to cover staircases and balconies and to frame windows.

Mini-climate 5 Cool, filtered sun.
Size Tree ivies can grow upright to a height of 1m with a similar spread. If allowed to wander over a support their growth will be unlimited.
Feeding Feed with standard liquid fertilizer every two weeks.
Potting Repot every spring using two-thirds soil-based potting mixture and one-third peat-moss. If you don't want to move an older plant into a larger pot topdress instead.

PEACOCK PLANT
Calathea makoyana

The leaves of peacock plants look as if they have been hand painted with dark-green patterns. They look best in a mixed group of foliage plants. Smaller plants can be used in bottle gardens and larger terraria.

Mini-climate 3 Warm, shady.
Size Peacock plants can grow to a height of 1m with a spread of about 60cm. Plants of all sizes are offered for sale.
Feeding Feed with standard liquid fertilizer every two weeks during spring and summer and once a month during autumn and winter.
Potting Repot every spring using a mixture of two-thirds soil-based potting mixture and one-third leaf mould or peat. Once plants are in 15cm pots topdress instead.
Special points Stand plants on trays filled with moist pebbles to increase humidity.

COMPOUND-LEAVED UPRIGHT PLANTS

FINGER ARALIA
Dizygotheca elegantissima

Also known as "false aralias", these plants are elegant, open shrubs made up of many narrow leaflets. Leaf colour changes with age from bronze to a very deep green and the leaf texture becomes coarser. The dark tracery of the palmate leaves makes a delicate background to set off bolder foliage, or several plants can be grouped together to create a lacy mass of leaves.

Mini-climate 2 Warm, filtered sun.
Size Finger aralias reach 2m in height with a spread of 60cm. Pinch out growing tips to encourage bushy growth. Plants of all sizes are offered for sale.
Feeding Feed with standard liquid fertilizer every two weeks in spring and summer.
Potting Repot every two years in spring using soil-based potting mixture. If you don't want to move an older plant into a larger pot topdress instead.
Special points Stand plants on trays filled with moist pebbles to increase humidity.

Upright plants 3

COMPOUND-LEAVED UPRIGHT PLANTS continued

NORFOLK ISLAND PINE
Araucaria heterophylla

Also known as "Christmas tree plants", these pines are at their best when four years old. Because of their starkness, they seldom look well mixed with other plants, but a most striking effect can be created by grouping several of these conifers together to give a Japanese look.

Mini-climate 5   Cool, filtered sun.
Size   Norfolk Island pines are slow-growing: a ten-year old plant rarely exceeds 1.8m in height and 1.2m width.
Feeding   Feed with standard liquid fertilizer every two weeks in spring and summer.
Potting   Repot every two or three years in spring using soil-based potting mixture. Once plants are in 24cm pots topdress instead.
Special points   Water more sparingly during the winter rest period.

SILK OAK
Grevillea robusta

Silk oaks are treelike evergreen shrubs with finely divided, fernlike leaves. The leaves are bronze when they first appear, turning green later. They look good grouped with other plants and, when they are large enough, displayed as specimen plants.

Mini-climate 4   Cool, sunny.
Size   Silk oaks are fast-growing and will reach 1.5m high in two or three years. Encourage bushy growth by stopping the main shoot when young. Young plants are offered for sale.
Feeding   Feed with standard liquid fertilizer every two weeks during spring and summer.
Potting   Repot every spring using lime-free soil-based potting mixture. If you don't want to move an older plant into a larger pot topdress instead.
Special points   Water more sparingly in winter.

UMBRELLA PLANT
Cyperus alternifolius "Gracilis"

The radiating grasslike bracts of these plants resemble the spokes of an open umbrella. The tall stems are very brittle and should be handled with care. Umbrella plants have a Japanese look and suit stark modern interiors.

Mini-climate 2   Warm, filtered sun.
Size   Umbrella plants will reach a height of 1.2m given suitably wet conditions.
Feeding   Feed with standard liquid fertilizer once every month.
Potting   Repot in spring using soil-based potting mixture with added charcoal, but only if the roots have completely filled the existing pot. Ensure plants are repotted at the same soil level. If you don't want to move an older plant into a larger pot topdress instead.
Special points   Stand permanently in a water-filled saucer to keep the roots saturated.

SPIKY-LEAVED UPRIGHT PLANTS

BOAT LILY
Rhoeo spathacea "Variegata"

These plants are also known as "Moses-in-the-cradle", referring to the boat-shaped cups which encase the small, white, three-petalled flowers. The long, rather stiff leaves are beautifully coloured, having yellow and cream stripes on their upper surface and purple on their lower surface. Boat lilies are best displayed on their own so that the unusual flower-cups can be seen.

Mini-climate 2   Warm, filtered sun.
Size   Boat lilies reach a maximum height of 30cm with a spread of 45cm. Plants of this size are offered for sale. Maintain as an upright plant by pinching off basal shoots.
Feeding   Feed with standard liquid fertilizer every two weeks in spring and summer.
Potting   Repot every second year in spring using soil-based potting mixture. If you don't want to move an older plant into a larger pot topdress instead.

Temperature 10°-15°C spring to autumn, 7°-10°C in winter | 10°-15°C | 15-21°C   Light sunny | filtered sun | shady   Humidity low | moderate | high   Watering sparingly | moderately | plentifully   Care easy | fairly easy | challenging

EUROPEAN FAN PALM
Chamaerops humilis

Also known as "dwarf fan palms", these handsome, low-growing palms have wide, fan-shaped fronds. These are made up of rigid, sword-shaped segments with split ends. There is no recognizable stem, except in very mature plants, the fronds being held upright on long leaf stalks. These are ornamental plants with an oriental look to them to be used as specimens or in groups depending on their size.

Mini-climate 2 Warm, filtered sun.
Size European fan palms are slow-growing, but will reach 1.5m in height with a similar spread when mature. Plants of all sizes are offered for sale.
Feeding Feed with standard liquid fertilizer once a month in spring, summer and autumn.
Potting Repot every two years in spring using soil-based potting mixture. Once plants are in 30cm pots topdress instead.
Special points Stand plants outside in a sheltered place in summer. Water more sparingly in winter.

MOTHER-IN-LAW'S TONGUE
Sansevieria trifasciata "Laurentii"

The upright leaves of this plant emerge in a cluster from an underground stem. The thick, leathery leaves are marbled with dark green and have golden bands along their margin. Display large plants as specimens or group them with other spiky-leaved plants in a modern setting.

Mini-climate 2 Warm, filtered sun.
Size The leaves of mother-in-law's tongues can grow to a height of about 1m. Plants of all sizes are offered for sale.
Feeding Feed with half-strength standard liquid fertilizer once a month.
Potting Repot in spring or early summer, using a mixture of one-third coarse sand or perlite and two-thirds soil-based potting mixture, but only when a mass of roots appears on the surface. If you don't want to move an older plant into a larger pot topdress instead.
Special points Water more sparingly in winter.

RAINBOW PLANT
Dracaena marginata "Tricolor"

The name "rainbow plant" is derived from the leaf markings, which form stripes of green, cream and pink. In mature plants, the topknot of leaves emerges from the bare, woody stem, giving plants a palmlike look. Three or four specimens planted in the same pot make a good display in a modern setting.

Mini-climate 2 Warm, filtered sun.
Size Rainbow plants will grow to 1.5m with a spread of 45cm. Plants of 30cm in height are offered for sale, but there is more demand for older plants with bare stems.
Feeding Feed with standard liquid fertilizer every two weeks in spring and summer, and once a month in autumn and winter.
Potting Repot every spring using soil-based potting mixture. If you don't want to move an older plant into a larger pot topdress instead.
Special points Water more sparingly in winter.

STICK YUCCA
Yucca elephantipes

These plants have a very distinctive appearance. Many are specially grown from logs which, when planted, produce roots and leaves. The leaves are long and narrow, and can appear in clumps at any point of the upright stem. Yuccas have a strong shape and should be displayed on their own, or with other spiky-leaved plants in a modern setting.

Mini-climate 1 Warm, sunny.
Size Yuccas up to 2m in height with a spread of 45cm are offered for sale. The spread increases as more leaves are produced. Plants can also be bought which are virtually stemless; these are known as "tip yuccas".
Feeding Feed with standard liquid fertilizer once every month.
Potting Repot every spring using soil-based potting mixture. If you don't want to move an older plant into a larger pot topdress instead.
Special points Water more sparingly in winter.

Arching plants 1

The overall shape of the plants in this category is determined by the way the stems, leafstalks or fronds branch out in an arch from the base of the plant. Because of this, most of the arching plants take up a great deal of space when fully grown and are best displayed on their own. Indeed, the largest arching plants, with their strong architectural shapes, make striking additions to the modern interior. Also in this category are three plants, the ponytail, West Indian holly and weeping fig, whose leaves hang downwards to give a "weeping" effect.

There is a great variety of leaf shape and texture in this category, ranging from the smooth, lance-shaped leaves of the white sails to the deeply cut leaves of some philodendrons and the delicate leaflets of the ferns and palms.

The diversity of leaf shape among arching plants compensates for the lack of colourful foliage in the group, and some species, such as the wax plant and white sails, produce very attractive flowers.

The graceful lines of the Boston and hare's foot ferns are produced by the arching fronds and are best appreciated when viewed at eye-level, as is the flat-topped button fern: display them in an urn, a tall terracotta pot or hanging basket. Plants such as the bamboo palm, the Kentia palm and the coconut palm can grow to quite a size and older plants are dominant enough to become the focal point of a room. Arching plants are among the most elegant of plants and should ideally be displayed in a position where they can be seen from all angles.

SMALL-LEAVED ARCHING PLANTS

WAX PLANT
Begonia fuchsioides

These delicate-looking begonias have small, oval leaves with a glossy texture. The leaves are borne on long, thin stems which begin to arch over as they get longer. Small, waxy, succulent-looking, shell-pink flowers appear in clusters between autumn and spring. Wax plants need some kind of support if they are to be seen to best effect. Display with green foliage groups in an informal setting.

They can look good if allowed to trail from a hanging basket.

Mini-climate 1 Warm, sunny.
Size Wax plants can grow to about 1m in height, with a spread of about 50cm. Pinch out growing tips to maintain bushy growth. Small plants are offered for sale.
Feeding Feed with standard liquid fertilizer once every two weeks during the flowering period.
Potting Repot every spring using an equal-parts mixture of soil-based and peat-based potting mixture. If you don't want to move an older plant into a larger pot topdress instead.
Special points Water more sparingly in winter.

BUTTON FERN
Pellaea rotundifolia

These unusual-looking ferns have low, spreading fronds making them one of the few ferns with an almost horizontal outline. The pinnae of the fronds are also most unfernlike, consisting of leathery, button-shaped leaflets arranged in a row, one on either side of a stiff midrib. These leaflets weigh the fronds down to give an arching appearance. Button ferns make excellent infill plants to hide foreground pots in groups of plants. Display with plants of varying leaf texture in a modern setting for best effect. They can also be used in bottle gardens and terraria.

Mini-climate 3 Warm, shady.
Size The individual fronds of button ferns grow to a maximum of 30cm long, giving the plant a wide but very flat shape.
Feeding Feed with standard liquid fertilizer every two weeks.
Potting Repot in spring using fern potting mixture in a shallow pot, but only if the roots have completely filled the existing pot. If you don't want to move an older plant into a larger pot, prune the roots to curb growth.
Special points Button ferns can be placed outside in a sheltered shady spot in summer. Stand plants on trays filled with moist pebbles to increase humidity.

Temperature 10°-15°C spring to autumn, 7°-10°C in winter / 10°-15°C / 15°-21°C Light sunny / filtered sun / shady Humidity low / moderate / high Watering sparingly / moderately / plentifully Care easy / fairly easy / challenging

LARGE-LEAVED ARCHING PLANTS

FINGER PLANT
Philodendron bipinnatifidum

The leaves of these plants are heart-shaped in outline with deeply cut edges. The leaves are borne on stout stalks radiating from a central stem and unlike most of the other philodendron species these plants do not climb. They make dramatic feature plants for a large room.

Mini-climate 3 Warm, shady.
Size Finger plants can reach a height and spread of about 1.2m. Plants of all sizes are offered for sale.
Feeding Feed with standard liquid fertilizer every two weeks in spring and summer.
Potting Repot in spring using half soil-based potting mixture and half leaf mould, but only if the roots have completely filled the existing pot. Once plants are in 30cm pots topdress instead.
Special points Destroy any scale insects you find.

WHITE SAILS
Spathiphyllum "Clevelandii"

The striking arumlike flower heads of the white sails are produced from May to August. Each flower lasts for six weeks or more, turning from white to an attractive pale green. Their elegant shape makes them ideal specimen plants for the modern interior.

Mini-climate 3 Warm, shady.
Size Mature white sails can reach a height and spread of 90cm. Plants in flower are offered for sale.
Feeding Feed with standard liquid fertilizer every two weeks from early spring to late summer.
Potting Repot every two years in spring using peat-based potting mixture. Once plants are in a 15-20cm pot root prune instead.
Special points Stand plants on trays filled with moist pebbles to increase humidity.

COCONUT PALM
Cocos nucifera

These most striking looking plants grow directly from the nut which sits on top of the potting mixture. From the nut sprout the upright stalks which bear the once-divided, arching fronds. These fronds are heavily ribbed. The coconut palm makes a striking specimen plant for a stark modern interior.

Mini-climate 2 Warm, filtered sun.
Size Coconut palms can reach more than 1.5m in height. Large plants are offered for sale.
Feeding Feed with half-strength liquid fertilizer every two weeks in spring and summer.
Potting Repotting is unnecessary.
Special points Coconut palms only last about two years in the home as they resent root disturbance.

COMPOUND-LEAVED ARCHING PLANTS

HARE'S FOOT FERN
Polypodium aureum "Mandaianum"

These plants derive their common name from the furry rhizome from which the fronds arise. The fronds are carried on long, arching stems and each bears up to ten silvery blue-green leaflets. Each leaflet has a ruffled edge. Since their colour is so attractive, hare's foot ferns should be displayed as feature plants when they are large enough. Smaller plants mix well with other ferns.

Mini-climate 3 Warm, shady.
Size The fronds of the hare's foot fern can grow to about 60cm in length giving the plant a large spread. Plants of all sizes are offered for sale.
Feeding Feed with half-strength standard liquid fertilizer once a week from spring to autumn.
Potting Repot in spring using half soil-based potting mixture and half leaf mould in a shallow container, but only if the rhizomes have completely filled the existing pot. Once plants are in 20cm pots root prune instead.
Special points Stand plants on trays filled with moist pebbles to increase humidity.

Arching plants 2

COMPOUND-LEAVED ARCHING PLANTS continued

KENTIA PALM
Howea belmoreana

These slender palms were great favourites in the 19th century, adding soft grace to large rooms. The arching fronds are borne on upright stems giving the plant an elegant look. Always specimen plants, Kentia palms can be difficult to place due to their large size but seem to thrive in a range of conditions found in the home.

Mini-climate 2 Warm, filtered sun.
Size Kentia palms can grow to 2.5m with a spread of 2m. Medium and large plants are offered for sale.
Feeding Feed with standard liquid fertilizer once a month from spring to autumn.
Potting Repot every second year in spring using soil-based potting mixture. Once plants are in 30cm pots topdress instead.
Special points Clean leaves with a damp sponge.

Similar-shaped species
Howea forsterana is very similar and can only be told apart by the greater, flat-topped spread and wider gaps between the frond leaflets of this species.

DWARF COCONUT PALM
Microcoelum weddellianum

These compact palms have shiny fronds which are deeply divided into many threadlike leaflets arranged in a herringbone fashion. Although the fronds look feathery they are quite tough to the touch. Dwarf coconut palms have no true trunk; the fronds arise from a short, thickened base. They are not as arching as the larger types and are therefore suitable for use on table tops or shelves.

Mini-climate 2 Warm, filtered sun.
Size Dwarf coconut palms reach a maximum height and spread of 90cm. Small plants are offered for sale all year.
Feeding Feed with standard liquid fertilizer once a month in summer.
Potting Repot every two years in spring using soil-based potting mixture. If you don't want to move an older plant into a larger pot topdress instead.

BAMBOO PALM
Rhapis excelsa

Also known as "little lady palms", these plants have stems which cluster together giving the plant a crowded look. The leaves are composed of five to nine, often blunt-tipped segments giving an overall fan-shaped look. Each segment is deeply cut. Display the bamboo palm with other dark-green foliage plants. Older plants lose their lower leaves making them suitable for displaying on their own.

Mini-climate 2 Warm, filtered sun.
Size Bamboo palms are slow-growing taking several years to reach a maximum height of 1.5m tall with a similar spread. Medium and large plants are offered for sale.
Feeding Feed with standard liquid fertilizer once a month during the active growing period.
Potting Repot every second year in spring using soil-based potting mixture. Once plants are in 30cm pots topdress instead.

BOSTON FERN
Nephrolepis exaltata "Bostoniensis"

These lush but graceful ferns have swordlike fronds which are available in several forms: some with crested fronds, others with very finely divided leaf sections. Boston ferns make elegant specimen plants, used either on a pedestal or in a hanging basket, and suit almost any type of setting.

Mini-climate 3 Warm, shady.
Size Boston ferns have fronds that are often 90cm long and can grow to 1.8m. Plants of all sizes are offered for sale.
Feeding Feed with standard liquid fertilizer every two weeks when actively growing, otherwise feed once a month.
Potting Repot in spring using fern potting mixture but only if the roots have completely filled the existing pot. If you don't want to move an older plant into a larger pot topdress instead.
Special points Stand plants on trays filled with moist pebbles to increase humidity.

Similar-shaped species
Nephrolepis cordifolia is smaller; its fronds will grow up to 60cm long.

Temperature 10°-15°C spring to autumn, 7°-10°C in winter | 10°-15°C | 15°-21°C   **Light** sunny | filtered sun | shady   **Humidity** low | moderate | high   **Watering** sparingly | moderately | plentifully   **Care** easy | fairly easy | challenging

·ARCHING PLANTS·

PARLOUR PALM
Chamaedorea elegans "Bella"

These palms have dainty, deeply divided fronds arching from the central stem. The fronds are fresh green when young and darken with age. Mature plants produce small sprays of tiny, yellow, beadlike flowers. Parlour palms thrive in the conditions of a bathroom, and small plants add interest to bottle gardens and terraria.

Mini-climate 2 Warm, filtered sun.
Size Parlour palms are dwarf palms reaching a height of about 90cm after several years, with a spread of 45cm. Young plants are offered for sale.
Feeding Feed with standard liquid fertilizer once a month from spring to autumn.
Potting Repot in spring using soil-based potting mixture but only if the roots have completely filled the existing pot. Once plants are in 15-20cm pots topdress instead.
Special points Water more sparingly in winter.

Similar-shaped species
Chamaedorea erumpens forms a clump of slender stems, knotted at intervals like bamboo and with sections of bare stem. They can grow to about 2-2.5m in height.

WEEPING ARCHING PLANTS

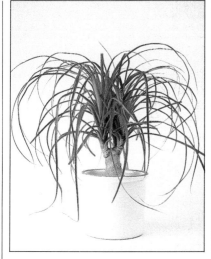

WEST INDIAN HOLLY
Leea coccinea

These plants have deep-green, holly-shaped leaves which are often tinged with a coppery-red. The plant has a very open appearance as the leaves are twice divided. West Indian hollies can be used as specimen plants or as a foil for low-growing foliage plants.

Mini-climate 2 Warm, filtered sun.
Size West Indian hollies reach a maximum height of about 1.5m with a similar spread. Plants of about 30cm tall with a similar spread are offered for sale.
Feeding Feed with standard liquid fertilizer every two weeks from spring to autumn.
Potting Repot every spring using soil-based potting mixture. If you don't want to move an older plant into a larger pot topdress instead.
Special points Water more sparingly in winter.

WEEPING FIG
Ficus benjamina

These plants are the most elegant of the ornamental figs with their graceful, grey-barked arching stems bearing the dangling, pointed leaves. The arrangement of the leaves gives the plant an open appearance; good for both modern and period interiors.

Mini-climate 3 Warm, shady.
Size Weeping figs have a maximum height of 1.5m with a spread of about 1.2m if given enough room. Medium-sized and large plants are offered for sale.
Feeding Feed with standard liquid fertilizer every two weeks in spring and summer.
Potting Repot in spring using a soil-based potting mixture but only if the roots have completely filled the existing pot. If you don't want to move an older plant into a larger pot topdress instead.
Special points Water more sparingly in winter.

PONYTAIL
Beaucarnea recurvata

These are most bizarre-looking plants, having a ponytail-like tuft of narrow, green leaves sprouting from the top of a fat or long, woody stem. The swollen base adds to the unusual appearance of the plant. Ponytails are ideal plants for displaying in a modern interior and will thrive in any centrally heated room.

Mini-climate 2 Warm, filtered sun.
Size Ponytails reach a maximum height of 1.5m with a spread of 60cm. Small and medium sized plants are offered for sale.
Feeding Feed with standard liquid fertilizer every month during summer.
Potting Repot every three or four years in spring using soil-based potting mixture. Ponytails thrive in small pots.
Special points Can easily be killed by overwatering.

Rosette-shaped plants 1

This category is made up of plants whose leaves radiate from a central growing point and overlap each other, forming a circular cluster of leaf bases, usually at potting mixture level. Plants can be small and low-growing, or tall with large leaves: the shape of the cluster varies from the flat-leaved rosette of low-growing plants, such as African violets and earth stars, to the tall, arching rosette of the bird's nest fern and the blue-flowered torch. Another variation is the spiky-leaved rosette formed by the variegated pineapple plant and the scarlet star. These plants look good displayed on their own as they have such strong shapes. Flat-leaved rosette-shaped plants should be massed together and placed where they can be seen from above.

Many of the plants in this category are from the brome-liad family and originate from tropical America. They are striking, exotic-looking plants which often have bold and unusual flower spikes, or leaves which become suffused with strong colour prior to, and during, the flowering period. The leaves of many bromeliads, such as the urn plant and the bird's nest bromeliad, form a cup-shaped central reservoir which should be kept topped up with fresh water if the plant is to remain in good condition.

Many bromeliads are epiphytic; in their native tropical environment they grow on trees—using them only as a means of support, not as a source of nutrients. An effective way to display them, therefore, is on a natural-looking support such as a dried branch covered in moist sphagnum moss, or attach them to a large piece of cork or bark.

ARCHING ROSETTE-SHAPED PLANTS

URN PLANT
Aechmea fasciata

When three or four years old, these plants produce a drumstick-shaped inflorescence which rises from the centre of the rosette. This flower head comprises many spiny, pink bracts through which peep short-lived, pale-blue flowers. The head remains attractive for about six months. The leathery leaves are marked with white cross-banding on a grey-green background. Display large plants as specimens, or grow small plants on a dried branch covered with sphagnum moss.

Mini-climate 1 Warm, sunny.
Size The leaves of urn plants reach 60cm long and the flower spikes grow 15cm above the leaves. Small plants grown from offsets and mature plants are offered for sale.
Feeding Feed with half-strength standard liquid fertilizer once a month in spring and summer. Apply feed to the centre of the rosette as well as the roots.
Potting Repot in spring using bromeliad potting mixture but only if the roots have completely filled the existing pot. Once plants are in 15cm pots topdress instead.
Special points Keep the centre of the rosette filled with fresh water. Change the water once a month.

FLAMING SWORD
Vriesea splendens

These bromeliads have exotically marked leaves; they are shiny green banded with deep purple. The leaves form an upright vase, from the centre of which a bright-red spike of bracts emerges when the plants are several years old. Small, yellow flowers poke through the red bracts. Several plants massed together make a spectacular display; alternatively, include the flaming sword with strong foliage plants or use small specimens on a dried branch covered with sphagnum moss.

Mini-climate 2 Warm, filtered sun.
Size Flaming swords can reach a height and spread of about 45cm. The flower spike can reach 60cm in height. Plants of all sizes are offered for sale.
Feeding Feed with half-strength standard liquid fertilizer once a month. Ensure the feed gets on the leaves, roots and the central cup.
Potting Repot in spring using bromeliad potting mixture but only if the roots have completely filled the existing pot. Once plants are in 15cm pots topdress instead.
Special points Keep the centre of the rosette filled with fresh water except when the flower bud first appears. Change the water once a month.

Similar-shaped species
Vriesea fenestralis is a little larger with paler green leaves covered in brown markings.
Vriesea psittacina has shorter leaves which are plain green with mauve shading towards the centre of the rosette.
Vriesea saundersii has a squat rosette of grey-green leaves with a dull rose-pink underside and a yellow flower spike.

Temperature 10°-15°C spring to autumn, 7°-10°C in winter | 10°-15°C | 15°-21°C **Light** sunny | filtered sun | shady **Humidity** low | moderate | high **Watering** sparingly | moderately | plentifully **Care** easy | fairly easy | challenging

QUEEN'S TEARS
Billbergia nutans

These plants have tough leaves with toothed edges. There may be many plants in the same pot, as production of offsets is prolific. During the short flowering season in May and June, the foliage is interspersed with trailing, bright-pink bracts which are very attractive. These bracts open to display the small yellow, green and purple flowers. Queen's tears are best displayed at eye-level as feature plants.

Mini-climate 1 Warm, sunny.
Size The leaves of queen's tears reach about 60cm in length. Spread depends on the number of offsets produced. Small plants are offered for sale.
Feeding Feed with standard liquid fertilizer once every two weeks during spring and summer.
Potting Repot every spring using bromeliad potting mixture. Once plants are in 15cm pots topdress instead.
Special points The rosette of leaves should be cut away at the base after flowering to allow the offsets around it to develop.

BLUE-FLOWERED TORCH
Tillandsia cyanea

These are medium-sized bromeliads with stiff, arching, grassy leaves arranged in a loose rosette. When mature, the plants produce a fleshy spear-shaped flower head, made up of pinky-green overlapping bracts. This unusual flower head is flat and wide and will remain decorative for some months. Three-petalled, bright violet-blue flowers appear in succession from between the bracts. Display blue-flowered torches as feature plants.

Mini-climate 1 Warm, sunny.
Size The leaves of blue-flowered torches reach about 30cm in length. Offsets give the plant a large spread. Small plants are offered for sale.
Feeding Feed with half-strength standard liquid fertilizer once a month. This can be applied to the leaves as a foliar feed.
Potting Repot every spring using bromeliad potting mixture. Once plants are in 10cm pots topdress instead.
Special points Place in a sheltered part of the garden in summer to encourage flowering.

BIRD'S NEST FERN
Asplenium nidus

These plants have shiny, apple-green fronds arranged in an upward-spreading rosette at whose base is a circle of young leaf fronds. These slowly unroll from the fibrous core of the plant. Large bird's nest ferns are too bold in shape to display with other ferns and look best either arranged on their own, or included in a mixed group of large-leaved foliage plants.

Mini-climate 3 Warm, shady.
Size The fronds of bird's nest ferns can reach 45cm long. Young plants are offered for sale.
Feeding Feed with standard liquid fertilizer once a month.
Potting Repot in spring using fern potting mixture but only when a mass of roots appears on the surface of the potting mixture. If you don't want to move an older plant into a larger pot root prune instead.
Special points Stand plants on trays filled with moist pebbles to increase humidity.

SPIKY-LEAVED ROSETTE-SHAPED PLANTS

VEITCH SCREW PINE
Pandanus veitchii

These plants get their name from the way the leaf bases spiral round the stem but, despite their name, they are unrelated to the pine family. The long, arching leaves are a rich dark green edged in cream and have a fine-toothed edge which can rasp the skin. Use these handsome specimens in a modern setting for a dramatic effect.

Mini-climate 1 Warm, sunny.
Size Screw pines can reach a height and spread of about 90cm. Plants of all sizes are offered for sale.
Feeding Feed with standard liquid fertilizer every two weeks during spring and summer and once a month during autumn and winter.
Potting Repot every spring using soil-based potting mixture. If you don't want to move an older plant into a larger pot topdress instead.
Special points Thick, stiltlike aerial roots form after two years and lift the plant base away from the potting mixture. These roots should be encouraged to grow into the potting mixture for improved anchorage.

Rosette-shaped plants 2

SPIKY-LEAVED ROSETTE-SHAPED PLANTS continued

VARIEGATED PINEAPPLE
Ananas comosus variegatus

These plants are prized for their stiff, spiny leaves which curve gracefully outward, giving them a symmetrical shape. When five or six years old they produce striking pink flower heads, followed by a pink fruit which is unlikely to ripen and be edible. Large plants displayed in an urn suit formal interiors.

Mini-climate 1 Warm, sunny.
Size Variegated pineapple plants grow to a maximum height of about 1m with a spread of up to 2m. Fruiting plants are offered for sale.
Feeding Feed with standard liquid fertilizer every two weeks during spring and summer.
Potting Repot in spring every two years using bromeliad potting mixture. Once plants are in 15-20cm pots topdress instead.
Special points In direct sunlight, a rich-pink hue enhances the variegation of the leaves.

Similar-shaped species
Ananas bracteatus striatus is the variegated form of the wild pineapple and has boldly striped leaves which become pink if grown in bright light.
Ananas nanus is much smaller with plain, dark-green leaves and produces small, inedible fruits. It can be bought in fruit in a 10cm pot.

FLAT-LEAVED ROSETTE-SHAPED PLANTS

SCARLET STAR
Guzmania lingulata

These winter-flowering bromeliads have centres made up of bright-orange or scarlet bracts filled with small, yellow flowers. The arching leaves are soft, glossy and bright green in colour. These are strongly coloured plants which suit bold, modern interiors. Mass several plants together in a shallow glass bowl or display in pairs for a symmetrical arrangement.

Mini-climate 2 Warm, filtered sun.
Size The scarlet star reaches about 25cm in height and has a spread of up to 30cm.
Feeding Feed with half-strength standard liquid fertilizer once a month. Ensure the feed gets onto the leaves and roots and into the central cup.
Potting Repot in spring using bromeliad potting mixture but only if the roots have filled the existing pot.
Special points Empty the central cup and fill with fresh water every month.

EARTH STAR PLANT
Cryptanthus bivittatus

These small plants have some of the most beautifully coloured foliage found in the bromeliads. The sharply pointed leaves have two distinctive cream stripes running along their length, which turn pink or even a strong red if placed in the direct sun. Clusters of small white flowers are hidden by the leaves. These stemless plants can be massed together in shallow bowls or terraria.

Mini-climate 1 Warm, sunny.
Size Earth stars are slow-growing and will reach 15-20cm across by the time they flower.
Feeding Feed occasionally by splashing with half-strength standard liquid fertilizer.
Potting Repotting is hardly ever necessary.
Special points Some time after flowering has finished cut away the parent plant to allow the offsets around its base to develop.

BLUSHING BROMELIAD
Neoregelia carolinae "Tricolor"

These flat-topped bromeliads have striking foliage; young leaves are a soft green striped with ivory white. As the plants mature the leaves become suffused with pink, and just before flowering the centre becomes bright red. Display within a group of bold foliage plants for best effect.

Mini-climate 2 Warm, filtered sun.
Size Mature blushing bromeliads grow to about 20cm in height with a spread of about 45cm.
Feeding Feed with half-strength standard liquid fertilizer once a month. Apply on to the leaves, into the cup and on to the potting mixture.
Potting Repot in spring using bromeliad potting mixture but only if the roots have completely filled the existing pot. Once plants are in 12cm pots topdress instead.

Temperature 10°-15°C spring to autumn, 7°-10°C in winter | 10°-15°C | 15°-21°C

Light sunny | filtered sun | shady

Humidity low | moderate | high

Watering sparingly | moderately | plentifully

Care easy | fairly easy | challenging

AFRICAN VIOLET
Saintpaulia hybrids

These plants have an impressive range of flower colours from white and pink to purple, magenta and violet. The flowers are held in clusters above the rosette of furry leaves. With this range of colour African violets can be used in both modern and period interiors. One of the most effective ways to display them is massed in a shallow bowl. Miniature varieties can be displayed in a terrarium.

Mini-climate 2 Warm, filtered sun.
Size African violets will form a flat rosette of about 20cm diameter. Flowering plants are available all year. Named varieties run into thousands.
Feeding Feed with specially prepared African violet liquid fertilizer, used at one-quarter strength, at each watering throughout the year.
Potting Repot only when the roots have completely filled the existing pot. Use a mixture of equal parts peat moss, perlite and vermiculite in half pots or shallow pans.
Special points Avoid wetting the hairy leaves when watering and feeding as they will become stained.

BIRD'S NEST BROMELIAD
Nidularium innocentii

These plants form low, spreading rosettes of straplike, dark-green leaves. The centre of the rosette becomes very dark red, sometimes almost black, at flowering time. The small, white flowers form a clump in the centre of the water-filled vase and last only a short time, although the coloured centre remains attractive for some months. Bird's nest bromeliads can be grouped with other bold-leaved plants.

Mini-climate 2 Warm, filtered sun.
Size Bird's nest bromeliads grow to a height of about 20cm with a spread of 40cm. Three or four year old plants about to flower are offered for sale.
Feeding Feed with half-strength standard liquid fertilizer once a month. Apply on to the leaves, into the cup and on to the potting mixture.
Potting Repot in spring using bromeliad potting mixture but only if the roots have completely filled the existing pot. Once plants are in 10cm pots topdress instead.
Special points Some time after flowering has finished cut away the parent plant to allow the offsets around its base to develop.

Similar-shaped species
Nidularium fulgens is of similar size with dark-spotted, spiky-edged leaves.

CAPE PRIMROSE
Streptocarpus "John Innes" hybrids

These small plants have primrose-like leaves and large, tubular flowers on long stalks. Flowers may be white, pink, red, mauve or blue. Attractive twisted seed pods appear but these are best cut off to encourage more flowers. These plants are best treated as annuals and discarded when flowering has finished. Like primulas and African violets, Cape primroses should be massed together in a shallow bowl placed on a low table.

Mini-climate 5 Cool, filtered sun.
Size Cape primroses grow to about 30cm in height with a spread of 45cm. Small plants in bud are offered for sale.
Feeding Feed with half-strength, high-phosphate liquid fertilizer every two weeks from early spring to late autumn.
Potting Repot every spring using an equal-parts mixture of sphagnum peat moss, coarse grade perlite and vermiculite. Add half a tablespoon of limestone chips to every cup of mixture. Once plants are in 15cm pots root prune instead.

GLOXINIA
Sinningia speciosa hybrids

The large, downy leaves have a bold pattern of veins on them but are eclipsed by the large, showy flowers. They are borne in a cluster on top of the rosette of leaves. Trumpet-shaped with frilled edges they can be white, pink, red or purple, and are often margined in white. Although gloxinias can be treated as annuals they have a tuber which can be dried off in autumn and repotted in spring. Gloxinias are best in period rooms, displayed either singly or massed together.

Mini-climate 2 Warm, filtered sun.
Size Gloxinias can attain a height and spread of about 30cm. Plants in bud are offered for sale.
Feeding Feed with high-phosphate liquid fertilizer once a month during the flowering period.
Potting Repot the tubers in spring using equal parts of peat-based potting mixture, vermiculite and perlite. Repotting once the plant is flowering is unnecessary.

Similar-shaped species
Sinningia pusilla is very small, no more than 3cm tall, but has relatively large, pale-lavender flowers. Many attractive named varieties exist.

Bushy plants 1

Bushy plants are difficult to describe precisely as this category covers a vast range of flowering and foliage plants. Their common feature is a tendency to grow outwards as much as they grow upwards. This gives them a spread nearly equal to their height, and is why they are often displayed on their own, or in twos, rather than in groups with different plants—although some of the more upright bushy plants can make good foils for trailing plants. Many of the flowering bushy plants look good when several of the same species are massed up in a shallow bowl. A large number of the flowering bushy plants are annuals, bought for their display of flowers and then discarded when flowering has finished. Many species branch naturally, regularly producing side shoots, others branch freely only if their growing tips are regularly pinched out. Form and size range from the small, low-growing peperomias and hypoestes to the tall and shrubby spotted laurel. Leaf texture, shape, size and colour are also well represented; from the smooth, fleshy leaves of the florist's cyclamen to the large and pimpled leaves of the painted-leaf begonia. Colourful leaves are found on plants such as the flame nettle, polka-dot plant, and angel wings. Bushy plants are well suited to period homes or places where an informal atmosphere prevails.

SMALL-LEAVED BUSHY PLANTS

AMETHYST VIOLET
Browallia speciosa

These are showy plants with violet-blue flowers which appear in autumn and continue into early winter. They are best treated as annuals and discarded when flowering has finished. Several strains are available, including tall-growing and dwarf types. The stems tend to droop with maturity so plants are best displayed in eye-level hanging baskets or massed together in groups on a low table.

Mini-climate 1 Warm, sunny.
Size Amethyst violets grow to 60cm tall with a similar spread. Pinch out growing tips to encourage bushy growth. Mature plants are offered for sale in autumn.
Feeding Feed with standard liquid fertilizer every two weeks.
Potting Repot in spring using soil-based potting mixture but only if the roots have completely filled the existing pot. Once plants are in 12cm pots topdress instead.
Special points Destroy any greenfly you may find.

Similar-shaped species
Browallia viscosa is only half the size of *B.speciosa*, with smaller leaves and flowers. The leaves are slightly sticky.

ELATIOR BEGONIA
Begonia "Elatior" hybrids

These begonias flower for most of the year. The large, roselike flowers range in colour from deep red, through pink, to yellow and white. They are best treated as annuals and discarded when flowering has finished. The foliage is usually pale green but plants with deep-red foliage are sometimes available. As their flowers are quite large these begonias can be displayed as specimen plants or grouped together in a shallow pan. Elatior begonias do best in light, well-ventilated rooms.

Mini-climate 2 Warm, filtered sun.
Size "Elatior" begonias are usually erect with a maximum height and spread of 35-40cm. Small bushy plants are offered for sale from mid-spring to early autumn.
Feeding Feed with standard liquid fertilizer every two weeks in spring and summer.
Potting Repot two or three times during summer and autumn using a mixture of half soil-based potting mixture and half leaf mould or coarse peat moss. If you don't want to move an older plant into a larger pot topdress instead.
Special points Protect from powdery mildew by supplying adequate ventilation.

Similar-shaped species
Begonia tuberhybrida has large, double flowers of red, pink, white or yellow.

WAX BEGONIA
Begonia semperflorens-cultorum

These are small plants grown for their profusion of flowers. Single- and double-flowered varieties are available. The white, pink or red flowers begin blooming in spring and continue well into the winter. They are best treated as annuals and discarded when flowering has finished. They make excellent display plants when grouped together in shallow containers or mixed with colourful foliage plants. These begonias do best in light, well-ventilated rooms.

Mini-climate 1 Warm, sunny.
Size Wax begonias never reach more than 30cm in height when fully grown. They are offered for sale in spring as seedlings and for the rest of the year as mature plants.
Feeding Feed with standard liquid fertilizer every two weeks in spring and summer.
Potting Repot as needed, perhaps two or three times during summer and autumn, using a mixture of half soil-based potting mixture and half leaf mould or coarse peat moss. If you don't want to move an older plant into a larger pot topdress instead.
Special point Protect from powdery mildew by supplying adequate ventilation.

Temperature 10°-15°C spring to autumn; 7°-10°C in winter | 10°-15°C | 15°-21°C

Light sunny | filtered sun | shady

Humidity low | moderate | high

Watering sparingly | moderately | plentifully

Care easy | fairly easy | challenging

LEMON GERANIUM
Pelargonium crispum "Variegatum"

These geraniums are grown for their aromatic leaves rather than the flowers they produce. The foliage is pale green with a cream-coloured wavy edge, and plants can be trained to many shapes by appropriate pinching out of the growing tips. Place in a position where the leaves will be brushed against for maximum aromatic effect. Geraniums have a pretty, "cottage" look and suit period rooms which are not too formal.

Mini-climate 4 Cool, sunny.
Size Lemon geraniums can grow to 60-90cm tall or be kept small and bushy. Small rooted plants are offered for sale.
Feeding Feed with half-strength standard liquid fertilizer twice in summer.
Potting Repot in spring using soil-based potting mixture on top of a small layer of rough drainage material, but only if the roots have completely filled the existing pot.
Special points Do not overwater in winter as plants become susceptible to black stem rot.

PAINTED NETTLE
Coleus blumei

These plants have soft-textured leaves in a range of vivid colours, from red and bronze to cream and purple, some incorporating three or more colours. Although the serrated leaves closely resemble those of the stinging nettle, the two plants are not related. Painted nettles are best treated as annuals and discarded after one year. Their brightly patterned foliage is suited to period rooms containing richly coloured fabrics.

Mini-climate 1 Warm, sunny.
Size Painted nettles will grow to a height of 45cm in one year with a similar spread. Pinch out growing tips to encourage bushy growth.
Feeding Feed with standard liquid fertilizer every two weeks in spring and summer, and once a month during autumn and winter.
Potting Repot every two months using soil-based potting mixture. If you don't want to move an older plant into a larger pot topdress instead.
Special points Leaf colour is stronger if plants are placed in a sunny position.

EGYPTIAN STAR CLUSTER
Pentas lanceolata

These attractive plants are winter-flowering shrubs, although they may flower at any time of year. They have lance-shaped, hairy leaves and clusters of tiny, star-shaped flowers which can be mauve, white or pink in colour. The almost flat-topped flower heads can be nearly 10cm across. Egyptian star clusters look best when several plants are massed together in an informal room.

Mini-climate 1 Warm, sunny.
Size Egyptian star clusters reach between 30cm and 45cm in height. Pinch out growing tips to encourage bushy growth. Small plants are offered for sale.
Feeding Feed with standard liquid fertilizer every two weeks during the flowering period.
Potting Repot every spring using soil-based potting mixture. If you don't want to move an older plant into a larger pot topdress instead.
Special points Water more sparingly in winter.

BUSY LIZZIE
Impatiens wallerana hybrids

The flower colour of these ubiquitous plants ranges from white, through pink, to red; some flowers are striped with another colour. The foliage and thick, succulent stems also vary in colour from pale green to bronze. Busy Lizzies will begin flowering when only six weeks old and continue throughout the summer. They are best treated as annuals and discarded when flowering has finished. These plants look particularly attractive if grouped in a hanging basket or window-box.

Mini-climate 1 Warm, sunny.
Size Busy Lizzies are fast-growing, the modern hybrids reaching a maximum height of 35cm. Pinch out growing tips to encourage bushy growth. Seedlings and small and medium-sized plants are offered for sale.
Feeding Feed with standard liquid fertilizer every two weeks in spring and summer.
Potting Repot every spring using soil-based potting mixture but only if the roots have completely filled the existing pot. Once the plants are in 12cm pots topdress instead.

Bushy plants 2

SMALL-LEAVED BUSHY PLANTS continued

CHINESE HIBISCUS
Hibiscus rosa-sinensis

Large, funnel-shaped flowers and glossy, dark-green leaves make Chinese hibiscuses spectacular plants. Flowers can be red, pink, white, yellow or orange and appear singly, usually in spring and summer. Use in a bright, sunny setting for an oriental look, either individually or by grouping several plants of different colours together.

Mini-climate 1 Warm, sunny.
Size Chinese hibiscuses are fast-growing, quickly reaching 1.5m in height. Plants with opening buds are usually offered for sale in spring.
Feeding Feed with high-potash liquid fertilizer every two weeks in spring and summer, and once a month in autumn and winter. If flowers are not produced freely, increase the frequency of feeding (not the strength of the fertilizer).
Potting Repot every spring using soil-based potting mixture. If you don't want to move an older plant into a larger pot topdress instead.
Special points Water more sparingly in winter.

GERMAN VIOLET
Exacum affine

Also known as "Persian violets", these are small, bushy plants covered in bright-blue flowers with yellow eyes and shiny, olive-green leaves. They bloom in summer and the flowers can last for up to two months. They are best treated as annuals and discarded when flowering has finished. To display German violets, mass them in a large bowl, as they make an eye-catching show in any setting—traditional or modern.

Mini-climate 2 Warm, filtered sun.
Size German violets will quickly grow stems up to 30cm long. Young, budding plants are offered for sale in early spring.
Feeding Feed with standard liquid fertilizer every two weeks while the plant is in flower.
Potting Repot using soil-based potting mixture but only if the plant was bought in a very small pot. Further repotting is unnecessary.
Special points Stand plants on trays filled with moist pebbles to maintain high humidity.

REGAL GERANIUM
Pelargonium domesticum hybrids

These geraniums have large flower heads that range in colour from white to red; many are bicoloured or tricoloured. The flowering season is short, lasting only from spring to midsummer, but the showiness of the flowers compensates for this. Very much at home in indoor window-boxes, they look equally good as specimen plants.

Mini-climate 4 Cool, sunny.
Size Regal geraniums can be grown as single-stemmed plants of up to 60cm tall, or as small bushy shrubs. Plants of all sizes are offered for sale.
Feeding Feed occasionally with standard liquid fertilizer during spring and summer.
Potting Repot every spring using a soil-based potting mixture. Once plants are in 15cm pots topdress instead.
Special points Cut off faded flower heads to encourage new growth.

Similar-shaped species
Pelargonium hortorum has ball-like clusters of flowers almost all year round.

RED HERRINGBONE PLANT
Maranta leuconeura erythroneura

Also known as "prayer plants" (because of the way pairs of leaves close together at night), they are remarkable for their beautiful leaves marked with deep-red, raised veins. The red midrib is surrounded by a pale-green stripe on the olive-green leaf. Red herringbone plants are amongst the showiest of plants and should be displayed in a prominent position. They can also be trained to grow up short, moss-covered poles.

Mini-climate 3 Warm, shady.
Size Red herringbone plants will grow to a maximum of 15-30cm tall with 40cm spread. Small plants are offered for sale.
Feeding Feed with standard liquid fertilizer every two weeks during spring, summer and autumn.
Potting Repot every spring using soil-based potting mixture in half-pots or other shallow containers. If you don't want to move an older plant into a larger pot topdress instead.

Temperature 10°-15°C spring to autumn, 7°-10°C in winter 10°-15°C 15°-21°C **Light** sunny filtered sun shady **Humidity** low moderate high **Watering** sparingly moderately plentifully **Care** easy fairly easy challenging

CINERARIA
Senecio cruentus hybrids

Cinerarias have large, daisy-shaped flowers which cluster together in the centre of the fleshy leaves. The flowers can be of orange, red, magenta, pink, blue or purple, often with a circle of white surrounding the central disc. The leaves are furry to touch and are often tinged with blue on their undersides. Cinerarias are best treated as annuals and discarded when flowering has finished. A bold display can be made with several cinerarias of the same colour massed together in a china dish or basket. They suit both traditional and modern rooms.

Mini-climate 4 Cool, sunny.
Size Budding cineraria plants up to 30cm tall and of similar spread are offered for sale throughout winter and spring.
Feeding Feeding is not required for these temporary pot plants.
Potting Repotting is unnecessary.
Special points To keep plants in a decorative state for as long as possible, ensure that the potting mixture does not dry out too much. Water is easily lost through the large leaves and the plant will collapse if the roots dry out. Destroy any aphids or whitefly you may find.

POINSETTIA
Euphorbia pulcherrima

With their flamboyant red, pink or creamy-white bracts, poinsettias are welcome at Christmastime. The bracts remain decorative for two months. After this they should be cut hard back and kept for their foliage alone, as it is not easy to get these plants to bloom for a second year. The poinsettia is essentially a specimen plant; the common red form is particularly striking, but can look good when mixed with dark-green foliage plants.

Mini-climate 1 Warm, sunny.
Size Poinsettias rarely grow larger than 30-35cm tall. They are offered for sale in autumn and winter.
Feeding Feed with standard liquid fertilizer once every month.
Potting Repotting of first year plants is unnecessary. If keeping the plant for a second year, repot in the same pot with fresh soil-based potting mixture.
Special points Poinsettias have a sap which can cause irritation of the skin in some people.

POLKA-DOT PLANT
Hypoestes phyllostachya

These are pretty plants with unusual foliage. The leaves, which range from olive-green to very dark green, are spotted with pale-pink dots. They are best treated as annuals and discarded after one year. New forms, as they are quite small, look more dramatic if several plants are grouped together, either in separate pots or planted in a shallow pan.

Mini-climate 2 Warm, filtered sun.
Size Polka-dot plants can grow quite tall but will become straggly, so it is advisable to limit growth to 30cm tall by pinching out the growing tips. Small, bushy plants of 5-7cm tall are offered for sale.
Feeding Feed with standard liquid fertilizer every two weeks from early summer to mid-autumn.
Potting Repot in spring but only if the roots have completely filled the existing pot. Once plants are in 12cm pots topdress instead.
Special points Spray leaves occasionally with tepid water to discourage red spider mites.

AZALEA
Rhododendron simsii

Azaleas produce clusters of brightly coloured flowers atop a mass of shiny, green leaves. Flower colour ranges from white to magenta, including almost every shade of red and pink. Some flowers are bicoloured. They are best treated as annuals and discarded when flowering has finished. Mass up azaleas in a shallow bowl and place in a prominent position in a hallway or other cool place.

Mini-climate 5 Cool, filtered sun.
Size Azaleas do not grow much larger than 30cm in height with a similar spread. Budding plants are offered for sale in winter and spring.
Feeding Feed with standard liquid fertilizer once every two weeks from spring to autumn.
Potting Repotting is unnecessary.
Special points To keep plants in a decorative state for as long as possible, keep the potting mixture permanently moist and display in a cool place.

Bushy plants 3

SMALL-LEAVED BUSHY PLANTS continued

FLORIST'S CYCLAMEN
Cyclamen persicum hybrids

Florist's cyclamens flower in late autumn, winter and early spring. Many varieties are available, with the colour of the swept-back flowers ranging from white, through red, to purple. Some varieties have frilled or perfumed flowers. Although usually treated as an annual, if the tubers are dried off in the late spring and rested during the summer months, cyclamens can last for many years. Cyclamens do not mix well with other plants. They are ideal for colourful displays in entrance halls or period rooms where conditions are not excessively hot.

Mini-climate 5 Cool, filtered sun.
Size Cyclamens rarely grow larger than 20-25cm tall. Budded plants are offered for sale from September until Christmastime.
Feeding Feed with standard liquid fertilizer every two weeks when in flower.
Potting Repotting of first year plants is unnecessary. Repot a rested tuber in soil-based potting mixture in September. Use the same pot each year.
Special points Never pour water directly onto the tuber; instead stand the pot in water for ten minutes.

CHRISTMAS CHERRY
Solanum capsicastrum

Marble-sized, orange-red berries make these small, shrubby plants an autumn favourite. The berries will last for several months if kept in a sunny but cool place; hot, dry air considerably shortens their lives. Placed on a low table or in a window-box, the Christmas cherry adds colour and interest to a group of foliage plants.

Mini-climate 4 Cool, sunny.
Size Christmas cherries reach a maximum height of 45cm. Plants bearing berries are offered for sale.
Feeding Feed with standard liquid fertilizer every two weeks.
Potting Repot in spring using soil-based potting mixture. To keep for a second fruiting season cut away half the growth and move them outside in 12cm pots for the summer.
Special points Mist-spray daily to increase humidity and aid pollination when in flower. The berries are not edible, so keep the plants away from small children.

EMERALD RIPPLE PEPEROMIA
Peperomia caperata

These small plants have very distinctive, deeply ridged, heart-shaped leaves. The low-growing form of the leaves is offset by the vertical, white flower spikes which emerge from the rosette of leaves. Peperomias look good when included in foliage groups with plants of contrasting sizes and textures.

Mini-climate 2 Warm, filtered sun.
Size Emerald ripple peperomias are compact plants, rarely growing taller than 15cm with a similar spread. Young plants and a miniature form for use in bottle gardens are offered for sale.
Feeding Feed with half-strength standard liquid fertilizer once a month from mid-spring to autumn.
Potting Repot in spring using a peat-based potting mixture but only if the roots have completely filled the existing pot.
Special points Do not overwater peperomias as they are liable to rot.

CHRISTMAS PEPPER
Capsicum annuum

An increasingly popular plant bearing brightly coloured fleshy berries which appear in autumn and remain decorative until after Christmas. The most familiar berries are orange-red in colour but white, yellow, green and purple-berried varieties are also available. They are best treated as annuals and discarded when the fruiting has finished. They make colourful Christmas displays and are striking massed together as a table decoration.

Mini-climate 1 Warm, sunny.
Size Christmas peppers are at their best when at 30-35cm height and spread, and fruiting plants of this size are offered for sale.
Feeding Feed with standard liquid fertilizer every two weeks in the fruiting season.
Potting Repotting is unnecessary.
Special points To keep plants in a decorative state for as long as possible, stand plants on trays filled with moist pebbles to increase humidity.

Temperature 10°-15°C spring to autumn, 7°-10°C in winter · 10°-15°C · 15-21°C
Light sunny · filtered sun · shady
Humidity low · moderate · high
Watering sparingly · moderately · plentifully
Care easy · fairly easy · challenging

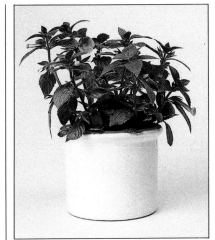

FLORIST'S CHRYSANTHEMUM
Chrysanthemum morifolium hybrids

Also known as "pot chrysanthemums", these plants are offered for sale with flowers of every colour but blue. The flowers and foliage have a distinctive scent. They will remain in flower for about six weeks, and are best treated as annuals and discarded when flowering has finished. Several plants grouped together in a shallow basket or pan on a low table look particularly attractive.

Mini-climate 5 Cool, filtered sun.
Size Florist's chrysanthemums have been specially cultivated to reach no more than 30cm in height. They are offered for sale in flower throughout the year.
Feeding Feeding is not required for these temporary plants.
Potting Repotting is unnecessary.
Special points When buying chrysanthemums make sure the flower buds show colour as tightly closed green buds often fail to open.

PRIMULA
Primula obconica

This is one of the prettiest flowering plants, blooming between Christmas and summer. The long-stalked clusters of flowers are white, pink, salmon or mauve with a distinctive green eye. Primulas are best treated as annuals and discarded when flowering has finished. Use singly or massed together in a shallow pan or basket in any cool area, such as a hallway or bedroom.

Mini-climate 5 Cool, filtered sun.
Size Primulas rarely grow taller than 30cm, with a spread of 25cm. Plants in flower are offered for sale.
Feeding Feed with standard liquid fertilizer every two weeks.
Potting Repotting is unnecessary.

Similar-shaped species
Primula malacoides is a very delicate plant with small white, rose pink or lilac flowers.

CUPID'S BOWER
Achimenes grandiflora

Also known as "magic flowers", these plants have hairy, upright, green or red stems and dull-green leaves which are also hairy. Flowers can be pink, purple or yellow in colour, with white throats. The flowering period lasts from June to October. These are very useful infill plants for an indoor window-box.

Mini-climate 1 Warm, sunny.
Size Cupid's bowers grow to 45cm in height. Small plants are offered for sale in spring.
Feeding Feed with phosphate-rich liquid fertilizer at one-eighth strength when watering during the flowering period.
Potting Repot every spring using an equal-parts mixture of peat moss, coarse sand or perlite, and vermiculite. Divide older plants every spring.
Special points Do not water in winter.

LARGE-LEAVED BUSHY PLANTS

JAPANESE FATSIA
Fatsia japonica

An evergreen shrub which has been used for over a century as an indoor and outdoor plant. It has attractive, shiny, fingered leaves whose colour and texture contrast with the stem which becomes gnarled and woody with age. The plant can be moved outside in summer, where the leaves become a deeper shade of green. Japanese fatsias can look extremely decorative in an architectural setting.

Mini-climate 5 Cool, filtered sun.
Size Japanese fatsias are fast-growing shrubs, reaching 1.5m in height and spread in two years. Small plants are offered for sale.
Feeding Feed with standard liquid fertilizer every two weeks during spring and summer.
Potting Repot every spring using soil-based potting mixture. Clay pots are best because fatsias tend to be top-heavy. If you don't want to move an older plant into a larger pot topdress instead.

Bushy plants 4

LARGE-LEAVED BUSHY PLANTS continued

SPOTTED LAUREL
Aucuba japonica "Variegata"

Also known as "Japanese laurels", these plants were much used by the Victorians in their shrubberies and greenhouses. The modern hybrids are more cheerful, having leaves strongly variegated with yellow. Spotted laurels can be used in window-boxes and in foliage arrangements for cool rooms as they tolerate a certain amount of neglect, poor light and draughts.

Mini-climate 5 Cool, filtered sun.
Size Spotted laurels can reach 90cm high. Plants of about 20cm high are offered for sale.
Feeding Feed with standard liquid fertilizer once a month in summer.
Potting Repot every spring using soil-based potting mixture. Once plants are in 20cm pots topdress instead.
Special points Clean leaves regularly with a damp sponge. Plants can be put outside in summer.

ANGEL WINGS
Caladium hortulanum hybrids

Angel wings send up long, fleshy stalks bearing the paper-thin, heart-shaped leaves. The variety of leaf colours and patterns is immense—besides green leaves with red veining, white and cream leaves veined with pink or green are also available. Angel wings are highly ornamental, especially if several different leaf colours are grouped together.

Mini-climate 3 Warm, shady.
Size The mainly green-leaved angel wings grow to a maximum height of 20-25cm. Varieties with coloured leaves may reach 45-60cm high. Plants in full leaf are offered for sale.
Feeding Feed with half-strength liquid fertilizer every two weeks in spring and summer.
Potting Repot a rested tuber in spring using peat-based potting mixture. Make provision for good drainage. Use 12cm pots and cover the tuber with 2-3cm of potting mixture.

SAFFRON SPIKE
Aphelandra squarrosa "Louisae"

These are dual-purpose flowering and foliage plants. For about six weeks the plant has unusual flower heads of overlapping yellow bracts. When flowering has finished, pinch off the dead blooms and use the saffron spike as a foliage plant. The leaves are large and glossy and marked with large, white veins. Mix with plain-leaved plants for a contrasting display in a modern living-room.

Mini-climate 2 Warm, filtered sun.
Size Saffron spikes grow to about 30cm in height with a similar spread. Plants already in flower are offered for sale.
Feeding Feed with standard liquid fertilizer every week from spring to early autumn.
Potting Repot every spring using soil-based potting mixture. Once plants are in 15cm pots topdress instead.

FLAMINGO FLOWER
Anthurium scherzeranum hybrids

The exotic flower heads consist of a bright scarlet bract encircling a tail-like flower spike. They last for several weeks and can appear at any time between February and July. When in flower, several plants grouped together make an attractive display; when not in flower, the leaves harmonize with those of other tropical plants suitable for shady spots.

Mini-climate 3 Warm, shady.
Size Flamingo flowers grow to about 60cm in height. Small plants are offered for sale.
Feeding Feed every two weeks with standard liquid fertilizer.
Potting Repot every spring using a mixture of one-third soil-based potting mixture, one-third coarse peat moss, and one-third coarse sand. Once plants are in 18cm pots topdress instead. Cover any exposed roots in peat moss.
Special points Water more sparingly in winter. Stand plants on trays filled with moist pebbles to increase humidity.

PAINTED-LEAF BEGONIA
Begonia rex-cultorum

Also known as "rex begonias", these are among the most handsome begonias, grown for their beautifully coloured leaves rather than their flowers, which tend to be insignificant. The heart-shaped leaves, which can be up to 30cm in length, bear striking patterns made up of variations of red, black, silver and green. Leaf texture also varies: some hybrids have smooth leaves; this one has a rippled or pimpled surface.

Mini-climate 3 Warm, shady.
Size Painted-leaf begonias can grow up to 30cm in height with a 90cm spread. Young plants 5-8cm high are offered for sale.
Feeding Feed with standard liquid fertilizer every two weeks in spring and summer.
Potting Divide overcrowded clumps and repot in spring every three years using peat-based potting mixture in a shallow container.
Special points Water more sparingly in winter. Destroy any powdery mildew you may find.

Similar-shaped species
Begonia masoniana has a deep-red, cross-shaped pattern in the middle of its pale-green leaves.

COMPOUND-LEAVED BUSHY PLANTS

MAIDENHAIR FERN
Adiantum raddianum

Maidenhair ferns have delicate, pale-green fronds borne on black, wiry stalks. They mix well with both foliage and flowering house plants and are useful for softening the outline of many arrangements. They also look very attractive on their own. Small plants can be planted in terraria.

Mini-climate 3 Warm, shady.
Size Maidenhair ferns grow to 30cm in height with a similar spread. Plants of all sizes are offered for sale.
Feeding Feed with standard liquid fertilizer once a month during spring and summer.
Potting Repot in spring using fern potting mixture but only when a mass of roots appears on the surface of the potting mixture.
Special points Stand plants on trays filled with moist pebbles to increase humidity.

Similar-shaped species
Adiantum raddianum microphyllum has minute, dark-green, wedge-shaped leaflets.
Adiantum hispidulum is very small and has fingerlike fronds.

ASPARAGUS FERN
Asparagus setaceus

Asparagus ferns have light, feathery foliage made up of tiny branchlets on wiry stems. Taller growing kinds may be trained up thin canes to form a delicate column shape. Trained around east- or west-facing windows they can give a charming "cottage" effect. They can also be included in fern groups in a hanging basket.

Mini-climate 2 Warm, filtered sun.
Size Asparagus ferns can produce stems up to 1.2m long. Small plants are offered for sale.
Feeding Feed with standard liquid fertilizer every two weeks in spring and summer, and once a month in autumn and winter.
Potting Repot every spring using soil-based potting mixture. If you don't want to move an older plant into a larger pot topdress instead.

Similar-shaped species
Asparagus asparagoides is a vigorous climbing vine with leaflet-like branchlets up to 5cm long.
Asparagus falcatus is similar but has sickle-shaped spines on its stems.

CRETAN BRAKE FERN
Pteris cretica

Also known as "table ferns", these plants form clumps of striped fronds which grow from short, underground rhizomes. Each frond is hand-shaped, the individual pinnae looking like fingers. Cretan brake ferns mix well with other plants, especially if used as pot hiders at the front of plant groupings. They are ideal for a north-facing conservatory or plant window collection.

Mini-climate 3 Warm, shady.
Size Cretan brake ferns grow to 35cm in height with a similar spread. Small plants of about 12cm in height are offered for sale.
Feeding Feed with half-strength standard liquid fertilizer once a month.
Potting Repot in spring using fern potting mixture but only if the roots have completely filled the existing pot. If you don't want to move an older plant to a larger pot topdress instead.

Similar-shaped species
Pteris tremula looks like bracken. It is fast-growing, with fronds up to 60cm long and 30cm wide.

Climbing plants 1

Climbing plants usually have stems which are too weak to grow unaided in an upright position, but will grow in any direction provided they have a support to cling to. Many climbing plants can be displayed equally effectively as trailers, and vice-versa. The species which bear aerial roots, such as the philodendrons and the Swiss cheese plant, usually produce quite thick stems and their fleshy leaves can be large and weighty, so they are best grown on a stout moss-covered pole. Some climbing plants naturally scramble through other plants, gaining some support by sending out tendrils or by just "leaning" on their neighbours. Others which produce curly leaf tendrils can be trained on canes, wire hoops and trellis work. Although the tendrils may look thin and frail they are usually very strong. Climbing plants can also be trained to frame windows, mirrors or archways or used to create a foliage screen dividing areas in a room. Many have attractive foliage, such as the scalloped leaves of the kangaroo vine and the yellow-and-green variegated leaves of the Cape ivy and Algerian ivy. A number of climbers have flowers, including the Cape leadwort whose blooms are a striking sky-blue and the jasmine, with its small but heavily scented white flowers. Most spectacular of all are the large, showy flowers of the passion flower.

SMALL-LEAVED CLIMBING PLANTS

ALGERIAN IVY
Hedera canariensis

Also known as "Canary Island ivies", these plants have slightly lobed dark-green leaves with patches of grey-green variegation. They are vigorous climbers and can easily be trained up any kind of support. They make good specimen plants when very large and are most suitable for use in cool places such as halls and stairways.

Mini-climate 5 Cool, filtered sun.
Size Algerian ivies are fast-growing with an unpredictable maximum height and spread; certainly 2m. Leaves can be as much as 12cm long and 15cm wide. Plants of all sizes are offered for sale.
Feeding Feed with standard liquid fertilizer every two weeks when actively growing.
Potting Repot in spring using soil-based potting mixture but only if the roots have completely filled the existing pot. Once plants are in 12-15cm pots topdress instead.
Special points Water more sparingly in winter.

CAPE IVY
Senecio macroglossus

These plants are very similar to the English ivies, but their leaves are smoother, softer and more fleshy. The leaves are borne on purple stems and are green marked with pale-cream streaks and patches. In some cases, where variegation is very strong, all the leaves on a shoot may be predominantly cream-coloured. Cape ivies should be trained around hoops of bamboo cane or wire, or planted in small hanging baskets.

Mini-climate 1 Warm, sunny.
Size Cape ivies grow up to 1m in height and spread. Pinch out growing tips to maintain bushy growth. Small plants are offered for sale.
Feeding Feed with standard liquid fertilizer every two weeks during spring and summer.
Potting Repot every spring using a mixture of one part coarse sand to three parts soil-based mixture. Once plants are in 15cm pots topdress instead.
Special points Water more sparingly in winter. Destroy any aphids you may find.

GRAPE IVY
Cissus rhombifolia

These plants have deeply toothed leaves. New leaf growth appears to be silver due to a fine covering of hairs on both surfaces. Older leaves have undersides covered in fine, brown hairs. Trained up a simple framework of bamboo canes, grape ivies can become quite large feature plants relatively quickly. They also make an excellent display in large hanging baskets.

Mini-climate 2 Warm, filtered sun.
Size Grape ivies grow to 1.8m in height in around two years and can reach 3m in ideal conditions. Pinch out growing tips regularly to encourage bushy growth. Plants of all sizes are offered for sale.
Feeding Feed with standard liquid fertilizer every two weeks in spring and summer.
Potting Repot every spring using soil-based potting mixture. Once plants are in 15-18cm pots topdress instead.

Temperature 10°-15°C spring to autumn; 7°-10°C in winter 10°-15°C 15°-21°C

Light sunny filtered sun shady

Humidity low moderate high

Watering sparingly moderately plentifully

Care easy fairly easy challenging

PASSION FLOWER
Passiflora caerulea

These exotic-looking plants have beautiful flowers. Each consists of five pinkish-white petals and five pinkish-white sepals encircling a ring of purple-blue filaments. These filaments encircle the golden anthers. The flowers may appear at any time during the summer and autumn. The foliage is dark green and stems should be trained over a wire support to make an attractive shape. Passion flowers make striking specimen plants for conservatories or large, bright windowsills.

Mini-climate 1 Warm, sunny.
Size Passion flowers have a maximum height and spread of about 10m. Plants of all sizes are offered for sale.
Feeding Feed with standard liquid fertilizer every two weeks during spring, summer and autumn.
Potting Repot every spring using soil-based potting mixture. Once plants are in 20cm pots topdress instead.
Special points To keep plants in a decorative state for as long as possible, prune heavily in spring.

WAX FLOWER
Stephanotis floribunda

These plants have dark-green, glossy leaves carried on woody stems, which twine readily round any support, and delightfully scented, waxy, white flowers. The flowers grow in clusters of ten or more and each is tube-shaped, flaring out into five pointed lobes. They appear from spring until autumn. Wax flowers may be trained to climb a trellis or, if space is more limited, round a hoop of wire or cane inserted into the pot.

Mini-climate 1 Warm, sunny.
Size Wax flowers are vigorous growers. Height and spread is variable, but is usually about 3m. Pinch out growing tips to encourage bushy growth. Plants of all sizes are offered for sale.
Feeding Feed with standard liquid fertilizer every two weeks during spring and summer.
Potting Repot every second year in spring using soil-based potting mixture. Once plants are in 20cm pots topdress instead.
Special points Stand plants on trays filled with moist pebbles to increase humidity. Water more sparingly in winter.

PLUSH VINE
Mikania ternata

These small plants have soft, slaty-green foliage covered in fine, purple hairs. The underside of the leaves and the stems are purple. Plush vines can be used in much the same way as ivies—either as trailers or climbers—although they do not grow as tall. Their unusual colouring provides a contrast to light-green plants in a mixed foliage arrangement.

Mini-climate 2 Warm, filtered sun.
Size Plush vines have a maximum height and spread of about 60cm. Small plants are offered for sale.
Feeding Feed with standard liquid fertilizer every two weeks from spring to autumn.
Potting Repot in spring using soil-based potting mixture. Discard the plant after the second repotting.
Special points Do not wet the hairy foliage.

BLACK-EYED SUSAN
Thunbergia alata

Black-eyed Susans have attractive bright-orange flowers with a characteristic deep chocolate-brown "eye". The large, round blooms are produced from spring to late autumn. Black-eyed Susans look particularly good when trained to climb up strings in front of a window.

Mini-climate 4 Cool, sunny.
Size Black-eyed Susans may reach over 2m in height. Young plants are offered for sale.
Feeding Feed with standard liquid fertilizer every two weeks.
Potting Repot in spring using soil-based potting mixture but only if the roots have completely filled the existing pot. Once plants are in 15cm pots top-dress instead.
Special points To keep plants in a decorative state for as long as possible, pinch out any faded flowers.

Climbing plants 2

SMALL-LEAVED CLIMBING PLANTS continued

KANGAROO VINE
Cissus antarctica

Relatives of the grapevine, these are scrambling foliage plants whose glossy, dark-green leaves have marked veining and a scalloped edge. They can be used in many different ways: either trained up poles, used as specimen plants or displayed in hanging baskets.

Mini-climate 2 Warm, filtered sun.
Size Kangaroo vines grow to 2m tall with a spread of 60cm in about two years. Plants of all sizes are offered for sale.
Feeding Feed with standard liquid fertilizer every two weeks in spring and summer.
Potting Repot every spring using soil-based potting mixture. Once plants are in 15-20cm pots topdress instead.
Special points Stand plants on trays filled with moist pebbles to increase humidity. Mist-spray plants in hanging baskets.

CAPE LEADWORT
Plumbago auriculata

These plants produce clusters of up to 20 pale-blue flowers from spring to autumn. A narrow, darker blue stripe runs down each of the five petals which flare from a 4cm long tube. Training these plants round a trellis produces an attractive display, or they can be trained to cover a wall.

Mini-climate 1 Warm, sunny.
Size The stems of the Cape leadwort can reach over 1m in length, but should be pruned every spring as the plants can become very straggly. Plants of all sizes are offered for sale.
Feeding Feed with tomato-type liquid fertilizer once every two weeks from spring until autumn.
Potting Repot every spring using soil-based potting mixture. Once plants are in 20cm pots topdress instead.
Special points Water more sparingly in winter.

WHITE-SCENTED JASMINE
Jasminum polyanthum

Clusters of white, scented flowers are produced by these attractive plants in winter and spring. Jasmine are most delicate-looking, but are very vigorous climbers, easily trained round wire hoops or any other fine support. If planted in a conservatory border, they can be trained to cover a wall.

Mini-climate 4 Cool, sunny.
Size White-scented jasmine can reach 6m if grown in a border, 1m if grown in a pot. Spread depends upon the support used. Plants in flower are offered for sale in winter.
Feeding Feed with standard liquid fertilizer once a month in summer and autumn.
Potting Repot every spring using soil-based potting mixture. Once plants are in 20cm pots topdress instead.
Special points Place plants outdoors in summer.

GOLDEN TRUMPET
Allamanda cathartica

These climbing plants produce bright, butter-cup-yellow flowers over a period of many weeks during the summer. The oval leaves which are carried on long stems are a glossy dark green colour. If grown in a conservatory border, or in a tub, golden trumpets can be trained to cover a wall. For the smaller room, they can be grown in pots and trained over a wire framework of any shape.

Mini-climate 2 Warm, filtered sun.
Size Golden trumpets are fast-growing and can attain a maximum height and spread of 2.5m. Plants should be cut back by as much as two-thirds in winter. Small plants are offered for sale in summer.
Feeding Feed with standard liquid fertilizer every two weeks in summer.
Potting Repot every spring using soil-based potting mixture. If you don't want to move an older plant into a larger pot topdress instead.
Special points Water more sparingly in winter.

Temperature 10°-15°C spring to autumn 7°-10°C in winter | 10°-15°C | 15°-21°C · Light sunny, filtered sun, shady · Humidity low, moderate, high · Watering sparingly, moderately, plentifully · Care easy, fairly easy, challenging

PAPER FLOWER
Bougainvillea buttiana

Armed with sharp spines, these plants are woody-stemmed. The small, creamy-white flowers are insignificant in themselves but are surrounded by large, decorative, papery bracts which can be white, yellow, orange, pink, red or purple. These are produced in clusters of between 10 and 20, mainly during spring and summer. Although they are naturally climbing plants, paper flowers can be trained to remain bushy indoors. They are best grown in very sunny rooms or conservatories, since they require a large amount of light to encourage them to flower.

Mini-climate 1 Warm, sunny.
Size Paper flowers can reach a maximum height and spread of about 2m. Pinch out growing tips to encourage bushy growth. Small plants are offered for sale.
Feeding Feed with standard liquid fertilizer every two weeks in summer.
Potting Repot every spring using soil-based potting mixture with extra peat moss mixed in. Once plants are in 20cm pots topdress instead.
Special points Water more sparingly in winter. Destroy any mealy bugs you may find.

LARGE-LEAVED CLIMBING PLANTS

BURGUNDY PHILODENDRON
Philodendron "Burgundy"

These large-leaved philodendrons have bright-red leaf stalks and undersides to their leaves. They will flourish if trained around a moss-covered pole. Large specimens look best displayed on their own.

Mini-climate 3 Warm, shady.
Size Burgundy philodendrons are slow-growing; they eventually reach a height of 2m.
Feeding Feed with standard liquid fertilizer every two weeks in spring and summer.
Potting Repot in spring using half soil-based potting mixture and half leaf mould, but only if the roots have filled the existing pot. Once plants are in 15-25cm pots topdress instead.

Similar-shaped species
Philodendron hastatum has deep-green leaves.

ARROWHEAD PLANT
Syngonium podophyllum "Imperial White"

These climbing plants are unusual in that the shape of the leaves changes as the plant matures. Young leaves have three deeply-cut lobes but, in older specimens, the leaves have five lobes. Arrowhead plants can be trained to climb up thin stakes, or up a moss-covered pole, or they can trail from a hanging basket.

Mini-climate 2 Warm, filtered sun.
Size The stems can grow up to 2m. The spread depends on the support system used.
Feeding Feed with standard liquid fertilizer every two weeks from spring to autumn.
Potting Repot in spring using an equal-parts mixture of soil-based potting mixture and leaf mould, but only if the roots have completely filled the existing pot. If you don't want to move an older plant into a larger pot topdress instead.

SWISS CHEESE PLANT
Monstera deliciosa

These plants have undivided, heart-shaped leaves when young; the characteristic split edges and holes appear with age. Train Swiss cheese plants up a moss-covered pole so that the pencil-thick aerial roots can be guided into the moss; never cut these roots off as they take in nutrients. The scale of a mature plant makes it a good foil for large pieces of furniture.

Mini-climate 3 Warm, shady.
Size Swiss cheese plants can reach a height in excess of 2.5m. Plants of all sizes are offered for sale.
Feeding Feed with standard liquid fertilizer every two weeks in spring and summer.
Potting Repot every spring using two-thirds soil-based potting mixture and one-third leaf mould. Once plants are in 20cm pots topdress instead.
Special points Clean older leaves regularly.

Trailing plants 1

Most of these plants look best displayed with their stems hanging downwards, although some, such as ivies and philodendrons, can be trained to climb as well. Trailing plants are best displayed in hanging baskets, on pedestals, or on shelves, so that the tumbling foliage can be appreciated. They can also be used to soften the outline of any arrangement or to disguise the edges of a hanging basket, shelf or table. Within the group there is a wonderful range of leaf textures, from the light, feathery fronds of the emerald fern to the bold, fleshy fronds of the staghorn fern, and the delicate, dripping foliage of the strawberry geranium. A dramatic hanging display can be made using the large foliage of the staghorn fern contrasted with the heart-shaped leaves of the sweetheart plant. For colour there are the red flowers of the columneas and the light-blue or white flowers of the Italian bellflower. The leaves of trailing plants can also provide colour and different textures: for example, the furry, purple foliage of the purple velvet plant and the beautiful, silver-marked foliage of the pothos vine.

SMALL-LEAVED TRAILING PLANTS

SWEETHEART PLANT
Philodendron scandens

These small-leaved philodendrons are the easiest members of this family to grow. The acutely pointed leaves are fleshy and attractively bronzed when they first appear, but become dark green and leathery with age. Sweetheart plants can be trained up a support, such as a moss-covered pole, as well as being left to trail. They make good fillers for the front of groups, and are ideal for warm rooms which don't get too much sun.

Mini-climate 3 Warm, shady.
Size Sweetheart plants are fast-growing; maximum size is unpredictable but a 2m length and a 50cm spread can be reached. Pinch out growing tips to encourage bushy growth. Small plants are offered for sale.
Feeding Feed with standard liquid fertilizer every two weeks in spring and summer, and once every month in autumn and winter.
Potting Repot every spring using half soil-based potting mixture and half leaf mould or peat moss. Once plants are in 25-30cm pots topdress instead.
Special points Stand plants on trays filled with moist pebbles to increase humidity.

POTHOS VINE
Scindapsus pictus "Argyraeus"

The most striking feature of these plants is their matt olive-green coloured leaves covered with silver spots. The heart-shaped leaves are carried on thick stems which occasionally produce aerial roots. Mass several small plants together or put a large specimen in a hanging basket near a sunny window. Pothos vines also make attractive feature plants when trained up moist, moss-covered poles.

Mini-climate 1 Warm, sunny.
Size Pothos vines are slow-growing, but mature plants can reach 1.5m in height with a similar spread. Pinch out growing tips in spring to encourage bushy growth. Plants of 10-15cm in height are offered for sale.
Feeding Feed with standard liquid fertilizer every two weeks from spring to autumn.
Potting Repot in spring using soil-based potting mixture but only if the roots have completely filled the existing pot. Once plants are in 15cm pots topdress instead.
Special points Water more sparingly in winter.

DEVIL'S IVY
Epipremnum aureum

These plants, also known as "Solomon Island's ivies", have yellowish-green, angular stems with aerial roots and large, bright-green leaves boldly and irregularly marked with yellow. Devil's ivy is impressive in hanging baskets, on high shelves, or when trained up moss-covered poles. Large specimens have large leaves and are best displayed on their own in a warm room.

Mini-climate 2 Warm, filtered sun.
Size The stems of devil's ivy grow to a maximum of 2m long with a 1m spread. Pinch out growing tips to encourage bushy growth. Young, small-leaved plants are offered for sale.
Feeding Feed with standard liquid fertilizer every two weeks in spring and summer.
Potting Repot every spring using soil-based potting mixture. If you don't want to move an older plant into a larger pot topdress instead.
Special points Water more sparingly in winter.

Temperature 10°-15°C spring to autumn; 7°-10°C in winter / 10°-15°C / 15°-21°C **Light** sunny / filtered sun / shady **Humidity** low / moderate / high **Watering** sparingly / moderately / plentifully **Care** easy / fairly easy / challenging

WANDERING JEW
Zebrina pendula

Wandering Jews are highly decorative plants with attractive leaf colouring. The oval leaves have a striped, iridescent upper surface and a deep-purple underside. In spring and autumn, clusters of small, purple-pink flowers are produced. Wandering Jews make a fine display when massed together in hanging baskets, but also look attractive trailing over the edge of a bowl in a mixed planting.

Mini-climate 1 Warm, sunny.
Size The stems of wandering Jews grow to 40cm long with a spread of 30cm. Pinch out growing tips to encourage bushy growth. Small plants are offered for sale.
Feeding Feed with standard liquid fertilizer once every two weeks.
Potting Repot in spring using soil-based potting mixture but only if the roots have completely filled the existing pot. Discard the plant after the second or third repotting.
Special points Remove stems with poorly coloured leaves should they appear.

MINIATURE WAX PLANT
Hoya bella

These are spreading plants with drooping stems and dull green, fleshy leaves. The pure white, strongly scented flowers are grouped in star-shaped clusters of eight to ten, each flower having a curious purple centre. Flowers appear through the summer. Miniature wax plants are best displayed in hanging baskets as the centres of the drooping flowers can only be seen from below. They look good in a sunny conservatory or modern interior.

Mini-climate 1 Warm, sunny.
Size Miniature wax plants grow to 30cm in height, the branches then begin to trail and produce a maximum spread of 45cm.
Feeding Feed with high-potash liquid fertilizer every two weeks from spring to early autumn.
Potting Repot every spring using soil-based potting mixture making provision for good drainage. Once plants are in 12-15cm pots topdress instead.
Special points Destroy any mealy bugs you may find.

COLUMNEA
Columnea "Banksii"

These plants have striking scarlet flowers borne amongst the small, waxy leaves on long trailing stems. The flowers may be produced at any time of year and a large plant may have up to 100 flowers at any one time. Use large plants as specimens in plain containers or hanging baskets in a warm room.

Mini-climate 2 Warm, filtered sun.
Size The trailing stems of columneas reach a maximum length of 1.2m. Young plants are offered for sale in spring.
Feeding Feed with one-quarter strength high-phosphate liquid fertilizer at every watering.
Potting Repot every spring using a mixture of equal parts peat moss, perlite and vermiculite. If you don't want to move an older plant into a larger pot prune the roots instead.
Special points Maintain high humidity throughout the year.

TRADESCANTIA
Tradescantia albiflora "Albovittata"

Tradescantias are very similar to zebrinas. The silver and green striped leaves are almost transparent. Mass plants together in a hanging basket or allow a large specimen to trail from a shelf. They are useful for inclusion at the front of mixed arrangements in a suitably warm room. Tradescantias will also climb.

Mini-climate 1 Warm, sunny.
Size Tradescantias are fast-growing, the stems reaching 30cm long. Pinch out growing tips to encourage bushy growth.
Feeding Feed with standard liquid fertilizer every two weeks from spring to autumn.
Potting Repot in spring using soil-based potting mixture but only if the roots have completely filled the existing pot. Discard the plant after the second repotting.
Special points Remove any dried or poorly coloured leaves.

Similar-shaped species
Tradescantia fluminensis "Variegata" has leaves which are a deep olive-green striped with cream and pink and covered with soft, velvety hairs.
Tradescantia sillamontana has peppermint-green leaves with long, white, woolly hair.

Trailing plants 2

SMALL-LEAVED TRAILING PLANTS continued

PICKABACK PLANT
Tolmiea menziesii

These plants, which are also known as "mother-of-thousands", derive their common names from the way that a number of mature leaves produce small plantlets on their upper surfaces. These weigh down the long leafstalks to give a trailing appearance. The fresh-green leaves and slender leafstalks are covered with soft hair. These are excellent plants to display in hanging baskets. They are easily kept in any cool place.

Mini-climate 5 Cool, filtered sun.
Size Pickaback plants are fast-growing and reach a height of about 30cm with a similar spread. Small plants are offered for sale.
Feeding Feed with standard liquid fertilizer every two weeks during spring and summer.
Potting Repot in spring using soil-based potting mixture but only if the roots have completely filled the existing pot. Discard the plant after the second or third repotting.
Special points Water more sparingly in winter.

SPIDER PLANT
Chlorophytum comosum "Vittatum"

These hybrids have a distinctive white or cream stripe down the centre of each leaf. The narrow leaves arch over but the true trailing effect is produced by long stems bearing numerous plantlets. Well-grown spider plants make striking feature plants when displayed from a height, either on pedestals or in hanging baskets.

Mini-climate 5 Cool, filtered sun.
Size The leaves of spider plants can grow up to 60cm long. The spread depends on the number of plants growing in the same pot. Plants of all sizes are offered for sale.
Feeding Feed with standard liquid fertilizer every two weeks.
Potting Repot in spring using soil-based potting mixture but only if the roots have completely filled the existing pot. If you don't want to move an older plant into a larger pot topdress instead.
Special points Allow a 3cm space at the top of the pot for the development of the fat roots.

STRAWBERRY GERANIUM
Saxifraga stolonifera

These plants produce many plantlets on threadlike stems. The mother plants are small and low-growing and the plantlets hang down from the centre of the plant giving a trailing effect. Strawberry geraniums are best displayed in hanging baskets so that the red undersides to their leaves may be seen. Display in cool places, such as hallways, and ensure the delicate trailing stems are not brushed against.

Mini-climate 5 Cool, filtered sun.
Size Strawberry geraniums are fast growing, but reach no more than 20cm high. The trailing stems grow to 60cm long.
Feeding Feed with standard liquid fertilizer once a month.
Potting Repot every spring using soil-based potting mixture. Discard the plant after the second repotting.
Special points Water more sparingly during the winter rest period.

ENGLISH IVY
Hedera helix hybrids

There are many hybrids of the English ivies, all forming low-growing bushy trailers, but with many variations in leaf shape and colour.
Ivies may be used in a variety of ways: to infill the fronts of groups, as trailers in hanging baskets, or displayed along shelves. They can also be trained to climb.

Mini-climate 5 Cool, filtered sun.
Size Ivies can grow very large and straggly so pinch out growing tips to encourage bushy growth. Plants of all sizes are offered for sale.
Feeding Feed with standard liquid fertilizer every two weeks in spring and summer and once a month in autumn and winter.
Potting Repot in spring using soil-based potting mixture but only if the roots have completely filled the existing pot. If you don't want to move an older plant into a larger pot topdress instead.
Special points Water more sparingly during the winter rest period.

Temperature 10°-15°C spring to autumn, 7°-10°C in winter / 10°-15°C / 15°-21°C

Light sunny / filtered sun / shady

Humidity low / moderate / high

Watering sparingly / moderately / plentifully

Care easy / fairly easy / challenging

EMERALD FERN
Asparagus densiflorus "Sprengeri"

These plants have arching fronds which begin to trail with age. Each frond is covered in tiny branchlets, giving the plants a delicate, fernlike appearance; in fact they are not true ferns but related to the lilies. Use them to soften the outline of arrangements, or group with true ferns in a hanging basket. Emerald ferns thrive in most conditions and have a fresh, informal look which makes them suitable for most types of setting.

Mini-climate 2 Warm, filtered sun.
Size The fronds of emerald ferns can grow up to 90cm in length. Small plants are offered for sale.
Feeding Feed with standard liquid fertilizer every two weeks in spring and summer, and once a month in autumn and winter.
Potting Repot in spring using soil-based potting mixture but only if the roots have completely filled the existing pot. If you don't want to move an older plant into a larger pot topdress instead.
Special points To keep plants in a decorative state for as long as possible, faded fronds should be cut out as they appear.

PURPLE VELVET PLANT
Gynura aurantiaca

The tooth-edged leaves of these plants are covered in fine, purple hair and are at their most colourful when the leaves first open. The stems are upright at first but sprawl as they get longer. The downy leaves are seen to full advantage when the plants are massed in hanging baskets and viewed against a sunny window. A large plant looks good displayed in a room containing richly coloured fabrics.

Mini-climate 1 Warm, sunny.
Size The trailing stems of purple velvet plants can reach 50-100cm in length. Small, compact plants are offered for sale.
Feeding Feed with standard liquid fertilizer once every month.
Potting Repot in spring using soil-based potting mixture. Discard the plant after the second repotting.
Special points Water more sparingly in winter. Unpleasantly scented orange flowers are produced and should be removed before they open.

ITALIAN BELLFLOWER
Campanula isophylla

Italian bellflowers produce clusters of delicate-looking white or pale-blue flowers in early August and continue flowering until November. The flowers are normally so numerous that they completely hide the pale-green foliage. They are best treated as annuals and discarded when flowering has finished. Italian bellflowers are useful plants for massing in hanging baskets or window-boxes. They look good in conservatories or informal rooms.

Mini-climate 4 Cool, sunny.
Size The slender stems of Italian bellflowers reach a maximum length of 30cm. Pinch out growing tips to encourage bushy growth. Small plants are offered for sale in summer.
Feeding Feed with standard liquid fertilizer every two weeks during the flowering season.
Potting Repot every spring using soil-based potting mixture. When plants are in 12cm pots topdress instead.
Special points Mist-spray plants in hanging baskets every day throughout summer and autumn.

LARGE-LEAVED TRAILING PLANTS

STAGHORN FERN
Platycerium bifurcatum

These are most unusual ferns. All plants have two types of frond: small fronds which clasp the plant's support and large, drooping fronds which give the fern its distinctive appearance. The fronds are dark green and covered with a fine, white, felty scurf. Staghorn ferns make striking specimen plants, particularly when displayed from a height.

Mini-climate 3 Warm, shady.
Size The fronds of the staghorn fern reach up to 90cm. Small plants are offered for sale.
Feeding Feed with standard liquid fertilizer once a month during active growth. Add feed to a bucket of water used to soak the pot or bark.
Potting Only small plants should be in pots—use fern potting mixture. Older plants should be grown on a piece of bark. Wrap the root ball in sphagnum moss and tie to the bark.
Special points Mist-spray regularly to maintain high humidity.

Creeping plants

These are plants with stems that grow just over the surface of the potting mixture, and this ground-hugging habit creates a carpeting effect when they are allowed to spread. Creeping plants can be used successfully as ground cover around upright plants and to break up the hard lines of large containers. Some creeping plants, such as the club moss, send roots down into the potting mixture whenever they touch it, virtually creating new plants; while others, such as the Swedish ivy, do no more than rest on the surface of the mixture.

Plants in this group tend to be small-leaved and most are small in overall size. Some will spread to become quite large with age, but will only do this if they are given adequate space. Certain species, like the versatile creeping fig, have a naturally creeping habit but can also be trained to climb up a support or trail from a hanging basket, as can the larger Swedish ivy.

Some of the plants in this category have unusual leaf-markings: the eyelash begonia has reddish-brown markings on lime-green leaves; the snakeskin plant has exotic, carmine-red leaf veins on a dark-green background; and the little snakeskin plant has silver leaf veins. The bead plant has pea-sized orange berries which remain decorative for several months. The colourful leaves and berries of the creeping plants compensate for the lack of flowers; any flowers which do appear are small and insignificant. Many of the creeping plants are particularly well suited to the humid atmosphere of bottle gardens and terraria.

SMALL-LEAVED CREEPING PLANTS

MIND-YOUR-OWN-BUSINESS
Soleirolia soleirolii

These pretty plants produce masses of tiny, bright-green leaves on thin stems, and will quickly carpet all available space in the pot. A number of these mossy mounds make an attractive display if they are massed together in a wicker basket They also look good filling in the front of foliage displays. Do not use them in bottle gardens or terraria as they quickly fill all the available space.

Mini-climate 4 Cool, sunny.
Size Mind-your-own-business plants will not exceed 5cm in height, but their spread is only limited by the size of the container in which they are grown. Trim the plant with a pair of scissors to maintain a neat shape. Small and medium-sized plants are offered for sale all year.
Feeding Feed with half-strength standard liquid fertilizer every two weeks in summer.
Potting Repot in spring using soil-based potting mixture. Discard the plant after the second repotting.
Special points Keep potting mixture damp at all times to prevent the leaves from turning brown.

BEAD PLANT
Nertera granadensis

The attractive bead plants have tiny, green leaves, but are prized for the profusion of pea-sized, bright-orange berries that develop from the insignificant, greenish-yellow flowers. The berries appear in late summer and last several months. They are best treated as annuals and discarded when the berries begin to die off. Bead plants make colourful table displays and are also suitable for growing in dish gardens, bottle gardens and terraria as long as they are kept small.

Mini-climate 4 Cool, sunny.
Size Bead plants form a low mound up to 8cm high, with a maximum spread of around 15cm. Small plants are offered for sale.
Feeding Feed with standard liquid fertilizer every two months while the berries are growing.
Potting Repot every spring using a mixture of two-thirds soil-based potting mixture and one-third peat moss. If you don't want to move an older plant into a larger pot topdress instead.
Special points Water more sparingly in winter. Bead plants can be placed outside, in a sheltered spot, in summer.

CLUB MOSS
Selaginella martensii

These unusual plants have decorative, medium-green leaves which are packed round the branches like the scales of a fish. The creeping stems of the club mosses form a dense mat of foliage with a pleasant, soft texture. Roots are put down into the potting mixture at intervals. A terrarium or bottle garden is the best environment in which to display these small plants as they will thrive in the humid atmosphere.

Mini-climate 2 Warm, filtered sun.
Size The creeping stems of club mosses may grow to 15cm in length. Small plants are offered for sale.
Feeding Feed with one-quarter strength standard liquid fertilizer every two weeks.
Potting Repot every spring using a mixture of two-thirds peat-based potting mix and one-third coarse sand. Once plants are in 15-20cm pots simply remove plants from their pots, clean and refill them with fresh mixture and replace the plants.
Special points Touch the plants as little as possible as this can damage the foliage.

Similar-shaped species
Selaginella apoda has shorter stems which branch more profusely, bearing fleshy, pale-green leaves.
Selaginella emmeliana has white-edged leaves which grow on erect stems of up to 30cm long.

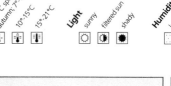

Temperature			Light			Humidity			Watering			Care		
10°-15°C spring to autumn; 7°-10°C in winter	10°-15°C	15°-21°C	sunny	filtered sun	shady	low	moderate	high	sparingly	moderately	plentifully	easy	fairly easy	challenging

EYELASH BEGONIA
Begonia "Tiger Paws"

Eyelash begonias derive their name from the short, coarse hairs which grow around the edge of each lopsided, heart-shaped leaf. The attractive foliage is bright lime-green in colour, marked with a bronze-red pattern which gives the leaves a patched or blotchy appearance. The stalks are also speckled with red and arise from a rhizome which creeps across the surface of the potting mixture. Mass these begonias together in a basket or mix them with other foliage plants.

Mini-climate 2 Warm, filtered sun.
Size Eyelash begonias grow to about 15cm in height with a 30cm spread. Small plants are offered for sale all year.
Feeding Feed with standard liquid fertilizer every two weeks during spring and summer.
Potting Repot every spring using an equal combination of soil-based potting mixture and leaf mould. If you don't want to move an older plant into a larger pot topdress instead. Discard the plant after several repottings.
Special points Stand plants on trays filled with moist pebbles to increase humidity. Protect from powdery mildew by supplying adequate ventilation.

SNAKESKIN PLANT
Fittonia verschaffeltii

These plants have oval, olive-green leaves which are covered by a network of fine, carmine-coloured veins creating a mosaic effect. Yellow flower spikes may occasionally be produced. These plants are suitable for massing together on a low table; they also look good in the forefront of a foliage group and are ideal for bottle gardens or terraria.

Mini-climate 3 Warm, shady.
Size Snakeskin plants reach a height of 15cm with a spread of about 30cm. Pinch out growing tips to encourage bushy growth. Small plants are offered for sale all year.
Feeding Feed with half-strength standard liquid fertilizer every two weeks in spring and summer.
Potting Repot every spring using peat-based potting mixture in half-pots or other shallow containers. Once plants are in 12cm pots simply remove plants from their pots, clean and refill them with fresh mixture and replace the plants.
Special points Stand plants on trays filled with moist pebbles to increase humidity.

Similar-shaped species
Fittonia verschaffeltii argyroneura "Nana" has smaller leaves with silver veins and reaches a maximum spread of only 15cm.

SWEDISH IVY
Plectranthus australis

Swedish ivies have fleshy, dark-green foliage borne on succulent, pink stems which lie flat on the potting mixture before they grow over the edge of the pot. The occasional pale-lavender flowers are insignificant and can be removed as they develop. Especially attractive in hanging baskets, the Swedish ivy also provides excellent ground cover for indoor window-boxes and other large groupings.

Mini-climate 1 Warm, sunny.
Size Swedish ivies are fast-growing; their stems quickly reach 90cm in length, with a height of 20cm. Pinch out the growing tips to encourage bushy growth. Small plants are offered for sale.
Feeding Feed with standard liquid fertilizer every two weeks from spring to autumn.
Potting Repot in spring using soil-based potting mixture but only if the roots have completely filled the existing pot. If you don't want to move an older plant into a larger pot topdress instead.
Special points Water more sparingly in winter.

Similar-shaped species
Plectranthus oertendahlii has bronze-green leaves covered in soft hairs. The leaves have prominent white veins and are rosy-purple underneath.

CREEPING FIG
Ficus pumila

These plants have small, heart-shaped, slightly wrinkled leaves borne on long, wiry stems which spread out across the surface of the potting mixture. Creeping figs look good in shallow hanging baskets. Alternatively, they can be used as ground cover in indoor window-boxes. Small plants make good fillers in bottle gardens.

Mini-climate 5 Cool, filtered sun.
Size The stems of the creeping fig can reach 60cm in length. Spread depends on the mode of growth. Small plants are offered for sale.
Feeding Feed with standard liquid fertilizer every two weeks.
Potting Repot in spring using peat-based potting mixture but only if the roots have completely filled the existing pot.
Special points Stand plants on trays filled with moist pebbles to increase humidity. Never allow the potting mixture to dry out as the leaves will shrivel and never recover.

Bulbs

Bulbs and corms are the food storage organs of plants which have a distinct dormant period when all top growth dies down and no further growth takes place. Bulbs are made up of tightly packed modified leaves surrounding an embryo shoot and usually a complete embryo flower. Corms consist of modified stem bases covered in thin, papery scales and do not contain the young plant, but a bud from which the shoots and roots appear. Most bulbs and corms are "hardy", in that they need a period of wintering. Hardy bulbs are bought in their dormant state during autumn and early winter and, when potted up and provided with the right growing conditions, they start to come into flower in a matter of a few weeks. These special cold, dark conditions are known as "wintering" and it is during this period that roots are produced. To produce good flowers, the wintering recommendations for each bulb should be

adhered to, as it is essential that adequate roots are established before flowering is induced. It should be noted that the care symbols for each entry refer to conditions applicable when the plant is in full flower. Some corms, such as crocuses, need to be kept cool right up to the stage when the flower buds start to show colour, and their early development cannot be enjoyed in the home. Most spring bulbs, such as tulips, narcissi and hyacinths, especially those treated by the nurseryman, can be potted up and most of their growth and development watched and enjoyed. The size of the plants produced ranges from the tiny crocus to the tall and elegant amaryllis.

Hardy bulbs and corms provide temporary house plants, but tender bulbs, such as the amaryllis, can be brought into flower season after season providing they are given a rest period in autumn.

DAFFODIL AND NARCISSUS
Narcissus hybrids

These bulbs have bright, graceful flowers, many of which are scented, with colours ranging through all shades of orange, yellow, cream and white. Many different shapes are available: trumpets, clusters, double-flowered and many other forms. Daffodils have trumpets which are longer than their outer petals, whereas narcissi have trumpets shorter than or as long as the outer petals. Daffodils and narcissi bloom naturally in late winter and early spring. Display them in bowls filled with potting mixture or bulb fibre, or grow them hydroponically in glass containers.

Mini-climate 5 Cool, filtered sun.
Size Daffodils and narcissi grow to 15-45cm in height, according to variety. Bulbs are offered for sale in three sizes; "rounds" which produce one flower, "double-nosed" which produce two flowers, and "mother" bulbs which will produce three. Bulbs which produce more flowers are more expensive. Specially prepared bulbs which will flower earlier in the year are also offered for sale.
Feeding Feeding is unnecessary.
Potting Plant in early autumn in peat-based potting mixture or bulb fibre. Plant several bulbs in each pot, with just the tip of the bulb showing. They can also be grown in gravel or shingle.
Special points Prepared bulbs should be "wintered" for six weeks, ordinary bulbs for ten weeks.

AMARYLLIS
Hippeastrum hybrids

These plants have spectacular trumpet-shaped blooms borne in groups of up to four on a bare stem. Straplike leaves develop after the flowers. A large bulb may produce two flower stalks. The flowers, which are produced in spring, can be white, red, orange or yellow, and are often striped or patterned. Mass several plants of the same colour together in a large bowl for a dramatic display.

Mini-climate 1 Warm, sunny.
Size The flower stems of the amaryllis grow to 45cm long, with flowers as much as 15-18cm in diameter. Ordinary bulbs are offered for sale in autumn. Specially prepared bulbs which will flower at Christmastime are also offered for sale.
Feeding Feed with standard liquid fertilizer every two weeks from the time the flowers fade until mid-summer. Switch to high-potash fertilizer to ripen the bulb and to ensure flowering the following year. Stop feeding from mid-September.
Potting Plant new bulbs by themselves in 12-15cm pots using soil-based potting mixture. Bury only half of the bulb in the mixture. Repotting should only be necessary every three or four years.
Special points These tender bulbs should not be "wintered". During the autumn rest period, leave the bulbs in their pots and water very sparingly. Stand them outside in a sunny spot during summer and early autumn to help induce flowering the following year.

MINIATURE IRIS
Iris reticulata

These lovely bulbous plants produce flowers early in the season, sometimes even before the leaves have developed, although the leaves eventually become taller than the flowers. The flowers are the typical iris shape and may be light or dark blue or mauve in colour, with bright-yellow markings. Each bloom rarely lasts more than two days, even if they are displayed in a cool place. However, their delicate fragrance makes it worth displaying them so that they can be appreciated close-up.

Mini-climate 5 Cool, filtered sun.
Size The flower stalks of miniature irises grow to about 15cm in height, with leaves which are slightly longer. The tiny bulbs are sold dry in autumn or planted up and in leaf in winter.
Feeding Feeding is unnecessary.
Potting Plant the bulbs in the autumn in a shallow container using bulb fibre. Good drainage is essential as these tiny bulbs rot very easily. Plant them 6cm deep and close together—about 12 in a 30cm pot.
Special points Bulbs should be "wintered" for six weeks. Miniature irises can be planted out in the garden when flowering has finished.

Temperature 10°-15°C spring to autumn, 7°-10°C in winter · 10°-15°C · 15°-21°C Light sunny · filtered sun · shady Humidity low · moderate · high Watering sparingly · moderately · plentifully Care easy · fairly easy · challenging

CROCUS
Crocus hybrids

The most commonly seen indoor crocuses are large-flowered Dutch hybrids which have green-and-white striped leaves and white, yellow, bronze, purple or striped blooms. These are cup-shaped and appear during winter and early spring. It is best to mass one variety of crocus in a shallow bowl.

Mini-climate 5 Cool, filtered sun.
Size Crocuses grow to about 12cm in height. Dry corms are offered for sale in late summer. Pre-planted pots are offered for sale at Christmastime.
Feeding Feeding is unnecessary.
Potting Plant several corms together in early autumn, using soil-based potting mixture or bulb fibre. Plant the corms just below the surface of the potting mixture.
Special points Corms must be "wintered" for ten weeks and only brought into a warm room when the flower buds are seen.

TULIP
Tulipa hybrids

Tulips have an extraordinary variety of shapes, colours and patterns; even the leaves can be plain or variegated. The flowers are produced during late winter and early spring. It is best to plant just one variety of tulip in a bowl, rather than mixing colours in the same container.

Mini-climate 5 Cool, filtered sun.
Size Tulips grow to about 35cm tall. Dwarf varieties grow to 10cm tall. Most tulip bulbs are "rounds", producing only one flower. Specially prepared bulbs which will flower earlier are also offered for sale.
Feeding Feeding is only necessary if the bulbs are to be planted outside the following season. Feed every ten days from the time the buds appear.
Potting Plant in early autumn using either peat-based potting mixture or bulb fibre. Five or six bulbs should be planted close together, with just the tips exposed above the potting mixture.
Special points Prepared bulbs should be "wintered" for eight weeks, ordinary bulbs for ten weeks.

GRAPE HYACINTH
Muscari sp.

The tiny bulbs of the grape hyacinth produce long narrow stalks topped with an elongated cluster of tiny blue or white flowers. Each individual flower is bell-shaped, and rimmed with a frilled white edge. The clusters of flowers open from the bottom upwards. The narrow leaves are strap shaped and channelled, meaning they have a definite rounded outer surface and a concave inner surface. Plant in small pots and display several of them along a windowsill.

Mini-climate 4 Cool, sunny.
Size Grape hyacinths reach a height of about 15cm, with leaves of nearly the same length. Bulbs already in leaf are offered for sale.
Feeding Feeding is unnecessary.
Potting Plant about twelve bulbs in a 15cm pot in soil-based potting mixture or bulb fibre. Leave the tips of the bulbs above the potting mixture.
Special points These bulbs should be "wintered" for ten weeks.

HYACINTH
Hyacinthus orientalis hybrids

Hyacinth flowers appear in spring and may be single or double, red, pink, yellow, blue or white. Their colour and distinctive scent make them really welcome in the home. A group known as Roman hyacinths may produce two or even three flower stalks, but these are less tightly packed with the bell-shaped flowers. These bulbs should be massed together in a shallow bowl for the best effect. They can also be cut and used in flower arrangements, combined with carnations, freesias and catkins, for example.

Mini-climate 5 Cool, filtered sun.
Size The single flower stalks are 20-30cm tall. Bulbs are sold according to size, from 16-19cm in circumference, and the size of the flower spike depends on the size of the bulb. Specially prepared bulbs which flower slightly earlier are offered for sale.
Feeding Feeding is unnecessary.
Potting Plant the bulbs "shoulder to shoulder" in soil-based potting mixture or bulb fibre. Leave the tips of the bulbs above the potting mixture. Hyacinths can also be grown in gravel, or water alone.
Special points Prepared bulbs should be "wintered" for six weeks, ordinary bulbs for ten weeks.

Cacti and succulents 1

Cacti and succulents add a different range of shapes and textures to a collection of house plants. Most of the cacti have abandoned leaves and developed their unusual body shapes to prevent excessive loss of water. Some are ribbed or segmented and they may be covered with decorative spines, bristles or hairs. One species, the old man cactus, is so closely covered with white hair that it resembles a ball of wool. Desert cacti (usually covered in spines), such as mammillarias and rebutias, have the added attraction of striking flowers. The jungle cacti (often without spines) such as the orchid and Christmas cacti, have stems which are notched at intervals and respectively produce brightly coloured flowers in early spring and mid-winter. Many cacti are relatively small,

reaching only a few centimetres in height; but others, such as the old man cactus, can grow to 3m tall.

Succulents are those plants which have fleshy stems or leaves that store water. They come in a range of shapes and sizes as diverse as those of the cacti. Succulents may be upright and treelike in shape, or have thin trailing stems, or be spherical or columnar in outline. Some are just a few centimetres high; others can grow to 2m tall and make large, striking plants. Leaf shape varies from the thick, succulent leaves of the Chinese jade and the silver crown to the thin, narrow leaves of the crown-of-thorns. Leaf colour also varies from the green of the lace aloe and Tom thumb to the silvery-mauve of the rosary vine or the green and white of the queen agave.

UPRIGHT PLANTS

SILVER CROWN
Cotyledon undulata

These most unusual plants have fleshy, fan-shaped leaves with undulating edges and a dense covering of fine, silver-white scurf. Although orange-yellow flowers may appear on older plants in summer, it is for their leaves that they are grown. Mass several plants together in a bowl on a low table.

Mini-climate 4 Cool, sunny.
Size Silver crowns are slow-growing reaching a height of about 50cm in three years. Plants of all sizes are offered for sale.
Feeding Feed with standard liquid fertilizer once a month from spring to early autumn.
Potting Repot every spring using two-thirds soil-based potting mixture and one-third coarse sand, making provision for good drainage. Once plants are in 15cm pots topdress instead.
Special points Avoid handling the plants as the meal will rub off. Water more sparingly in winter.

Similar-shaped species
Cotyledon orbiculata grows taller and has grey-green leaves edged with red, with just a little meal. Orange flowers appear in summer.

CROWN-OF-THORNS
Euphorbia milii

These succulent shrubs have horizontal branches bearing many sharp spines and relatively few leaves. The clusters of yellow or red "flowers" are in fact bracts which last for months, appearing in greatest profusion from February to September. Their interesting form and colourful bracts make them excellent specimen plants for the modern interior.

Mini-climate 1 Warm, sunny.
Size Crown-of-thorns can grow to about 90cm in height with a similar spread. Plants of all sizes are offered for sale.
Feeding Feed with standard liquid fertilizer once a month from spring to autumn.
Potting Repot young plants every second year in spring using half soil-based potting mixture and half coarse sand, making provision for good drainage. If you don't want to move an older plant into a larger pot topdress instead.
Special points These plants "bleed" a white latex if damaged: this latex should not be allowed to touch the eyes or the mouth.

TOM THUMB
Kalanchoe blossfeldiana hybrids

These attractive succulents flower in late winter and early spring, and remain in flower for about three months. The small flowers are grouped in closely packed flower heads borne on long stems. Each head has between 20 and 50 flowers. Colour ranges from pink, through red, to orange and yellow. The fleshy leaves are dark green and often edged in red. Tom thumbs are best treated as annuals and discarded when flowering has finished. Use massed together on a low table for a splash of winter colour.

Mini-climate 1 Warm, sunny.
Size Tom thumbs reach a maximum height of about 35cm tall. A dwarf form is available and reaches 20cm in height. Plants in flower are offered for sale all year but are particularly common around Christmastime.
Feeding Feed with standard liquid fertilizer once a month whilst in flower.
Potting Repotting is unnecessary.
Special points To keep plants in a decorative state for as long as possible remove flowers as they fade.

Temperature 10°-15°C spring to autumn, 7°-10°C in winter | 10°-15°C | 15°-21°C **Light** sunny | filtered sun | shady **Humidity** low | moderate | high **Watering** sparingly | moderately | plentifully **Care** easy | fairly easy | challenging

OLD MAN CACTUS
Cephalocereus senilis

The common name of these cacti is derived from the long, fine, white hair that shrouds the fleshy columnar body and hides the sharp spines. Flowers are only produced on older plants. Old man cacti look best massed with other cacti in a cactus garden.

Mini-climate 4 Cool, sunny.
Size Old man cacti are slow-growing and unlikely to grow taller than 25-30cm. Plants of all sizes are offered for sale.
Feeding Feed with tomato-type fertilizer once a month from spring to mid-autumn.
Potting Repot in spring using three parts soil-based potting mixture and one part coarse sand, but only if the plant has completely filled the existing pot. If you don't want to move an older plant into a larger pot topdress instead.
Special points Do not water during the winter rest period. The long hairs may be washed in a weak solution of detergent to keep them clean.

PERUVIAN APPLE CACTUS
Cereus peruvianus "Monstrosus"

These cacti have bright-green columnar bodies which are twisted and contorted into most unusual shapes. They are in fact mutations of the true species. The yellow spines are short and inconspicuous. Large but short-lived white, scented flowers are produced in summer on older specimens. Their sculptural quality can be quite spectacular when several plants are grouped in a modern interior.

Mini-climate 4 Cool, sunny.
Size The Peruvian apple cactus is slow-growing and each mutation varies in maximum height and spread. Small plants are offered for sale.
Feeding Feed with tomato-type fertilizer once a month from spring to early autumn.
Potting Repot every spring using two-thirds soil-based potting mixture and one-third coarse sand. If you don't want to move an older plant into a larger pot topdress instead.

RABBIT'S EARS CACTUS
Opuntia microdasys

These arresting cacti are made up of flattened, oval segments which fit on top of one another. These segments are densely covered in tufts of tiny, yellowish spines. Yellow flowers are produced very occasionally. Rabbit's ears cacti have a spectacular outline and larger ones can be used as specimen plants. Group smaller plants in a cactus garden.

Mini-climate 4 Cool, sunny.
Size Rabbit's ears cacti can reach a maximum height of about 90cm and spread of about 60cm. Plants of all sizes are offered for sale.
Feeding Feed with tomato-type fertilizer once a month from spring to autumn.
Potting Repot in spring using two-thirds soil-based potting mixture and one-third coarse sand, but only if the plants have completely filled the existing pot.
Special points The tiny spines can be very painful if they touch the skin. Water more sparingly during the winter rest period.

CHINESE JADE
Crassula arborescens

These succulents have fleshy, almost round leaves which are grey in colour and rimmed with red. These are borne on thick, branching, woody stems which are symmetrical in shape when the plant is mature. Small Chinese jades can be used as "trees" in dish gardens or miniature oriental gardens.

Mini-climate 4 Cool, sunny.
Size Very young Chinese jades are offered for sale; they will eventually reach 1.2m in height, when the stems will resemble gnarled tree trunks.
Feeding Feed with standard liquid fertilizer once a month from spring to early autumn.
Potting Repot every spring using three parts soil-based potting mixture and one part coarse sand. Once plants are in 20cm pots topdress instead.
Special points Water more sparingly in winter.

Similar-shaped species
Crassula ovata has shiny, jade-green succulent leaves and symmetrical branches.

Cacti and succulents 2

SPHERICAL PLANTS

FISH-HOOK CACTUS
Ferocactus latispinus

These cacti are noted for their fierce-looking spines which are grouped in clusters. Spines within individual clusters vary in size, shape and colour, with one being broader and more prominently hooked than the others. Really mature plants can produce violet-coloured flowers in summer. Large plants make good specimens—otherwise mix them with cacti of contrasting shapes in a cactus garden.

Mini-climate 4 Cool, sunny.
Size Fish-hook cacti can reach a maximum of 30cm in height and 20cm across. Plants of all sizes are offered for sale.
Feeding Feed with tomato-type fertilizer once a month from spring to autumn.
Potting Repot in spring using a combination of two-thirds soil-based potting mixture and one-third coarse sand, but only if the plant has completely filled the existing pot.
Special points Do not water during the winter rest period or plants will rot.

BISHOP'S CAP
Astrophytum myriostigma

These spherical cacti are divided into wide segments, each covered with a silvery meal instead of thorns. They look rather like de-spined sea urchins. The bright-yellow flowers resemble daisies and appear from the top of the plant in summer. Bishop's caps look good in cactus gardens or massed in a shallow bowl with a gravelly surround.

Mini-climate 4 Cool, sunny.
Size Bishop's caps are slow-growing, reaching about 25cm in height with a spread of 12cm. Plants of all sizes are offered for sale.
Feeding Feed with tomato-type fertilizer once a month from spring to autumn.
Potting Repot in spring using two-thirds soil-based potting mixture and one-third coarse sand, but only if the plant has completely filled the existing pot.
Special points Water more sparingly during the winter rest period.

GOLDEN PINCUSHION
Mammillaria rhodantha

These spherical cacti have bright-green bodies covered in small knobs which bear long, yellow-orange spines. These are arranged in circular groups over the whole body. Pink, daisylike flowers appear in a ring around the top of the body in summer. Display the golden pincushion in a cactus garden or group with other cacti.

Mini-climate 4 Cool, sunny.
Size Golden pincushions grow to about 10cm in height and 7cm in spread. Small plants are offered for sale.
Feeding Feed with tomato-type liquid fertilizer once a month from spring to autumn.
Potting Repot in spring using two-thirds soil-based potting mixture and one-third coarse sand, but only if the plant has completely filled the existing pot.
Special points Water more sparingly during the winter rest period.

RED CROWN
Rebutia minuscula

These small, white-spined cacti are almost completely round and quickly become surrounded by many offsets. They flower when very young and are crowned with red, funnel-shaped flowers from spring through the summer. The flowers open in the morning and close in the afternoon. Mass flowering red crowns together for a spectacular display in a modern setting.

Mini-climate 4 Cool, sunny.
Size Red crowns are fast-growing and can make clumps 15cm across in a year or two.
Feeding Feed with tomato-type fertilizer once a month from spring to mid-autumn.
Potting Repot in spring using three parts soil-based potting mixture and one part coarse sand, but only if the roots have completely filled the existing pot.
Special points Do not water during the winter rest period or plants will rot.

Temperature 10°-15°C spring to autumn; 7°-10°C in winter / 10°-15°C / 15°-21°C **Light** sunny / filtered sun / shady **Humidity** low / moderate / high **Watering** sparingly / moderately / plentifully **Care** easy / fairly easy / challenging

·CACTI AND SUCCULENTS·

ROSE PINCUSHION
Mammillaria zeilmanniana

The spherical body of the rose pincushion is densely covered in regularly arranged yellow and brown spines. The numerous flowers are produced in summer and form a ring at the top of the body. They are reddish-purple in colour. Allow the rose pincushion to form large clumps.

Mini-climate 4   Cool, sunny.
Size   Individual rose pincushions grow to 5cm in height but will form clumps of 25cm across in around five years. Small plants are offered for sale.
Feeding   Feed with tomato-type fertilizer once a month from spring to autumn.
Potting   Repot in spring using two-thirds soil-based potting mixture and one-third coarse sand, but only if the plant has completely filled the existing pot.
Special points   Water more sparingly during the winter rest period.

GOLDEN BARREL CACTUS
Echinocactus grusonii

These cacti are armed with stout, golden-yellow spines arranged in rows on the ribbed stems. Older plants develop the typical pattern of raised vertical ribs. Golden barrel cacti can be displayed with other cacti or foliage plants.

Mini-climate 4   Cool, sunny.
Size   Golden barrel cacti grow quickly to 8-10cm across, then it takes many years for the plant to double its size, though they can eventually reach a diameter of 20cm. Small plants are offered for sale.
Feeding   Feed with tomato-type fertilizer once a month from spring to autumn
Potting   Repot in spring using two-thirds soil-based potting mixture and one-third coarse sand, but only if the plant has completely filled the existing pot. When repotting is not necessary topdress instead.
Special points   Do not water during the winter rest period or plants will rot.

OLD LADY CACTUS
Mammillaria hahniana

These globular cacti get their name from the white, silky hairs which cover and hide the greyish-green body and the sharp spines. When the cacti are about four years old, crimson flowers appear in early May. Group several old lady cacti together for a dramatic display or use in a cactus garden.

Mini-climate 4   Cool, sunny.
Size   Old lady cacti grow to 10cm tall with a spread of 7cm. Small plants are offered for sale.
Feeding   Feed with tomato-type fertilizer once a month from spring to autumn.
Potting   Repot in spring using two-thirds soil-based potting mixture and one-third coarse sand, but only if the plant has completely filled the existing pot.
Special points   Water more sparingly during the winter rest period.

SPIKY-LEAVED PLANTS

LACE ALOE
Aloe aristata

These stemless succulents are made up of many fleshy leaves arranged in tight rosettes. The triangular leaves are dark green and covered with raised white spots. The small orange-red flowers are borne on a long stalk which appears from the centre of the rosette in summer and last only a few days. Offsets are readily produced from the base of mature plants. Group plants together and place them so that they are seen from above for maximum effect.

Mini-climate 1   Warm, sunny.
Size   Lace aloes reach a maximum height of 15cm. If offsets are left to develop in the same pot as the parent, spread is only limited by the size of the pot.
Feeding   Feed with standard liquid fertilizer once a month from spring to autumn.
Potting   Repot every spring using soil-based potting mixture. If you don't want to move an older plant into a larger pot topdress instead.
Special points   Water more sparingly in winter. Avoid trapping water in the rosette of leaves.

Cacti and succulents 3

FLAT-LEAVED ROSETTE-SHAPED PLANTS

PAINTED LADY
Echeveria derenbergii

These pretty succulents have tightly packed bluish-grey leaves with a coating of silvery scurf and red margins. Yellow and orange bell-shaped flowers borne on spikes are produced in winter and early spring. They make good, small specimen plants for the kitchen windowsill all year round.

Mini-climate 4   Cool, sunny.
Size   Painted ladies form cushions 10-15cm across. Young single plants are offered for sale.
Feeding   Feed with half-strength standard liquid fertilizer once a month from spring to autumn.
Potting   Repot every second spring using four parts soil-based potting mixture and one part coarse sand. If you don't want to move an older plant into a larger pot topdress instead.
Special points   Water more sparingly in winter.

MOULDED WAX PLANT
Echeveria agavoides

These succulents have triangular fleshy leaves which are light green with brown tips. Yellow flowers tipped with red are produced in spring. Moulded wax plants should be viewed from above for best effect—place them on a low table, or use in a succulent garden.

Mini-climate 4   Cool, sunny.
Size   Moulded wax plants grow to about 7cm in height with a spread of about 15cm. Plants of all sizes are offered for sale.
Feeding   Feed with half-strength standard liquid fertilizer once a month from spring to autumn.
Potting   Repot plants every second spring using four parts soil-based potting mixture and one part coarse sand. If you don't want to move an older plant into a larger pot topdress instead.
Special points   Water more sparingly in winter.

QUEEN AGAVE
Agave victoriae-reginae

These succulents have three-dimensional scalelike leaves. Each fleshy leaf is dark green with a white margin and bears a sharp black spine at its tip. Queen agaves are the most attractive of agaves and should be displayed so that they can be seen from above.

Mini-climate 4   Cool, sunny.
Size   Queen agaves are slow-growing, reaching a maximum height of 20cm, but they can attain a spread of about 45cm. Small plants are offered for sale.
Feeding   Feed with standard liquid fertilizer once a month during spring and summer.
Potting   Repot every second year in spring using two-thirds soil-based potting mixture and one-third coarse sand. If you don't want to move an older plant into a larger pot topdress instead.
Special points   Water more sparingly in winter.

TRAILING PLANTS

CLAW CACTUS
Schlumbergera truncata

These jungle cacti have flattened, segmented stems which are notched at intervals. Bright-magenta, pink or white flowers are produced in late autumn. The stems are erect at first but begin to trail as more segments are produced. They make good specimen plants for hanging baskets or shelves.

Mini-climate 2   Warm, filtered sun.
Size   The stems of claw cacti can grow to about 30cm in height and spread. Plants of all sizes are offered for sale.
Feeding   Feed with tomato-type fertilizer once a month from early November to the end of flowering.
Potting   Repot every second year in spring using two-thirds peat-based potting mixture and one-third coarse sand. Once plants are in 15cm pots repot every year.
Special points   Water more sparingly during the rest period following flowering.

Similar-shaped species
Schlumbergera **"Bridgesii"** is very similar but blooms later and has less sharply defined notches.

Temperature 10°-15°C spring to autumn, 7°-10°C in winter | 10°-15°C | 15°-21°C **Light** sunny | filtered sun | shady **Humidity** low | moderate | high **Watering** sparingly | moderately | plentifully **Care** easy | fairly easy | challenging

ROSARY VINE
Ceropegia woodii

These small, tuber-forming succulents have trailing threadlike stems bearing heart-shaped leaves. These fleshy leaves, which appear in pairs at intervals along the stems, are marbled with silvery-grey and have purple undersides. Small, tube-shaped flowers appear amongst the leaves in summer. Several rosary vines displayed together in a small hanging basket in a warm room make an unusual display. Position them where they will not be brushed against. Alternatively, the stems may be coiled in the pot so the flowers stand upright.

Mini-climate 1 Warm, sunny.
Size Rosary vine stems do not usually grow longer than 90cm. Cut back any bare stems to encourage leafy growth. Small plants are offered for sale.
Feeding Feed mature plants with standard liquid fertilizer once a month in spring and summer.
Potting Repot young plants every spring using an equal-parts combination of soil-based potting mixture and coarse sand. Older plants thrive in 8-10cm half pots. Hanging baskets should have a 2cm layer of drainage material at the bottom.
Special points Water more sparingly in winter.

RAT'S TAIL CACTUS
Aporocactus flagelliformis

These cacti have long streamers of narrow, fleshy stems covered with many rows of fine, prickly spines. Striking crimson-pink flowers appear in spring; each bloom lasts several days and the flowering season extends for up to two months. Display them in hanging baskets or on shelves, and position them where they will not be brushed against, as the spines are very difficult to remove from the skin. They can also be displayed in a cactus garden, with their long stems trailing through an arrangement of rocks.

Mini-climate 4 Cool, sunny.
Size Rat's tail cacti are fast-growing and their stems can reach 90cm long (occasionally much more) in three or four years. Plants of all sizes are offered for sale.
Feeding Feed with tomato-type fertilizer once a month from late December to the end of flowering.
Potting Repot every spring after flowering using soil-based potting mixture. Once plants are in a 15-25cm pot topdress instead.
Special points Water more sparingly during the rest period following flowering.

Similar-shaped species
Aporocactus mallisonii has stouter stems and flowers ranging from soft pink to deep crimson.

DONKEY'S TAIL
Sedum morganianum

These most unusual-looking plants have trailing stems which are densely packed with small, fat, succulent leaves. Each stem takes on the appearance of a rope as it is so thick. The individual leaves are a pale green, covered with a fine white bloom. Pink flowers may appear at the end of each "rope" in spring, but these plants do not flower readily in the home. Ideal plants for hanging baskets, donkey's tails should be displayed in a place where they will not be brushed against, as the leaves drop off very easily.

Mini-climate 1 Warm, sunny.
Size The stems of donkey's tails can grow to a maximum of 1m in length. Plants of all sizes are offered for sale.
Feeding Feeding is unnecessary.
Potting Repot every spring using a combination of one-third coarse sand and two-thirds soil-based potting mixture. Donkey's tails grow best in half-pots or hanging baskets where they have room to spread. Once the plants have grown too big for a 20cm pot, discard the plant and grow a new one from a cutting.
Special points Water more sparingly in winter.

The colour guide to flowering house plants
Whites, creams and yellows

We all respond to the colours found in nature; bring them inside and they cannot fail to enhance almost any type of setting. Concentrate on related or contrasting schemes: mass together plants in various shades of the same colour for a subtle effect, or use exciting complementaries for a bold effect. Before you buy any flowering plants to decorate your home, always think about the location you have chosen for them and make sure that, however beautiful their colour, they will enhance and harmonize with your existing colour scheme.

The most colourful part of a plant is not always the flower itself: in some plants, such as the poinsettia and flamingo flower, it is the bract, or petal-like leaf, which surrounds the flowers; in others, such as the bead plant and Christmas pepper, it is the berries and fruits which appear after the flowers have faded.

WHITE SAILS
Spathiphyllum "Clevelandii" (see p.169)
White arumlike flower heads which turn pale green with age. The colour of this plant suits any kind of interior decoration.

PRIMULA
Primula obconica (see p.181)
Pure white flowers with green centres, also available with pink, red and mauve flowers. Use either singly, or massed up in a bowl using different shades from white through to mauve.

ITALIAN BELLFLOWER
Campanula isophylla (see p.191)
Star-shaped white flowers, also available in several shades of blue. Use plants of one colour, or mix blue and white together, and place on a high shelf or in a hanging basket.

WAX BEGONIA
Begonia semperflorens-cultorum (see p.176)
Small white flowers, also available with pink and red flowers. Mass plants of the same colour together or mix them with exotic-coloured leaves.

MADAGASCAR PERIWINKLE
Catharanthus roseus
White flowers with carmine-red centres, also available with pink or all-white flowers. Use in groups with other plants or mass together in a bowl or basket.

YELLOW ELATIOR BEGONIA
Begonia "Elatior" hybrids (see p.176)
Primrose-yellow double flowers, also available in many other colours. Mass plants of one colour together for a bold effect.

CHRISTMAS PEPPER
Capsicum annuum (see p.180)
The bright fruits may be orange, red or yellow and will change colour as they ripen. Use massed to make a colourful winter table decoration.

WHITE ELATIOR BEGONIA
Begonia "Elatior" hybrids (see p.176)
Cream-coloured double flowers, also available in many other colours.

YELLOW BEGONIA
Begonia tuberhybrida (see p.176)
Deep-yellow flowers, also available with white, pink, red or orange flowers.

BLACK-EYED SUSAN
Thunbergia alata (see p.185)
Bright orange-yellow flowers with a black central eye. Leave them to ramble through other plants or train them up a support to create a cascade of colour.

See below left
AFRICAN VIOLET
Saintpaulia hybrids (see p.175)
Pure white flowers and white flowers edged with purple, also available in many shades of pink, blue and purple. Mass plants of one colour, or in various shades of the same colour, in a shallow bowl on a low table.

YELLOW CHRYSANTHEMUM
Chrysanthemum morifolium hybrids (see p.181)
Pale yellow daisylike flowers, available in many other colours.

WHITE BEGONIA
Begonia tuberhybrida (see p.176)
Ivory-coloured flowers, also available with pink, red, yellow or orange flowers. Display individually or in groups of one, or several, colours.

GOLDEN CHRYSANTHEMUM
Chrysanthemum morifolium hybrids (see p.181)
Dense golden flowers, available in many other colours.

WHITE CHRYSANTHEMUM
Chrysanthemum morifolium hybrids (see p.181)
Dense creamy-white flowers, available in many other colours. Mass in a large basket and display so they can be seen from above.

YELLOW FLOWERING MAPLE
Abutilon hybridum (see p.162)
Bell-shaped, creamy-yellow flowers, available in many other colours. Group several different colours together or display as feature plants when full grown.

See following page

·203·

Oranges and reds

CHRISTMAS PEPPER
Capsicum annuum (see p.180)
The bright fruits may be orange, red or yellow and
will change colour as they ripen. Use massed to make a
colourful winter table decoration.

WHITE ELATIOR BEGONIA
Begonia "Elatior" hybrids (see p.176)
Cream-coloured double flowers, also
available in many other colours.

BEAD PLANT
Nertera granadensis (see p.192)
Beadlike, deep-orange berries cover the plant.
Make a formal display on a table or low shelf.

YELLOW TOM THUMB
Kalanchoe blossfeldiana hybrids (see p.196)
Long-lasting deep-yellow flowers, also available with
orange, pink and red flowers. Mass plants together
on a sunny windowsill for winter colour.

ORANGE TOM THUMB
Kalanchoe blossfeldiana
hybrids (see p.196)
Long-lasting orange flowers,
also available in yellow, pink
and red.

PINK TOM THUMB
Kalanchoe blossfeldiana
hybrids (see p.196)
Long-lasting pink flowers
also available in yellow,
red and orange.

**GOLDEN
CHRYSANTHEMUM**
*Chrysanthemum
morifolium* hybrids
(see p.181)
Dense golden flowers,
available in
many other colours.

RED TOM THUMB
Kalanchoe blossfeldiana hybrids (see p.196)
Long-lasting scarlet flowers, also
available with yellow, orange and
pink flowers.

CHINESE HIBISCUS
Hibiscus rosa-sinensis
hybrids (see p.178)
Large deep-red flowers with a protruding stamen, also
available with white, yellow, pink or orange flowers.
Use either singly or in a group with different-coloured forms.

PINK BUSY LIZZIE
Impatiens wallerana hybrids (see p.177)
Deep-pink single flowers, also available with white, red, orange or bicoloured flowers. Mass plants of the same colour together in a hanging basket or window-box.

SCARLET STAR
Guzmania lingulata (see p.174)
Scarlet bracts surround small white flowers. Mass plants together in a container or use them in a symmetrical arrangement. They may also be cut and wired for use in large floral arrangements.

BEDDING GERANIUM
Pelargonium hortorum hybrids (see p.179)
Tight clusters of scarlet flowers, also available with white, mauve or pink flowers. Display in a row along a windowsill or group with foliage geraniums.

GLOXINIA
Sinningia speciosa hybrids (see p.175)
Red trumpet-shaped flowers, also available with white or violet flowers. Mass plants together and display on a low table.

PINK ELATIOR BEGONIA
Begonia "Elatior" hybrids (see p.176)
Deep-pink double flowers, also available in many other colours.

RED FLOWERING MAPLE
Abutilon hybridum (see p.162)
Scarlet bell-shaped flowers, available in many other colours. Group several different colours together or display as a feature plant when full grown.

See following page

Pinks, mauves and purples

PINK BUSY LIZZIE
Impatiens wallerana hybrids (see p.177)
Deep-pink single flowers, also available
with white, red, orange or bicoloured
flowers. Mass plants of the same
colour together in a hanging basket
or window-box.

FLAMINGO FLOWER
Anthurium andreanum hybrids (see p.182)
A salmon-coloured, shield-shaped bract surrounds
the central flower spike, also available with white or red flower
heads. Mass plants together for an exotic display.

RED WAX
BEGONIA *Begonia semperflorens-cultorum* (see p.176)
Scarlet flowers with yellow centres, also available with pink or white
flowers. Mass plants of the same colour together or mix with exotic-coloured leaves.

PINK BUSY LIZZIE
Impatiens "New Guinea" hybrids (see p.177)
Pinky-orange flowers and strongly variegated leaves, also available
with white, pink, orange
and bicoloured flowers.

SHRIMP PLANT
Justicia brandegeana
White flowers emerge from
pink, shrimp-shaped
bracts. Mass plants
together in a shallow
basket for a subtle
colour effect.

PINK ELATIOR BEGONIA
Begonia "Elatior"
hybrids (see p.176)
Deep-pink double flowers,
also available in many
other colours.

CAPE LEADWORT
Plumbago auriculata (see p.186)
Clusters of small, blue flowers, also
available with white flowers.
Use trained round a window or
up a support.

PINK WAX BEGONIA
Begonia semperflorens-cultorum (see p.176)
Strong-pink flowers with yellow eyes,
also available in red and white.

PURPLE AFRICAN VIOLET
Saintpaulia hybrids (see p.175)
Intense violet-coloured flowers with yellow centres, also available with pink, blue or white flowers. Mass plants of one colour, or several shades of the same colour, in a shallow bowl on a low table.

ITALIAN BELLFLOWER
Campanula isophylla (see p.191)
Star-shaped, bluish-mauve flowers, also available in other shades of blue and white. Use plants of one colour, or mix blue and white together, and place on a high shelf or in a hanging basket.

GLOXINIA
Sinningia speciosa hybrids (see p.175)
Purple blooms banded with white, also available with white or red flowers. Mass plants of the same colour together on a low table.

PINK AFRICAN VIOLET
Saintpaulia hybrids (see p.175)
Deep-pink flowers with yellow centres, also available with blue, purple or white flowers.

PASSION FLOWER
Passiflora caerulea (see p.185)
Curious white-petalled flowers with purple-fringed filaments, also available with pink and purple petals. Train round a sunny window or up a support.

URN PLANT
Aechmea fasciata (see p.172)
Short-lived, pale-blue flowers emerge from pink bracts. Use as feature plants or in a bold arrangement.

GERMAN VIOLET
Exacum affine (see p.178)
Tiny lilac-coloured flowers with gold centres, also available with white flowers. Mass plants together in a large bowl or group with golden flowers for counterpoint.

PINK BUSY LIZZIE
Impatiens wallerana hybrids (see p.177)
Sugar-pink single flowers, available with white, red, orange or bicoloured flowers.

The seasonal guide to flowering house plants

Key

Winter Spring Summer Autumn

Plant	Jan	Feb	Mar	Apr	May	Jun	Jul	Aug	Sep	Oct	Nov	Dec	Comments
Egyptian star cluster (see p.177)	■								■	■	■	■	Can flower at other times
Christmas cherry (see p.180)	■								■	■	■	■	Fruit
Tulip (see p.194)	■	■										■	Can flower at other times
Claw cactus (see p.200)	■	■										■	Can flower at other times
Poinsettia (see p.178)	■	■	■							■		■	
Hyacinth (see p.195)	■	■	■									■	
Daffodil and Narcissus (see p.194)	■	■	■									■	
Crocus (see p.194)	■	■	■										
Scarlet star (see p.174)	■	■	■										
Florist's cyclamen (see p.180)	■	■	■	■						■		■	
White-scented jasmine (see p.186)	■	■	■	■									
Tom thumb (see p.196)	■	■	■	■								■	Can flower at other times
Miniature iris (see p.194)	■	■	■	■									
Amaryllis (see p.194)	■	■	■	■	■								
Primula (see p.181)	■	■	■	■	■	■							Can flower at other times
African hemp (see p.164)		■	■	■									
African violet (see p.175)		■	■	■	■	■	■	■	■				Can flower continuously
Powder-puff cactus (see p.198)			■	■	■	■							
Rat's tail cactus (see p.201)			■	■	■								
Azalea (see p.179)			■	■	■								Can flower at other times
Grape hyacinth (see p.195)			■	■	■								
Saffron spike (see p.182)			■	■	■	■							
Rose pincushion (see p.198)			■	■	■	■							
Regal geranium (see p.179)			■	■	■	■	■						
Bird-of-paradise (see p.164)			■	■	■	■	■						Only mature plants will bloom
Wax begonia (see p.176)			■	■	■	■	■	■	■				Can flower continuously
Columnea (see p.189)			■	■	■	■	■	■	■	■			Can flower continuously
Crown-of-thorns (see p.196)			■	■	■	■	■	■	■	■			Can flower continuously
Cineraria (see p.178)				■	■	■							
Red crown (see p.198)				■	■	■	■						
White sails (see p.169)				■	■	■	■						Can flower at other times
Wax flower (see p.185)				■	■	■	■						
Bishop's cap (see p.198)				■	■	■	■	■					
Chinese hibiscus (see p.178)				■	■	■	■	■	■				Can flower at other times
Flaming sword (see p.173)				■	■	■	■	■	■				Only mature plants will bloom
Paper flower (see p.186)				■	■	■	■	■	■	■			
Busy Lizzie (see p.177)				■	■	■	■	■	■	■			Can flower continuously
Cape leadwort (see p.186)				■	■	■	■	■	■	■			
Calamondin orange (see p.162)					■	■	■	■					Can flower at other times
Bird's nest bromeliad (see p.174)						■	■	■	■				Only mature plants will bloom
Cape primrose (see p.175)					■	■	■	■	■	■			
Black-eyed Susan (see p.185)					■	■	■	■	■	■			
Gloxinia (see p.175)						■	■	■					
Blue-flowered torch (see p.172)						■	■	■	■				Only mature plants will bloom
Flowering maple (see p.162)						■	■	■	■				
Urn plant (see p.172)						■	■	■	■				Can flower at other times
Cupid's bower (see p.181)						■	■	■	■				
Flamingo flower (see p.182)						■	■	■	■				Can flower at other times
Elatior begonia (see p.176)						■	■	■	■				
Queen's tears (see p.173)						■	■	■	■				Can flower at other times
German violet (see p.178)						■	■	■	■				
Miniature wax plant (see p.189)						■	■	■	■				
Passion flower (see p.185)						■	■	■	■	■			
Bead plant (see p.192)							■	■	■	■			Fruit
Golden trumpet (see p.186)							■	■	■	■			
Blushing bromeliad (see p.174)							■	■	■	■			Only mature plants will bloom
Christmas pepper (see p.180)							■	■	■	■	■	■	Fruit
Amethyst violet (see p.176)								■	■	■	■		
Italian bellflower (see p.191)								■	■	■	■		
Florist's chrysanthemum (see p.181)									■	■	■		Can flower continuously

THE CUT-FLOWER GUIDE

Displays of cut flowers can transform a room with their shapes, colours and scents, and bring the freshness of the garden indoors at any time of the year. Arrangements need not be lavish; a few flowers arranged in an appropriate container can look just as effective as a large, complicated display.

On the following pages you will find a seasonal guide to the flowers, berries and blossoms which are most useful to the flower arranger. Foliage is another essential ingredient of flower arrangements and, since much of it is available from spring to autumn, it has been grouped according to its colour. Many of the types of foliage and flowers shown mix well together for striking seasonal arrangements. The entry for each featured plant contains advice on how to prepare the cut stems, and suggests how it can be used in arrangements.

Spring flowers and blossoms 1

A quick appraisal of late winter and early spring colour is of a ubiquitous dull brown, but on closer inspection you will find many interesting colours and textures. Quite early in the year the garden becomes infused with spots of white, lemon and pale green. As the season moves properly into spring, the colours intensify—and, against the fresh green of the new foliage, you see the many yellows of narcissi, followed by the subsequent rainbow colours of other cultivated bulbs and flowering trees.

Many garden shrubs also flower early; the sprays of the bright yellow forsythia, the white foam of May blossoms and the green clusters of guelder rose flowers can be cut and used to extend the outline of a simple spring arrangement. Later in the season, fruit blossoms, such as apple and pear, come into their own too, along with the earliest of the perennial material from the garden. These early perennials include some types of iris, violets, spurges, lilacs and rhododendrons.

LILY-OF-THE-VALLEY
Convallaria majalis

These delicate, bell-shaped flowers are easily grown in a shady spot in the garden. As they grow from a creeping rhizome, they quickly spread. They are also easy to force and can be obtained at most times of year. They look best arranged in simple bunches, with their own pale-green foliage, in a small glass vase. The heady scent of the flowers adds to their attraction. The white varieties are also very beautiful when mixed with other white flowers in a bridal bouquet.

Colours available White and pink.

Preparation Cut the stems on a slant and make a 5cm slit with a sharp knife. Strip any foliage from the floral stems and give a drink in warm water for about an hour before arranging in deep water.

Daffodils and narcissi **1** "Golden Ducat"
2 "Pheasant's Eye" **3** "Mrs Backhouse"
4 "Inglescombe" **5** "Cheerfulness" **6** "Mary Copeland"

DAFFODIL AND NARCISSUS
Narcissus sp.

This group of hardy spring bulbs includes many different species and hybrids. Daffodil is the common name used for most members of the genus, although some kinds are referred to as narcissi, especially those whose flowers have short centre trumpets. Dwarf species are available, while the tallest varieties are nearly 60cm in height. The bulbs must be planted in the autumn but then reappear each spring. Use the flowers in country-style spring arrangements. They also go well with forsythia or catkins and look good when massed in a simple container for a bold colour effect.

Colours available Daffodils and narcissi are available in a wide range of combinations of white, cream, yellow, orange and peach.

Preparation Cut the stems on a slant and make a 5cm slit with a sharp knife. Pass the cut ends through a flame to seal them. Give a deep drink for about an hour before arranging in shallow water.

FRITILLARY
Fritillaria sp.

Fritillarys are not easily grown in the garden, but ones raised in a cool greenhouse can be bought from florists' shops. The size and shape of the fritillary flower depend upon the species—some have clusters of large flowers at the top of a tall stalk, others have small bell-shaped flowers which are borne singly on drooping stems. The leaves resemble those of a tulip in shape, although some plants can have very long, narrow leaves. Fritillarys are amongst the first long-stemmed flowers to bloom in spring and the clustered flowers look good in large arrangements. The smaller species have drooping heads, so look better arranged in a simple vase on their own.

Colours available Red, orange, yellow, white, maroon and purple. The flowers of the smaller species are usually checkered or spotted with another colour.

Preparation Cut the stems with a sharp knife to avoid bruising. Give a deep drink in cool water before arranging.

Lilacs **1** "Katherine Havemeyer" **2** "Maud Notcutt"
3 "Massena"

LILAC
Syringa sp.

Lilacs are woody shrubs, easily grown in the garden, which flower profusely in late spring. Forced lilac is also readily available in florists' shops in winter and early spring. It should only be bought on long stems, as short-stemmed flowers do not last as well. The tiny, highly fragrant flowers are arranged in elongated clusters and the full blossom heads look good mixed with other pastel-coloured flowers, such as pale-coloured poppies and paeonies, in a simple vase. The yellow and white varieties can be used in soft-yellow and cream spring arrangements.

Colours available Purple, pink, white, whitish-green and yellow.

Preparation Cut the stems on a slant and make a 5cm slit with a sharp knife. Strip any foliage from the floral stems and dip into boiling water before giving a deep drink in cold water overnight. Arrange on long stems in deep water.

Lily-of-the-valley

Additional features
Long-lasting
Useful foliage
Fragrant
Suitable for drying

Rhododendrons

Lilies

LILY
Lilium hybrids

Lilies are amongst the loveliest of flowers, having an extremely elegant shape. Despite their fragile appearance, some lilies can be grown in the garden, although many are imported. They should be arranged simply, with nothing to detract from the flower itself. Ivory-coloured lilies are useful for wedding bouquets or church decoration.

Colours available Lilies are available in all colours except blue. Many flowers have two or more colours and most have dots or stripes of another colour.

Preparation Cut the stems on a slant and make a 5cm slit with a sharp knife. Strip any foliage from the floral stems and give a deep drink overnight in cold water before arranging.

TULIP
Tulipa hybrids

The vast range of colour and shape makes the tulip useful for many different types of arrangement. Apart from the traditional single, cuplike form, tulips may be double, feathered, vase-shaped or shaped like a lily. Tulip stems have a tendency to twist and bend once they are cut so they are not suitable for very formal arrangements. Tulips mix well with many types of flowers and have colours to suit most arrangements. Possibly the best way of displaying them is to mass flowers of the same colour in a vase with their own foliage.

Colours available Tulips are available in most colours, ranging from almost black to pure white. Many are streaked with another colour.

Preparation Cut off any white ends to the stems and all foliage, and roll the bunch in newspaper. Place the bundle in deep warm water for a few hours. This will straighten any curved stems. Prick each stem just below the head with a pin and arrange in water containing a teaspoonful of sugar.

RHODODENDRON
Rhododendron sp.

Rhododendrons are large, robust flowers. Use flowers on long stems to give a focal point to large, textured arrangements; shorter-stemmed flowers can be used in small vases of snowdrops or primroses. The heads can be floated in shallow dishes of water.

Colours available White, pink, red and purple.

Preparation Cut the stems on a slant and make a 5cm slit with a sharp knife. Strip any foliage from the floral stems and leave overnight in hot water. Arrange in fresh water containing a little household bleach.

Tulips

"White Triumphator"

"Aster Neilson"

"Dyanito"

"Blue Parrot"

"West Point"

"Flying Dutchman"

"Black Parrot"

"Greenland"

"May Blossom"

"Captain Fryatt"

"China Pink"

Spring flowers and blossoms 2

Freesias

FREESIA
Freesia hybrids

Freesias are very delicate in appearance and can become "lost" in very large, fussy arrangements. Their elongated shape is best seen when a small spray is displayed on its own in a vase, although the large white freesias can be used in bridal bouquets. The double variety lasts longer than the single variety.

Colours available White, yellow, mauve, pink, red and orange.

Preparation Cut the stems on a slant and make a 5cm slit with a sharp knife. Give a deep drink before arranging in deep water.

SPURGE
Euphorbia sp.

These small shrubby plants should be included in every flower arranger's garden, as they last well when cut and add an unusual range of colours, shapes and textures to country-style flower arrangements. The large

inflorescences are made up of tiny flowers surrounded by papery bracts and look good contrasted with feathery grasses or foliage.

Colours available Orange, red, yellow and green.

Preparation Cut the stems on a slant and make a 5cm slit with a sharp knife. Scald the ends in boiling water or pass them briefly over a flame to staunch the flow of latex from the cut stem. Give a deep drink in cold water before arranging.

IRIS
Iris sp.

These are very useful flowers, particularly if you grow them in your garden, as the foliage is as decorative as the flowers. The flowers are amongst the first to appear in spring. There are many varieties available, giving an enormous range of shapes, colours and sizes. Some irises grow very tall and have large flower heads suitable for large-scale flower arrangements. The smaller, wild irises can be arranged with some of their own foliage and a few tulips.

Colours available Mauve, purple, yellow, brown, orange, grey and white. The flowers are usually spotted or striped with another colour.

Preparation Cut the stems on a slant and make a 5cm slit with a sharp knife. Strip any foliage from the floral stems and give a deep drink in cool water.

MIMOSA
Acacia dealbata

These delicate, fluffy flower heads mix well with all kinds of spring flowers. They can be used in formal bouquets, but look equally lovely massed in a terracotta pot with a few golden daffodils and their own foliage. The

feathery, grey-green leaves make good background material in many arrangements and the strong, heady scent adds to the attractiveness of this plant.

Colours available Yellow.

Preparation Keep wrapped in polythene to exclude air for as long as possible before arranging. Just prior to arranging, remove the polythene and dip flower heads in cold water for a few moments. Cut the stems on a slant and make a 5cm slit with a sharp knife. Dip the stems in boiling water for a few seconds, then give a deep drink in warm water until the heads are dry.

Stocks **1** "Parma Violet" **2** "Yellow of Nice"
3 "Princess Alice"

STOCK
Matthiola incana

Stocks are widely available in both gardens and florists' shops. Those grown under glass are available for many months of the year.

Euphorbia wulfenii

Spurges

Euphorbia robbiae

Euphorbia griffithii "Fireglow"

Euphorbia characias

Euphorbia polychroma

Additional features

Long-lasting · Useful foliage · Fragrant · Suitable for drying

Their short spikes are packed with small, round flowers which can act as the focal point, or as filler material, in informal country-style arrangements.

Colours available White, yellow, crimson, mauve, purple, pink and orange.

Preparation Cut the stems on a slant and make a 5cm slit with a sharp knife. Strip any foliage from the floral stems. Dip in boiling water for a few minutes before giving a deep drink in cold water. Arrange in deep water.

POLYANTHUS
Primula vulgaris

These small, bushy plants have tubular flowers which flare out into a round face with a prominent, coloured eye. The variety of colours is immense, as new hybrids are being produced all the time. They can be grown in the garden but, for instant colour, it is often easier to buy them in florists' shops in early spring. Choose polyanthus with short stems, as the longer ones wilt very easily. Simple bunches bound with their own foliage look good in plain containers. Alternatively, they can be used with other similarly coloured flowers, such as hellebores or heathers, in a miniature arrangement.

Colours available Polyanthus are available in all colours including blue. Many varieties have a yellow ring surrounding the eye.

Preparation Cut the stems short with a sharp knife. Dip the ends in boiling water for a few minutes and then give a deep drink. Prick each stem just below the head to allow any air bubbles to escape. This helps the water to rise freely up the stem.

BABY'S BREATH
Gypsophila paniculata

These delicate sprays of flowers were once looked upon as foils for other, more robust flowers. They do add a pretty, hazy effect to arrangements of roses and carnations, but a generous amount massed in a glass vase or urn can look very striking in a modern setting. Baby's breath is commonly used in bouquets.

Colours available White and pink.

Preparation Cut stems on a slant and make a 5cm slit with a sharp knife. Strip any foliage from the floral stems and give a deep drink in hot water before arranging. Spray the arrangements with setting spray as the flowers fall easily. Change the water regularly to prevent fouling.

Baby's breath

Peruvian lily

PERUVIAN LILY
Alstroemeria pelegrina

These elegant, eye-catching flowers are hard to grow in the garden but are available in florists' shops for most of the year. They have stiff, upright stems at the top of which are the groups of flowers, making them ideal for massing in a vase, with just a few of their own leaves, for a striking display.

Colours available White, pink, red, orange and lilac. Some may be marked with red-purple dots.

Preparation Cut the stems on a slant and make a 5cm slit with a sharp knife. Strip any foliage from the floral stems and give a deep drink in cool water before arranging.

ARUM LILY
Zantedeschia aethiopica

It is possible to grow these beautiful flowers outside in a sheltered spot, but the best specimens come from the greenhouse. They have thick, fleshy flowers borne on erect stalks. The heart-shaped leaves are a rich green and just a few blooms, displayed with their own foliage in a round glass bowl, make an elegant display. The strong shape of arum lilies makes them a good focal point in any green group; they are also useful for formal displays which need to be seen from a distance.

Colours available White, yellow, green and pink.

Preparation Cut the stems on a slant and make a 5cm slit with a sharp knife. Give a deep drink in warm water before arranging. Soak the leaves in a starch solution for twenty-four hours to make them last longer.

Fruit blossoms **1** *Prunus serrulata* **2** *Prunus serrulata* "Ukon" **3** *Pyrus calleryana* "Chanticleer" **4** *Malus eleyi* **5** *Prunus serrulata* "Shirotae" **6** *Prunus serrulata* "Kwanzan"

FRUIT BLOSSOM
Prunus sp. and Malus sp.

This is a large group of ornamental and fruiting trees which bear delicate clusters of blossoms in early spring. Masses of blossoms make excellent background material for displays of pink tulips or yellow daffodils. A Japanese effect can be created by displaying a few stems of a white-blossomed variety in a red and black setting.

Colours available Red, pink and white.

Preparation Cut the stems on a slant and make a 5cm slit with a sharp knife. Give a cool drink before arranging in deep water.

PANSY
Viola wittrockiana

Pansies are pretty flowers whose round heads are usually marked with appealing, facelike blotches. Their small, delicate size suits them to table-top or miniature arrangements in small containers. Many are subtly scented.

Colours available Pansies are available in all colours, including blue and black. There are many plain-coloured varieties and many marked types.

Preparation The soft stems should be cut with a sharp knife to avoid bruising them. Dip the heads in water for a few minutes before arranging.

Other spring flowers

Crocus	Honesty
Hawthorn	Blazing star
Rosemary	Corn lily
Bluebell	Wallflower
Forsythia	Magnolia
Clematis	Arctic poppy
Spirea	Buttercup
Kafir lily	Primrose
Alyssum	Love-in-mist
Jasmine	Broom
Hyacinth	Jew's mallow
Cowslip	Quince

Summer flowers 1

Summer brings flowers and foliage in abundance, of every shape, size, colour and texture. The overall colours of summer move from the pale yellows, pastel pinks, peaches and white of the carnations and foxgloves, to the deeper tones and warmer colours of paeonies and sweet Williams. Many summer flowers, such as the poppy, sweet pea and rose, are available in a wide range of colours, and can be used in many different arrangements. Moreover, flowers are often accompanied by an equally wide range of different shaped and coloured foliage—of which the hostas, ivies and privets must be among the most useful.

While much available material is herbaceous or perennial, there is an equally large range of flowering shrub material: use these branches either on their own or with cut flowers for bigger, grander displays, choosing from weigela, viburnum or mock orange, amongst many others.

Summer arrangements should make use of this abundance of material, and flowers should be arranged *en masse*. Most summer flowers have a heady fragrance which makes them doubly welcome in the home.

LADY'S MANTLE
Alchemilla mollis

These plants are easily grown in the garden but are not commonly seen in florists' shops. Lady's mantle is very versatile: the blooms can be used in both formal and informal arrangements, and the lovely, yellow-green heads mix well with almost every colour of flower and foliage. They also look good massed on their own or arranged with feathery grasses and foliage in a simple glass or dull metal container. The round, umbrella-like leaves are soft and downy and contrast beautifully with red or bronze leaves in an arrangement.

Colours available Yellow-green.

Preparation Cut the stems on a slant and make a 5cm slit with a sharp knife. Strip any foliage from the floral stems and arrange in deep water immediately. This will prevent air bubbles forming in the stem.

Paeonies **1** *Paeonia lactiflora* **2** *Paeonia officinalis* "Rubra-plena" **3** *Paeonia officinalis*

PAEONY
Paeonia sp.

The most commonly seen paeony is the large-flowered, deep-magenta variety. Although very beautiful, it needs to be used thoughtfully as it can be dominating in flower arrangements; it looks good arranged with red or yellow-green foliage. There are many other kinds of paeony, all of which can be used as focal points in arrangements. Red paeonies mix well with other red flowers, and the delicate pinks look devastating with the salmon-pink spikes of foxgloves or gladioli. Larger paeonies can be used in large arrangements which are meant to be seen from a distance.

Colours available Shades of pink, red, magenta, orange and white.

Preparation After cutting, paeonies can be left out of water for several days if placed in a cold room. If put in polythene bags in a cold room they will keep fresh for some weeks. Prior to arranging, cut the stems on a slant and make a 5cm slit with a sharp knife. Give a long, warm drink before arranging.

FOXTAIL LILY
Eremurus sp.

These long spikes are covered in densely packed, small, star-shaped flowers. The flowers open from the bottom of the stem upwards and, as the stems can range in height from 60cm to 2m, they can look majestic arranged in a long, narrow vase with some stiff, lance-shaped leaves.

Colours available White, yellow, pink and orange.

Preparation Cut the stems on a slant and make a 5cm slit with a sharp knife. Give a deep drink in cool water before arranging.

CARNATIONS AND PINKS
Dianthus caryophyllus

Carnations and pinks present a great challenge to the grower, as they hybridize very easily and new hybrids are always appearing on the market. These new hybrids may be bigger, smaller, more fragrant, have brighter colours, or be formed with a new mixture of colours—the range to choose from is vast. Although pinks and carnations look very similar, they can be told apart by the fact that carnations have larger flowers, wider leaves and longer stems than the pinks. Carnations and pinks are very formal flowers, especially the shop-bought ones with very straight stems. They can be used in all kinds of summer arrangements, but do look good on their own in a simple, tall-necked vase. Use the delicate pink or white flowers with grey foliage such as eucalyptus or artemisia.

Colours available Available in almost every colour except blue. Many are marked with another colour.

Preparation Cut the stems on a slant between the nodes (bumps on the stems). Make a 5cm slit with a sharp knife and strip any foliage from the floral stems. Give a long deep drink before arranging them in warm water.

"Purple Frosted"

"Crowley Sim"

Lady's mantle

Additional features
Long-lasting Useful foliage Fragrant Suitable for drying

Sword lilies **1** "Albert Schweitzer" **2** "White Angel" **3** "Madam Butterfly"

SWORD LILY
Gladiolus hybrids

With their elegant shape, gladioli are extremely useful for all types of arrangement. They are also easy to grow in the garden. There are many varieties of gladiolus, varying in size, colour and floret type, although all the florets face the same way on the flower spike. Arrange the smaller, soft-coloured gladioli with pink roses or other small flowers. Three or four spikes of the tall, bright-red gladioli look good in a long, elegant vase in a prominent position.

Colours available A wide variety of colours including red, orange, yellow, pink and white.

Preparation Cut the stems on a slant and make a 5cm slit with a sharp knife. Cut stems under water and, to make the blooms last longer, cut off a small piece of the stem every four or five days. If you don't want to use these flowers immediately, keep them in a cold place for about a week.

POPPY
Papaver sp.

The popular conception of the poppy is of a bright-red, large-petalled flower. There are, however, many hybrids and cultivars available in a wide range of colours and sizes. Poppies have very delicate petals so they are not really suitable for formal arrangements. They are very short-lived, usually lasting only one day. Use the bright-red flowers with dark-green foliage. All the pastel shades mix well with other muted flowers—lilacs, roses and delphiniums.

Colours available Many shades of red, pink, orange, yellow, cream and white.

Preparation Cut the stems with a sharp knife. Dip the ends in boiling water or pass them over a flame to seal them and prevent the sap from clouding the water. Give a long, deep drink before arranging.

Sweet Williams

SWEET WILLIAM
Dianthus barbatus

The many varieties of sweet William are available in florists' shops and are very easy to cultivate in the garden. Their round, flat heads consist of many small flowers tightly packed together. The bright colours mix very well with other summer flowers in informal arrangements, and they look particularly attractive when massed together in a wicker basket.

Colours available Flowers are usually a mixture of two or more of the following colours: red, pink, crimson and white, arranged in rings of colour around the centre of the flower.

Preparation Cut the stems on a slant and make a 5cm slit with a sharp knife. Strip any foliage from the floral stems. Give a long, cool drink before arranging.

Carnations and pinks

"Zebra"

"Joker"

"Portrait"

"Allwood's Cream"

"Arthur Sim"

"Fragrant Ann"

"Comoco Sim"

"Inchmery"

Summer flowers 2

Delphinium

DELPHINIUM
Delphinium sp.

Delphiniums are popular as both florists' flowers and garden plants, and many new hybrids are coming on to the market, extending the range of colours and sizes available. The long spikes are laden with small, fragrant flowers and are good for arrangements in tall vases. Use the tall, white varieties for large-scale decorations. If you don't have room for large arrangements, there are shorter hybrids available in all the colours, and these can look

Foxgloves

Digitalis purpurea

D. purpurea "Alba"

D. grandiflora "Ambigua"

very attractive massed together with some of their own feathery foliage.

Colours available Many shades of blue and mauve. Also pink, white and cream.

Preparation Cut the stems on a slant and make a 5cm slit with a sharp knife. Give a long drink in cool water before arranging. To make the flowers last longer for a special occasion, it is worth filling the hollow stems with water and plugging the ends with cotton wool.

DECORATIVE ONION
Allium sp.

These members of the onion family bear numerous tiny flowers in large, ball-like clusters. Use as focal points in an arrangement of large-headed flowers.

Colours available Yellow, purple, pink and white.

Preparation Cut the stems on a slant and make a 5cm slit with a sharp knife before arranging in deep water. Add a teaspoonful of bleach to the water to remove the onion smell.

FOXGLOVE
Digitalis sp.

These beautiful wild flowers are becoming more popular in gardens but are still fairly difficult to find in florists' shops. Try to grow your own foxgloves as they should not be taken from the wild. They are excellent for arrangements, as they retain their petals for some considerable time after cutting. The delicate colours of the foxglove mix well with any other pastel-coloured flowers and their elongated shape makes them good for outlining the shape of large, formal arrangements. They can also look lovely arranged informally in a basket or terracotta pot.

Colours available Mauve, purple, white, cream, red, yellow and gold. Most are spotted with another colour within the bell.

Preparation Cut the stems on a slant and make a 5cm slit with a sharp knife. Strip any foliage from the floral stems and give an overnight drink in warm water before arranging.

Tea rose hybrids **1** "Message" **2** "Goldgleam" **3** "Pascali" **4** "Margaret Merrill"

HYBRID TEA ROSE
Rosa sp.

The variety of roses available is ever-increasing as new hybrids and cultivars come on the market. The only drawback has been the loss of fragrance from some cultivars. Hybrid tea roses are compact roses with high-centred double flowers. They can be used in formal arrangements and bouquets. Roses of one colour, massed in a plain container or basket, can look lovely.

Colours available Roses are available in just about every shade of every colour except blue.

Preparation Cut the stems on a slant and make a 5cm slit with a sharp knife. Strip any foliage from the floral stems and dip stems in boiling water for a minute. Give a long drink in cold water before arranging.

Yarrow "Coronation Gold"

YARROW
Achillea filipendulina

These informal-looking, flat-headed flowers are available in a range of sizes as well as colours. They are easily grown in the garden and commonly found along roadsides and in hedgerows. Use large, bright-gold heads as

Additional features
Long-lasting
Useful foliage
Fragrant
Suitable for drying

focal points in large arrangements and smaller, pale-yellow or white heads in arrangements of white flowers, such as roses, or with variegated hosta lily leaves. As the petals do not fall and the flowers dry well, they can be included in dried-flower arrangements whilst still fresh.

Colours available Many shades of yellow and gold, and white.

Preparation Cut the stems on a slant and make a 5cm slit with a sharp knife. Strip any foliage from the floral stems and give a deep drink before arranging.

TRANSVAAL DAISY
Gerbera jamesonii

These large, brightly coloured, daisy-shaped flowers have soft, furry petals and soft, grey-green stems which are leafless. They can be greenhouse-grown and are becoming more readily available in florists' shops. The yellow and orange flowers look good arranged with white spider chrysanthemums and eucalyptus leaves, and can also be used to effect in autumnal dried-flower arrangements, as their colour complements the warm tones of the dried material. Contrast the round heads with iris spikes, gladioli, or delphiniums of the same colour.

Colours available Purple, crimson, red, pink, white, yellow and orange.

Preparation Cut the stems on a slant and make a 5cm slit with a sharp knife. Dip the ends of the stems in boiling water, then give a long drink in cool water before arranging.

Sweet peas
Colour varieties

Transvaal daisies
Colour varieties

African lily

AFRICAN LILY
Agapanthus africanus

These evergreen plants have smooth, lance-shaped leaves and tall, succulent stems. The individual flowers are small and borne in a ball-shaped cluster at the top of the stem, giving a large inflorescence. They can be grown in the garden in a sheltered spot and are readily available in florists' shops. African lilies can be used in large arrangements and make a lovely, cool, summer arrangement if their round heads are mixed with tall, white, spiky flowers such as irises or gladioli.

Colours available Blue and white.

Preparation Cut the stems on a slant and make a 5cm slit with a sharp knife. Arrange in deep water.

SWEET PEA
Lathyrus odoratus

These delicate flowers are well known for their sweet scent which can quickly fill a room. They are easily grown in the garden, where their climbing stems will need to be supported if they are to bloom profusely. They are also found in florists' shops during summer. There are usually four or five blooms to a stem and a large bunch of flowers of the same colour can be very eye-catching. Sweet peas also look lovely arranged informally with roses of the same colour. This gives a very fragrant display.

Colours available A wide range of shades of red, pink, purple, apricot and white.

Preparation Sweet peas should be handled as little as possible. Cut long stems with a sharp knife and give a deep drink in cool water for several hours before arranging.

Other summer flowers

Bells-of-Ireland	Snapdragon
Gentian	Lupin
Angelica	Candytuft
Cornflower	Marigold
Columbine	Clarkia
Brodiaea	Loosestrife
Zinnia	Lavender
Anthemis daisy	Hollyhock
Marguerite daisy	Petunia
Geranium	Clary
Bellflower	Californian poppy
Mock orange	Livingstone daisy

Autumn flowers and berries 1

The colours of autumn flowers are deeper than those of spring and summer. Purples, reds, browns and golds predominate among both flowers and foliage. Deep-yellow sunflowers and coneflowers, and fiery red-hot pokers provide rich and vibrant colours, while the many types of dahlia offer a splendid range of hues and shapes. When the flowers are over, the fruits, berries and vegetables of autumn can be used in arrangements. Vegetables such as globe artichokes can add interesting texture and colour to a display. Berries and fruits, such as rose hips and crab apples,

add rich colour to arrangements and can look very attractive displayed informally by themselves or with some foliage. Autumn foliage is well worth using as the supply of home-grown flowers diminishes. Some foliage changes colour, turning to shades of red, orange, coppery-brown and deep purple. Towards the end of the season it may be worth investing in some flamboyant imported material. One or two of the large South African nodding pincushion heads are enough to prolong the displays of autumnal flowers for a little longer, adding variety in shape and colour.

CONEFLOWER
Rudbeckia sp.

These pretty, daisy-shaped flowers have lovely, rich colouring. The round face is centred by a dark cone. Single and double flowers are available, and flowers of different colours massed in a terracotta pot bring the colours of autumn indoors. Coneflowers look equally good with red or yellow foliage.

Colours available Yellow, orange and brown; often ringed with red. The centres are dark brown.

Preparation Cut the stems on a slant and make a 5cm slit with a sharp knife. Strip any foliage from the floral stems and dip the cut ends into boiling water for a few minutes. Give a deep drink before arranging.

CAPE LILY
Crinum powellii

These elegant plants have clusters of trumpet-shaped flowers borne at the top of a thick, succulent stem. The flowers are produced in succession and should be picked off as they fade. Use the Cape lily in large, formal arrangements where a certain elegance is required. The white variety is ideal for wedding displays. It also looks good arranged in a simple, white, porcelain vase with sprays of delicate flowers, such as twigs of lime from which all the foliage has been removed.

Colours available Pink and white.

Preparation Cut stems on a slant and make a 5cm slit with a sharp knife. Give a long drink before arranging. The hollow stems can be filled with water and the ends plugged with cotton wool to make the flowers last longer.

Cape lily

Crab apple "John Downie"

CRAB APPLE
Malus sp.

The fruits of the crab apple tree are small and round and usually inedible when raw. More often found in the garden or hedgerow than in florists' shops, the attractive colouring of the fruits and the coppery tones of the autumn foliage make them useful for autumn groups. Mix them with flowers of autumnal shades, such as dahlias, red-hot pokers or coneflowers, or with woody shrubs such as the flowering maple or spindle tree. The undried fruits also look good in dried arrangements, although they will begin to shrivel after a time.

Colours available The fruits and leaves take on the shades of autumn—reds, yellows and oranges. The spring blossoms are red, pink or white.

Preparation Scrape the stems and make a 5cm slit with a sharp knife. Give a long drink in deep water before arranging.

ST JOHN'S WORT
Hypericum elatum

A popular garden shrub which is very easy to grow. Although common in gardens, it is not often seen in florists' shops. St John's wort is a semi-evergreen shrub: the leaves are retained in the winter but, instead of remaining green, turn a greenish-red and are aromatic if crushed. The yellow flowers are very delicate but will last until October, when they are followed by

the clusters of oval berries. The sprays are most useful as background material in all kinds of arrangements and the berries look good in arrangements of autumn fruits and flowers.

Colours available Summer flowers are yellow and foliage green; autumn berries are red and the foliage a greenish-red.

Preparation Cut the stems on a slant and make a 5cm slit with a sharp knife. Strip any foliage from the floral stems. Give a deep drink before arranging in cool water.

FLOWERING MAPLE
Abutilon hybridum

These woody shrubs are common in gardens, but the cut branches are often difficult to find in florists' shops. The delicate, papery flowers are a wide-funnel shape and hang down from the leaf axils. The woody branches and pale green, often mottled, leaves interspersed with the colourful flowers look good arranged on their own in a plain vase or with other delicate material.

Colours available The flowers are combinations of red, yellow, mauve and pale blue.

Preparation Cut the stems on a slant and make a 5cm slit with a sharp knife. Strip any foliage from the floral stems and give a deep drink before arranging.

Flowering maple

Additional features
Long-lasting   Useful foliage   Fragrant   Suitable for drying

Spindle tree

SPINDLE TREE
Euonymus panipes

The berries of this shrub are most unusual—they are round and fleshy, suddenly bursting open into a flowerlike shape to reveal a mass of bright-orange seeds. The foliage is deep green, fading to a green speckled with white and yellow. The spindle tree is best used at the back of an arrangement.

Colours available   The berries may be red, pink or white, with bright-orange seeds.

Preparation   Scrape the ends of the stems and make a 5cm slit with a sharp knife before arranging.

MICHAELMAS DAISY
Aster nova-belgii

Michaelmas daisies have upright main stems which bear shorter stems topped with the flower. Due to their ragged appearance, they do not mix well with other flowers. For best effect, mass up flowers of one colour and place in a large copper pan, then position the arrangement so it reflects the autumn sun.

Colours available   White, purple and pink.

Preparation   Cut the stems on a slant and make a 5cm slit with a sharp knife. Strip any foliage from the floral stems and dip the ends into boiling water for a few seconds, then give a deep drink for twelve hours.

Michaelmas daisy hybrids   **1** "Ada Ballard"
2 "Blandie"

GLOBE ARTICHOKE
Cynara scolymus

Globe artichokes are most useful in all stages of their development. Apart from being good to eat, the flower buds are made up of fresh-green, overlapping bracts which add textured interest to the base of autumnal groups. The tufts of purple flowers emerge later. The seed heads and the beautiful, fernlike foliage are also most useful.

Colours available   The flower buds are pale green; the flowers are purple.

Globe artichoke

Preparation   The flower heads need no special preparation. The leaves last much longer if the stems are held in boiling water for thirty seconds and then the whole leaf submerged in cold water for an hour.

STRAW FLOWER
Helichrysum bracteatum

These flowers, which are most often seen dried, can also be used in fresh flower arrangements. The daisylike flower heads are surrounded by papery bracts giving the illusion of being dried, when in fact they are quite fresh. The colours of the flowers are ideally suited to informal autumn arrangements and look good with almost all types of flower. Mass up the flowers, in baskets, then use them to fill alcoves or unused fireplaces. As the petals do not fall, allow the flowers to dry out, to provide a dried arrangement.

Colours available   Yellow, red, orange, magenta, purple and combinations of these colours.

Preparation   Cut the stems with a sharp knife, and dip in boiling water. Allow a long drink in cool water before arranging.

Straw flowers

Colour varieties

Autumn flowers and berries 2

Sunflower

SUNFLOWER
Helianthus annuus

Sunflowers are favourites in the garden as they are so easy to grow, and most rewarding as they reach such a size. The large heads can easily unbalance an arrangement of small flowers, so use them as a focal point with large flowers, or mix them with foliage and berries.

Colours available Golden-yellow petals with dark-brown central discs.

Preparation Cut stems on a slant and make a 5cm slit with a sharp knife. Dip the ends of the stems into boiling water and give a long drink before arranging.

Bear's breeches

BEAR'S BREECHES
Acanthus spinosus

These unusual, tall spikes are formed by small flowers enclosed in leafy bracts all the way up the succulent stem. The spikes give a good outline to large, formal and informal arrangements of autumn flowers and foliage. They can also be contrasted with large, round flowers such as sunflowers and dahlias. The spiky foliage is very attractive and looks good arranged in a vase with pink flowers.

Colours available Purple-pink flowers hidden amongst purple-green, leafy bracts.

Preparation Cut the stems on a slant and make a 5cm slit with a sharp knife. Dip the cut ends in boiling water and give a deep drink in cold water for several hours. Leaf stalks should also be dipped in boiling

water for a few moments. The whole leaf should then be submerged in a weak solution of starch for about twelve hours.

DAHLIA
Dahlia hybrids

Dahlias are popular, easily grown garden flowers which are becoming more readily available in florists' shops. They come in many sizes, shapes and colours. All the various shapes have a different name—"cactus", "pompom", "quilled" and "fancy", to name but a few, and the range is ever expanding as growers experiment with new crosses and hybrids. Dahlias mix well in all types of arrangements as they have an attractive, round shape and a predominant "face", so that you know which way round to place them in an arrangement. Use the peach- and apricot-coloured flowers with autumn foliage arrangements and the vibrant reds in a vase of red roses or red-hot pokers. Mix the whites with other white flowers and deep-green foliage for a striking effect, or mass up dahlias of the same colour but different shapes for a textured, informal arrangement.

Colours available Dahlias are available in many different colours, and many shades of the same colour, as new hybrids produce increasingly subtle tones. The only colour not yet produced is blue.

Preparation Cut the stems on a slant and make a 5cm slit with a sharp knife. Strip any foliage from the floral stems and dip the ends in boiling water for a few minutes. Give a cool drink overnight before arranging in deep water. For special occasions or formal arrangements, when the flowers have to look good for as long as possible, arrange in deep water containing a teaspoonful of sugar and an aspirin.

Dahlias

"Rokesley Mini"

"Authority"

"Little Conn"

"Glorie van Heernstede"

"Super"

Guelder rose berries

Rose hips **1** *Rosa* sp. **2** *R. moyesii* **3** *R. rugosa*

ROSE HIPS
Rosa sp.

Autumnal hedgerows were once full of the bright-red hips of wild roses, but the supply of these is decreasing. Hips will form on all garden roses, but are often not given the chance as the plants are pruned back. They are, however, very beautiful and come in many different shapes and sizes, according to the type of rose. Rose hips look good in all autumn arrangements, especially those incorporating dark-red flowers and foliage. Hips can also be used to add a splash of colour to arrangements of dried foliage and seed heads.

Colours available Rose hips may be many different shades of red, depending on the time of cutting.

Preparation Cut the stems on a slant and make a 5cm slit with a sharp knife. Strip any foliage and thorns from the stems. Dip the cut ends into boiling water for a minute before giving a long drink.

TOBACCO PLANT
Nicotiana affinis

These plants are grown commercially for their leaves which are used in tobacco production. The garden varieties are cultivated for their colourful flowers which are heavily scented. The flowers are tubuiar, flaring out into a star-shaped face. Their myriad colours make them useful in all kinds of informal arrangements. Use the vibrant colours with red flowers or foliage, or make a truly autumnal arrangement using the orange- and yellow-coloured varieties. The lime-green flowers can add interest to a vase of delicate green foliage.

Colours available White, red, orange, yellow, crimson, lime-green, cream and pink.

Preparation The stems are very soft and should be cut with a sharp knife. Place in warm water before arranging in deep water.

RED-HOT POKER
Kniphofia uvaria

These easily grown garden plants are not often seen in florists' shops. They make good cut flowers, although their large size makes them a little difficult to arrange. Their colours are ideally suited to autumnal arrangements

and they add spiky interest to large, informal displays. The succulent stems of red-hot pokers tend to grow on, even when cut; this causes the stems to twist, so you will have to rearrange the flowers if you want to retain a particular shape.

Colours available The heads of red-hot pokers are green when they first appear, but then turn red. Hybrids are now available in cream-and-yellow and cream-and-pink.

Preparation Cut the stems on a slant and make a 5cm slit with a sharp knife, then give a long drink in cool water before arranging.

Red-hot poker

GUELDER ROSE BERRIES
Viburnum opulus

The translucent, golden berries which appear in autumn are as useful as the fragrant blossom which appears in spring. The berries are held in small clusters on branches which retain their leaves even when quite dry. This makes the guelder rose useful for background sprays in arrangements of fresh or dried materials.

Colours available Berries may be red, yellow, gold or blue. Spring flowers are white, green or pink. Foliage is bright green.

Preparation Scrape the stems and cut on a slant. Make a 5cm slit with a sharp knife and dip the cut ends into boiling water for a few moments. Give an overnight drink in cool water before arranging.

NODDING PINCUSHION
Leucospermum nutans

These spectacular flower heads are members of the protea family and are imported from South Africa. The heads have a rounded shape covered with yellow spikes with red bulbous tips. Nodding pincushions add a focal point to large arrangements of fresh or dried materials.

Colours available Yellow-red.

Preparation Cut the stems on a slant and make a 5cm slit with a sharp knife. Give a deep drink before arranging in cool water.

Other autumn flowers

Japanese anemone	Red valerian
Clematis	Chinese lantern
Hydrangea	Fleabane
Marigold	Montbretia
Sedum	Floss flower
Statice	Forget-me-not
Phlox	Rose mallow
Cotoneaster	Verbena
Lilyturf	Autumn crocus
Shasta daisy	Scabious

Winter flowers and berries

In winter, evergreens come into their own, producing masses of beautifully textured foliage and glowing berries. The term evergreen covers a multitude of foliage colours, including many variegated types, as well as textures—so that you can make up quite a bright arrangement using only evergreen foliage throughout the winter.

Towards the end of winter, many of the deciduous shrubs become covered with the palest of flowers—many of which have a deep scent which is released when twigs are cut and brought into the warmth. Winter camellias flower in white and pink at this time. Also, pushing through the grass or soil come the snowdrops, followed by the yellow winter aconites, some crocuses, and the earliest of the narcissi. The choice of blooms is increased with commercially grown anemones, lilac, early carnations and roses. Orchids are imported at this time of year too. All these flowers are plentiful in the shops, if somewhat expensive so, for larger arrangements, rely on evergreens or well-shaped bare twigs. You will find that some of these may burst into leaf in the warmth of the home.

COMMON HOLLY
Ilex aquifolium

The glossy, dark-green leaves with their wavy, spined edges and clusters of red berries are a familiar sight in winter, both in gardens and florists' shops. Holly can grow as small bushes or as trees, and is as colourful in the garden as it is in the home. Traditional winter arrangements using holly include Christmas wreaths and garlands, but it is also useful as background material to deep-red flowers.

Colours available Holly leaves may be deep green or variegated. Berries may be bright red, orange-red or yellow.

Preparation When cutting, use a pair of secateurs. Holly lasts longer if kept out of water.

Common holly

Wattle

WATTLE
Acacia longifolia

This delicate-looking shrub is related to the spring-flowering mimosa and has very similar yellow flowers. However, unlike the mimosa, the grey-green leaves of the wattle are undivided and willowlike in shape. The fragrant flowers contrast well with the foliage and the sprays are a welcome addition to winter arrangements of flowers and foliage.

Colours available Yellow ball-like flowers and grey-green foliage.

Preparation Keep wrapped in polythene to exclude air for as long as possible before arranging. Just prior to arranging, remove the polythene and dip flower heads in cold water for a few moments. Cut the stems on a slant and make a 5cm slit with a sharp knife. Dip the stems in boiling water for a few seconds, then give a deep drink with warm water until the heads are dry.

ANEMONE
Anemone coronaria

These delicate flowers are available in a wide variety of shapes and sizes, although the ones pictured here are the most familiar. Their fragile flowers are made up not of petals but of sepals (these are usually green and are the leaflike structures which surround the flower), and these form a cup shape round a deep-blue central disc. In the garden, anemones of different species can be found in spring, summer and autumn but, in florists' shops, they are available throughout the year. Although they can be mixed with other flowers, they look best massed in a glass vase. Pack them in tightly, as their stems have a tendency to bend and this can make a vase look untidy.

Colours available Red, blue, mauve, pink, white, yellow, magenta and scarlet. Many have a central disc ringed with another colour.

Preparation Cut the stems on a slant and make a 5cm slit with a sharp knife. Dip the cut ends in boiling water for a few seconds. Give a long, cool drink before arranging.

Anemones Colour varieties

CHINCHERINCHEE
Ornithogalum thyrsoides

Imported in winter, these flowers are a useful addition to the range available at this time of year. The tightly packed flowers will open from the bottom upwards and the spike is soon a mass of small, white, star-shaped flowers. They look good when used with colourful sprays of holly or cotoneaster at Christmas.

Colours available White.

Preparation Some chincherinchees come with wax sealing their ends. Cut this off and make a 5cm slit with a sharp knife. Give a deep drink of warm water and then put them in cool water for several days to allow all the flowers to open.

Additional features

Long-lasting · Useful foliage · Fragrant · Suitable for drying

Orchid

ORCHID
Dendrobium sp.

These exotic flowers are imported from the Far East. Orchids come in many different sizes and shapes, all with the usual "lip" surrounded by a ring of sepals and petals. The flowers need to be seen close up to be appreciated, so these orchids are best displayed very simply, either on their own or with the bare, red stems of the dogwood, in an uncluttered setting.

Colours available Red, orange, yellow, white and purple. The flowers are usually marked or patterned with another colour.

Preparation These orchids are usually bought with their stems fixed in a small tube of water. The stems can be left in this tube if the water is changed every two or three days.

WINTER-FLOWERING JASMINE
Jasminum nudiflorum

These shrubs are easily grown in the garden, and cut stems are available in florists' shops. In summer, the bush is covered in dark-green leaves, but during the winter it is covered with tubular, yellow flowers. Display a few sprays in a plain terracotta container or mix with early flowering narcissi.

Colours available Yellow.

Preparation Cut the stems on a slant and make a 5cm slit with a sharp knife. No other treatment is required before arranging.

CHRYSANTHEMUM
Chrysanthemum hybrids

At a time when substantial, brightly coloured flowers are not abundant, these flowers are a great addition to winter flower arrangements. Chrysanthemums grow in gardens in autumn but are now commercially forced and can be bought in florists' shops throughout the year. They are available as single heads and sprays in many different shapes and sizes. The single blooms are easier to arrange as focal points in a vase. The sprays are a little more difficult, as there are many flowers on each stem. These should be massed together in a large vase, or the individual flowers can be picked off and used in miniature arrangements.

Colours available Chrysanthemums are available in a wide range of colours—red, orange, rust, pink, white, yellow, lime-green, peach and cream. Many of the daisy-shaped flowers have a central disc of a different colour.

Preparation Cut the stems at a slant and make a 5cm slit with a sharp knife. Dip the cut ends in boiling water for a few seconds. Immerse the whole stem in cool water and give a long drink before arranging in deep water.

Cotoneaster

COTONEASTER
Cotoneaster "Cornubius"

The dark-green, lance-shaped leaves of this evergreen shrub are deeply veined and slightly matt, giving them an attractive texture. The red berries are borne in large clusters. Use small sprays in seasonal table decorations or in place of holly in wreaths and garlands. Cotoneaster can also be used as colourful background material in large arrangements.

Colours available Deep-green leaves, red berries in winter, cream flowers in summer.

Preparation Cut the stems on a slant and make a 5cm slit with a sharp knife. Give a long, cool drink before arranging.

WINTER ACONITE
Eranthis hyemalis

These beautiful flowers appear in gardens in February. The small, yellow flowers resemble buttercups in shape and are ringed by lime-green sepals. Display them with their own foliage in a miniature arrangement.

Colours available Yellow.

Preparation Cut the stems on a slant and make a slit with a sharp knife. Arrange in cool water.

Chrysanthemums

Thread-petalled florist's chrysanthemum

Single-flowered spray chrysanthemums

Other winter flowers

Snowdrop	Mahonia
Hellebore	Toadflax
Winter sweet	Algerian iris
Cymbidium	Cyclamen
Chionodoxa	Squill
Winter camellia	Hepatica
Witch hazel	Hyacinth
Grape hyacinth	Snowflake
Skimmia	Lenten rose
Firethorn	Heather
Barberry	Snowberry

Foliage 1

Foliage plays as great a part in flower arranging as flowers themselves. Individual leaves or sprays can either be used as background or filler material in mixed arrangements, or the foliage can be used on its own to make an attractive display. While the choice of foliage available in florists' shops may be limited, gardens and woods can provide an enormous variety of leaves with a fascinating range of colours, shapes and textures with which to experiment. Plain-green leaves range from the forest-green of the pittosporum to the apple-green of the hosta lily; or leaves may be variegated with white, cream or yellow— they may be completely coloured, like the golden-yellow leaves of the spindle tree, or marked only at the margins, like the variegated holly. Silver and grey foliage looks particularly attractive with yellow or pink flowers and can be used on its own—many different textures massed together in a monochromatic arrangement look very striking. Red and bronze leaves are usually associated with autumn, but many leaves have this colour all year round. When planning arrangements, try to utilize the natural outline of the leaves or sprays as an integral part of a design. Use spikes of leaves as outline material, soft, arching ivies and ferns to add curves—either within the arrangement or trailing down from an arrangement placed on a pedestal—and bold leaves such as those of the hosta lily and elephant's ear, to make a dramatic, modern display. Arrangements made up entirely of foliage can be just as attractive as arrangements of flowers.

To prepare cut foliage for display, condition it first by soaking it in water—overnight for older leaves and about two hours for younger leaves. Do not soak silver or grey foliage as it has a tendency to become soggy. Wash evergreen foliage in a solution of mild detergent to restore its shine. All foliage can be pressed; individual entries state which items can be air-dried or dried in glycerine.

GREEN FOLIAGE

VIBURNUM
Viburnum rhytidophyllum

These deep-green leaves have a distinctive wrinkled texture caused by the heavy veining on the upper surface. They mix very well with pansies and white or red dahlias, and can be used to vary texture in an all-green display. The evergreen leaves dry particularly well in air or glycerine.

SOFT SHIELD FERN
Polystichum setiferum

The leaves of this handsome fern have a soft texture and a good, bright-green colour. They are finely divided and gently arching, providing an excellent foil for cut flowers. They mix well with teazel and driftwood in a modern arrangement. Soft shield fern is an evergreen which does not dry well.

MAGNOLIA
Magnolia grandiflora

These shiny, green leaves have a leathery texture and a rust-coloured, feltlike underside. They can be used as a background for deep-red flowers. The evergreen leaves do not dry well.

HOSTA LILY
Hosta sp.

The leaves of the hosta lily are large and broad and are a bright-green colour. Their size and deeply grooved, glossy texture makes them ideal for modern arrangements, and they combine well with large flowers such as lilies or poppies. These leaves are at their best during the spring.

COTONEASTER
Cotoneaster horizontalis

Tiny, delicate, dark-green leaves are arranged on stiff stems. The leaves have a glossy upper surface, and are grey and hairy beneath. The long, narrow spikes of leaves are suitable for establishing the outline of an arrangement; the tiny leaves complement larger and more dominant elements with their delicate appearance. This foliage is evergreen but turns red in autumn. These leaves can be air-dried or dried in glycerine.

JAPANESE ANGELICA
Aralia chinensis

The oval-shaped leaves are a rich-green colour, and there is also a yellow-and-green variety. The number of leaflets on each spray makes them useful as filler material in all types of arrangement. They are deciduous leaves which can be air-dried.

ELEPHANT'S EAR
Bergenia sp.

The large, dark-green leaves of the elephant's ear have a smooth, shiny texture with bold ribbing. They are good for focal interest and are suitable for large-scale modern arrangements. These leaves are at their best during the winter months.

PITTOSPORUM
Pittosporum tobira

These attractive, tear-drop shaped leaves are a lustrous green and have a prominent central vein. Their thick, leathery texture contrasts well with rough or hairy leaves. As the leaves are small, pittosporum makes a good background material to cut flowers. This plant is an evergreen and can be used all year round.

Green foliage **1** Viburnum **2** Soft shield fern
3 Magnolia **4** Hosta lily **5** Cotoneaster
6 Japanese angelica **7** Elephant's ear **8** Pittosporum

Green-and-yellow foliage

Honeysuckle

Indian bean tree

California privet

Cut-leaf elder

Japanese maple

Japanese spindle tree

Locust tree

Mock orange

GREEN-AND-YELLOW FOLIAGE

HONEYSUCKLE
Lonicera nitida "Baggesen's Gold"

The rows of tiny, golden and pale-green leaves are borne in upright spikes. This shrubby form of honeysuckle can be used for outline, or as filler material in flower and foliage arrangements, and looks good with yellow roses. The evergreen leaves can be used fresh or air-dried at any time of year.

INDIAN BEAN TREE
Catalpa bignonioides

With its large, heart-shaped, pale yellow-green leaves, this foliage is useful for large-scale arrangements—though it does exude a pungent smell if crushed. Beanlike seed pods are produced in autumn. The leaves are at their best during summer. They do not dry well.

CALIFORNIA PRIVET
Ligustrum ovalifolium "Aureum"

This variety of privet is a pale-green colour with wide borders of deep yellow. Other varieties of privet may be green or white and green. The leaves have a soft texture. The evergreen leaves are borne in bushy spikes, and are useful in many types of arrangement, but do not dry well.

CUT-LEAF ELDER
Sambucus racemosa "Plumosa Aurea"

These unusual golden-yellow and green leaves have deeply serrated margins. The leaves are borne in sprays which are useful for giving a soft outline shape to a large arrangement. The cut-leaf elder produces berries in autumn, but the leaves are at their best in spring or summer. They do not dry well, but are very useful for fresh arrangements.

JAPANESE MAPLE
Acer japonicum "Aureum"

Deeply serrated margins give these large leaves a beautiful shape. The fresh, bright colouring and unusual "fan" shape make them a suitable focal point for a foliage display and are seen at their best in simple displays. The yellow leaves turn a rich crimson in autumn. They are especially attractive when pressed.

JAPANESE SPINDLE TREE
Euonymus japonicus "Ovatus Aureus"

The small, oval leaves are golden-yellow or yellow-green in colour and have an attractive glossy texture. They grow in dense sprays and make good filler material in arrangements of small, yellow flowers. These are evergreen leaves which do not dry well.

LOCUST TREE
Robinia pseudoacacia

When they first appear, the leaves are golden-yellow, turning into a pale yellow-green in the summer. The "Frisia" variety has golden-yellow leaves throughout the season. The small leaflets are arranged in very regular pairs on thin branchlets. Display these leaves so that the natural fan shape and interesting texture can be used to best effect.

MOCK ORANGE
Philadelphus coronarius "Aureus"

When young, the foliage of this plant is bright golden-yellow, becoming dark green with age. The round leaves have a pointed tip and roughly toothed margins, and are at their best in spring. Use them to complement large flowers of any colour.

Foliage 2

GREEN-AND-WHITE FOLIAGE

DOGWOOD
Cornus alba "Elegantissima"

This mid-green foliage is irregularly edged with white and grows on red stems. The plain-green varieties often turn red or orange in autumn. All provide useful colour for flower or foliage groups, mixing especially well with white flowers. The leaves are at their best in autumn. They do not dry well.

EUROPEAN ELDER
Sambucus nigra "Albo-variegata"

These slender, dark-green, pointed leaves are finely edged with pale yellow. They exude a disagreeable odour if bruised, but are an ideal background to a vase of yellow flowers. The leaves are at their best during spring and summer. They do not dry well.

COMMON PRIVET
Ligustrum vulgare "Aureo-variegatum"

These long, elegant leaves grow on densely packed branches which have an elongated overall shape. The smaller leaves are more prominently yellow, so a good colour range is present on each stem. These evergreen leaves air-dry well.

ENGLISH HOLLY
Ilex aquifolium "Golden Queen"

The sharp, spiky, dark-green leaves have white or silver edging. Holly is an evergreen foliage traditionally used in Christmas garlands and wreaths. It can also be usefully combined with hellebores, red or white carnations, or ivy. Holly lasts longer if arranged without water and air-dries well.

GREATER PERIWINKLE
Vinca major "Variegata"

These leaves are oval in shape and are mid-green edged with white. They are arranged in pairs on slender, curving stems which can be allowed to trail or twine. Use these evergreen leaves as trailing material in a pedestal arrangement.

ENGLISH IVY
Hedera helix hybrids

These small, heart-shaped leaves are mid-green with irregular, white edging. Ivies are evergreen trailers but can also be used to twine up through an arrangement. They contrast well with snowdrops and catkins in a winter arrangement, and can also be used effectively with freesias or foxgloves in shades of yellow for a fresh-looking display. The leaves are suitable for drying in glycerine.

Green-and-white foliage

Dogwood

European elder

Greater periwinkle

English ivy

Algerian ivy

Golden privet

Common privet

English holly

Variegated hosta lily

Pittosporum

ALGERIAN IVY
Hedera canariensis "Variegata"

These large, leathery leaves are dark green edged with white. The heart-shaped leaves grow on red stems and look good in displays of large flowers, such as daffodils or yellow Transvaal daisies. Whole stems of these evergreen leaves can trail from arrangements. The leaves are suitable for drying in glycerine.

VARIEGATED HOSTA LILY
Hosta sp.

These large, broad leaves have a prominent pale-yellow margin. Their size and deeply grooved, glossy texture make them ideal for modern arrangements. They also combine well with large flowers, such as roses, or with ferns in a foliage display. They are at their best in spring.

PITTOSPORUM
Pittosporum tenuifolium "Garnettii"

These pale-green leaves have narrow, irregular yellow margins and are borne on black stems. They have an open appearance and make excellent filler material at any time of year. The leaves can be dried in glycerine.

GOLDEN PRIVET
Ligustrum ovalifolium "Albo-marginatum"

These glossy, mid-green leaves have wide, irregular, creamy-white borders. The spikes of leaves are good filler material, and a useful addition to a green foliage arrangement at any time of year.

GREY FOLIAGE

EUCALYPTUS
Eucalyptus gunnii

The distinctive young foliage of this evergreen plant encircles the thin grey stems. (The leaves become elongated as they get older). The colour varies between blue-green and silvery-white. Eucalyptus leaves look good with pink or blue flowers in a modern setting, or with grasses and ferns in a dried arrangement. The fragrance is also attractive. These leaves can be used throughout the year but look best when still young. They can be dried in glycerine.

SEA KALE
Crambe maritima

The leaves of this spring vegetable are large, fleshy and brittle, and have a distinctive blue-green colour. They have a crinkly outline that provides an interesting contrast with more formal shapes, or they can be used to good effect in more abstract arrangements of leaves of different textures. They are at their best in summer. They do not dry well.

COMMON WORMWOOD
Artemisia "Powis Castle"

A sprig of common wormwood resembles a tiny tree in shape. The delicate silver-grey leaves are deeply dissected into slender filaments which have a silky texture and provide an unusual outline for small groups. These are evergreen leaves which may prove difficult to dry.

GROUNDSEL
Senecio "Sunshine"

Two distinct colours and textures are displayed by these small, oval leaves. They have a dark-green, leathery upper surface and a pale-green and densely felted lower surface. They look good in both flower and foliage arrangements as both sides of the leaves can be displayed to effect. Although the leaves are evergreen, they are at their best in winter. They do not dry well.

WHITE WILLOW
Salix alba

These two-tone leaves are deep-green above and silky-white beneath. The leaves are long and narrow and borne in pairs on the woody stems. Used thoughtfully, the sprays of leaves can add interest to both flower and foliage groups. The leaves are at their best in summer. They do not dry well.

MULLEIN
Verbascum sp.

These large, pale-grey leaves have a soft texture and gentle shape that combines well with other soft-textured foliage. They look attractive when mixed with flowers, particularly with pale-pink, blue or green flowers for a pastel-coloured arrangement. The evergreen leaves are at their best in summer. They do not dry well.

SENECIO
Senecio maritima

A fine, white down covers both surfaces of these deeply dissected leaves and gives them an attractive, silvery appearance. The leaves have a soft texture and they are ideal for adding an interesting shape to a small arrangement. They mix particularly well with pink roses and statice. The leaves are evergreen and are at their best in summer. They do not dry well.

ORNAMENTAL OATS
Helicotrichon sempervirens

These long, thin and slightly arching leaves are an intense blue-grey colour. They provide dramatic definition and contrast and go well with bright-blue flowers, such as irises, delphiniums and larkspur in a stark, modern arrangement. Although evergreen, the leaves are at their best in summer.

BALLOTA
Ballota pseudodictamnus

The very unusual leaves of this plant grow densely on slim, upright stems. They are heart-shaped with slightly scalloped edges and are "woolly-grey" in colour; they provide excellent textural variation for a fresh or dried all-foliage arrangement. The leaves are evergreen but are at their best in spring and summer. They do not dry well.

SAGEBRUSH
Artemisia "Douglasiana"

The linear leaves are borne on tall spikes and have a pale-grey underside with a slightly darker upper surface. The long, slender shape of the stems provides graceful lines and strong definition for mixed groups, whether used as focal point or as a background for pink or blue flowers such as roses, larkspur or cornflowers. These leaves are at their best in summer and are suitable for air-drying.

Grey foliage **1** Eucalyptus **2** Sea kale **3** Common wormwood **4** Groundsel **5** White willow **6** Mullein **7** Senecio **8** Ornamental oats **9** Ballota **10** Sagebrush.

Foliage 3

BRONZE FOLIAGE

ORNAMENTAL GRAPE VINE
Vitis vinifera "Purpurea"

These crimson-red leaves turn to a richer claret-red in the autumn. Pretty red-and-green variegated types are also available. The butterfly shape of the leaves is an attractive feature and as such should be arranged thoughtfully. The ornamental grape vine is useful in autumnal arrangements, mixing well with yellow and orange flowers and foliage of autumnal shades. The leaves do not dry well.

COPPER BEECH
Fagus sylvatica "Purpurea"

The delicate oval leaves have toothed edges and are a rich-copper colour. They blend well with other foliage, provide an excellent backing for large displays, and look especially striking when arranged with white or red flowers. Use older foliage, as young foliage is green. The leaves are at their best in spring and dry well in glycerine.

JAPANESE BARBERRY
Berberis thunbergii "Atropurpurea"

Small, rich, dark-bronze leaves grow in clusters on long tapering stems. They turn bright red in autumn, as does the variety which is mid-green for the rest of the year. This excellent and colourful outline foliage can be combined effectively with wood and pine cones in modern arrangements. The leaves are at their best in autumn and air-dry well.

NEW ZEALAND FLAX
Phormium tenax "Purpureum"

These straplike, stiff, leathery leaves may be red or green, and some varieties may be striped with yellow. They can grow to 3m long, but at this length become rather unusable. The young, shorter leaves provide elegant lines for arrangements. The leaves have good colour all year but do not dry well. They can, however, be used in short-term dried arrangements whilst still fresh.

NORWAY MAPLE
Acer platanoides "Goldsworth Purple"

Apart from the deep purple-crimson of this foliage, there are white-margined, pale-green and red varieties. The bold, pointed outline of maple leaves makes them suitable for large arrangements, and they make excellent filling material, combining well with large flowers such as yellow tulips or chrysanthemums. The leaves are at their best in autumn and can be dried in glycerine.

SMOKE TREE
Cotinus coggygria

These elliptical leaves grow in dense clusters. They are green with red veins, and assume a rich-red colour in autumn. The delicate mass of flower stems emerging from these clusters creates an unusual "smoky" effect which can be used effectively in Japanese-style arrangements. They also mix well with orange flowers. The leaves are at their best in autumn. They do not dry well.

PURPLE-LEAVED FILBERT
Corylus maxima "Atropurpurea"

These large, round leaves grow on slim arching stems and are deep-purple in colour. They make good foliage for large arrangements and combine well with round flowers of red, purple or mauve. They are at their best in autumn, but may prove difficult to dry.

STONECROP
Sedum maximum "Atropurpureum"

The green-and-red fleshy leaves are matched by clusters of tiny flowers of similar shades. Use them to instil texture and colour in an arrangement of fresh or dried flowers of autumnal shades. They are at their best during late summer and can easily be air-dried.

Bronze foliage

Ornamental grape vine

Copper beech

Japanese barberry

New Zealand flax

Smoke tree

Norway maple

Purple-leaved filbert

Stonecrop

THE DRIED-FLOWER GUIDE

Dried flowers have a charm that is independent of season, and create an appealing palette of pale and bright colours and of brittle and soft forms.

Flowers are not the only suitable materials; many other sorts of dried matter can be used, offering a great variety of shapes, textures and colours. The soft, neutral colours of grasses and cereals are a useful foil to flowers. The rich colours of autumnal foliage can be mixed with flowers and grasses, and both familiar and exotic seed heads offer unusual shapes and textures.

On the following pages you will find a selection of dried flowers (arranged according to their colour), foliage, cereals, grasses, seed heads and fruits, all of which can be used to make attractive and long-lasting displays. Advice is offered on how to use each item of dried material and, for each entry, the most effective method of drying is given.

Dried flowers 1
Whites and yellows

This range of colours, from the muted tones of the greenish-whites to the brilliant snow-whites and vibrant yellows, adds freshness and light to any arrangement. They mix well with other colours, and can be used either to evoke the brilliance of summer sunshine, when used with other brightly coloured dried flowers, or to reflect the mellow tones of autumn, when combined with flowers, foliage and grasses in shades of orange and brown. Their colours blend well with wicker baskets, terracotta and frosted glass.

Methods of drying

Air-drying   Glycerine   Silica/borax   Pressing

TUMBLEWEED
Amaranthus sp.
These green spikes look good in both flower and foliage arrangements.

LADY'S MANTLE
Alchemilla mollis
The delicate, yellow-green flowers blend well with grasses, cereals and seed heads.

WHITE BUTTON FLOWERS
Chrysanthemum hybrids
When the petals have been removed the central parts of the flowers can be dyed to any colour.

STATICE
Limonium sinuatum
The yellow, white, purple, pink or red flowers look attractive massed together in a terracotta container.

TANSY
Tanacetum vulgare
The bright-yellow, buttonlike flowers add a splash of colour to an arrangement.

HELIPTERUM
Helipterum roseum
White flowers with yellow centres add delicate colour to small arrangements and wreaths.

STRAW FLOWER
Helichrysum bracteatum
The yellow, white, orange or red daisylike flowers should be wired before drying.

〔∫∫∫〕

ACROLINIUM
Acrolinium sanfordii
These attractive bright-yellow flowers add colour to winter arrangements.

〔∫∫∫〕

PEARL EVERLASTING
Anaphalis margaritacea
Clusters of ivory-white flower heads which may be sprayed or dyed for display.

〔∫∫∫〕

GOLDEN MARGUERITE
Anthemis tinctoria
These versatile yellow flowers can be dyed or sprayed to any colour.

〔▲〕 〔∫∫∫〕

YARROW
Achillea filipendulina
The flat-headed yellow or white flowers provide focal point in a group.

〔∫∫∫〕

BABY'S BREATH
Gypsophila paniculata
The white or pink flowers are often used in bouquets and wreaths, but also look good on their own.

〔∫∫∫〕

Dried flowers 2
Pinks, reds and oranges

The colours in this group range from pale, delicate pinks to deep reds and flame oranges. Red flowers are perhaps the boldest and most eye-catching of all, but they attain a more subtle appeal when toned with brown, yellow or blue. Shades of pink add a light and delicate quality to an arrangement, and are seen at their best when contrasted with white and green. Deep, rich-orange flowers are especially lovely if used with the yellows and reds of autumnal foliage.

ROSE
Rosa sp.
Mass roses together in low baskets or tall containers to create an intense focal point of colour.

STRAW FLOWER
Helichrysum bracteatum
The orange, daisylike flowers should be wired before drying.

SAFFLOWER
Carthamus tinctorius
Red-orange flowers and grey-green leaves provide a stiff outline shape for arrangements.

MARSH ROSEMARY
Limonium suworowii
The long, narrow clusters of rose-pink flowers add unusual lines to any group.

CELOSIA
Celosia argentea "Cristata"
The purple or pink blooms have a mossy texture and provide a dramatic focal point for a large arrangement.

CHINESE LANTERN
Physalis alkekengi
The orange and green flower pods can be used in mixed autumnal arrangements, but also look good on their own.

Methods of drying

Air-drying Glycerine Silica/borax Pressing

BOTTLE BRUSH
Callistemon citrinus
The bright-orange heads look good in both flower and foliage arrangements.

STATICE
Limonium sinuatum
The pink, purple, yellow, white or red flowers look attractive massed together in a terra-cotta container.

HELIPTERUM
Helipterum roseum
Pink flowers with yellow centres add delicate colour to small arrangements and wreaths.

DECORATIVE ONION
Allium sp.
The flowers may be pink, blue or yellow. Mass them together in a tall container.

LARKSPUR
Delphinium consolida
Pink, mauve, blue or white flowers add height to arrangements of delicate flowers and are excellent for small wreaths.

GLOBE AMARANTH
Gomphrena globosa
These delicate, cloverlike flowers should be wired before drying.

STRAW FLOWER
Helichrysum bracteatum
The pink, daisylike flowers should be wired before drying.

HEMP AGRIMONY
Eupatorium purpureum
Use these delicate rose-pink flowers as filler material in larger flower arrangements.

ROCK CRESS
Arabis alpina "Rosea"
The tiny pink flowers can be used in bouquets and wreaths, but also look good on their own in a delicate container.

Dried flowers 3
Blues and purples

These dried flowers have colours ranging from cool and pale silvery-blue to the rich, warm tones of mauve and deep purple. The cool colours can be bright and stimulating when mixed with the complementary colours of yellow and orange; they can also be juxtaposed with white or used in a monochromatic arrangement. Mauve and purple flowers can add a touch of richness to a room if arranged with red flowers and foliage.

Methods of drying

Air-drying · Glycerine · Silica/borax · Pressing

DELPHINIUM
Delphinium elatum
Use single spikes to give height to an arrangement.

BLAZING STAR
Liatris spicata
These long spikes of tiny flowers can be used for outline in an arrangement.

LARKSPUR
Delphinium consolida
Blue, mauve, pink or white flowers add height to arrangements of delicate flowers and are excellent for small wreaths.

HYDRANGEA
Hydrangea macrophylla
Dense clusters of blue, white or pink flower heads can be used in wreaths and garlands, or in wide-necked glass bottles filled with other dried flowers.

ASTILBE
Astilbe japonica
The feathery plumes look good in arrangements of flowers or grasses. The ornamental foliage can be pressed.

STATICE
Limonium sinuatum
The purple, red, yellow, white or pink flowers look attractive massed together in a terracotta container.

DOCK
Rumex acetosa
These rust-purple plants make
excellent filling material, or can
be used to make a rustic group
if massed in a rush basket.

XERANTHEMUM
Xeranthemum annuum
These purple, lilac, white or pink
flowers should be wired together in
bunches for use in arrangements.

LAVENDER
Lavandula officinalis
The fragrant purple flowers may be
used in small bouquets, wreaths,
pot-pourris and herbal pillows.

GLOBE THISTLE
Echinops ritro
The rounded blue heads mix well
with yellow flowers.

SEA HOLLY
Eryngium maritimum
The silver-blue stems and heads
can be used to add texture to an
arrangement.

THRIFT
Armeria maritima
The ball-like, silver-pink flowers
provide focal point in a group.

GLOBE AMARANTH
Gomphrena globosa
These delicate, cloverlike flowers
should be wired before drying.

Dried foliage, cereals and grasses

Foliage, cereals and grasses should be con-
sidered essential dried-flower arranging
materials. Certainly, very few arrangements are
produced without one or more of these ingredients
to add some variation in shape, colour or texture. But
they are more than a mere foil to brightly coloured
flowers; with a little imagination they can provide
an attractive display by themselves.

PLATYLOBIUM
Platylobium angulare
The unusual foliage can be used as
background material in arrangements
of delicate flowers.

REED MACE
Typha latifolia
The hard-edged spikiness of
this relation of the bullrush is
useful in large groups.

BRISTLE BENT
Agrostis curtisii
This grey-green grass has a dense
flower head and is suitable for many
arrangements, including wreaths.

HARESTAIL GRASS
Lagurus ovatus
This delicate grass can be used with flowers or
with leaves, seed heads and other grasses.

QUAKING GRASS
Briza media
The delicate, nodding flower heads
add lightness to small arrangements.

EUCALYPTUS
Eucalyptus sp.
The red or brown
leaves add strong
shape and colour to
foliage arrangements.

GREVILLEA
Grevillea triternata
These interesting fernlike
leaves have an unusual
spiky quality which adds variety
to an arrangement.

PAMPAS GRASS
Cortaderia selloana
A useful background material for
large groups, pampas grass looks attractive
when displayed on its own in an urn.

Methods of drying

Air-drying Glycerine Silica/borax Pressing

BEECH
Fagus sylvatica
These attractive, copper-coloured leaves provide an excellent background for large displays.

BROME GRASS
Bromus sp.
This wild grass adds an attractive feathery texture to any dried arrangement.

BARLEY
Hordeum vulgare
This grass provides traditional arrangements with an interesting variation in shape and texture.

OATS
Avena sp.
This pale-green grass can be mixed with other grasses and foliage or used in flower arrangements.

BENT GRASS
Agrostis sp.
This pale grass adds a delicate lightness to grass or foliage arrangements.

BRACKEN
Pteridium aquilinum
All ferns add a delicate outline to dried-flower groups.

233

Dried seed heads and fruits

Dried material is not restricted solely to flowers, grasses and foliage; seed heads and fruits add to the already extensive range. Many plants have attractive seed heads which are only revealed when the flower itself has died. These are extremely useful, providing exciting variations of shape, colour and texture. Fruits can be wired for use in an arrangement or can be placed to create interest around the base of a container.

ORNAMENTAL GOURD
Cucurbita pepo ovifera
Many colours, shapes and textures are available. Dried gourds can be waxed or varnished and can be massed in a bowl or mixed with real fruits. Gourds retain their shape by varnishing.

POPPY
Papaver sp.
A great assortment of differently shaped pods is available. The heads can be wired and used in wreaths.

PROTEA
Protea sp.
These heads are for large, dramatic arrangements. Several heads massed together in a rush basket look effective.

COTTON
Gossypium sp.
These fluffy, white tufts are an unusual and interesting addition to displays of grasses or foliage.

BANKSIA
Banksia menziesii
These deep-brown seed heads are excellent for inclusion in modern abstract arrangements.

Methods of drying

Air-drying Glycerine Silica/borax Pressing

BEECH NUTS
Fagus sylvatica

These rich-brown nuts can be contrasted with delicate grasses in an arrangement or wired for use in wreaths.

SCABIOUS
Scabiosa caucasica

These delicate heads can be used in autumn foliage arrangements, or mixed with dried flowers for a light effect.

CHILLI PEPPER
Capsicum annuum

These red, orange or yellow fruits add outline shape and vivid colour to autumn foliage arrangements. Wire the heads for use in wreaths.

CARDOON BALLS
Cynara cardunculus

The handsome, fluffy heads provide height and texture for large arrangements.

MAIZE
Zea mays

The whole stems can be used in large seed pod and foliage arrangements or the heads can be wired for smaller arrangements.

LOVE-IN-A-MIST
Nigella damascena

The rosebud-shaped heads may have red or purple streaks. The frilly foliage around the heads adds a misty look to delicate arrangements.

TEASEL
Dipsacus fullonum

Distinctively shaped heads which may be cut in half to provide a starlike "flower". The heads can be wired for use in wreaths.

·239·

7.
PLANT CARE

Outdoors, plants are able to fend very much for themselves, needing only occasional assistance on our part. In the indoor garden, however, plants depend on us to meet all their needs: we decide what level of light and humidity they are given, the quantity and regularity of watering and feeding, how big a root-run they should be allowed, and what the minimum winter temperature should be. Successful gardeners and those whose house plants thrive are said to have green fingers or, at the very least, a green thumb. Certainly, some people seem to have a built-in feel for what plants need, and how they should be cared for, while others fail totally with their charges. There is, however, no mystery about growing plants successfully; good results can be achieved by anyone who is prepared to understand the needs of particular plants and establish a routine for looking after them. Always remember that you are dealing with living things; unhealthy specimens are a sorry sight and act as a reproach to us for failing to give them enough attention. Caring for plants is more likely to be a joy—as opposed to a chore—if you choose them carefully. Decorative qualities are, of course, important, but you should also be confident of your ability to look after the plant and be sure that it is capable of flourishing under the conditions you have to offer in your house.

Potting up your own plants
Plant care need be neither complicated nor time-consuming. Potting up young plants, such as these variegated bedding geraniums (*Pelargonium* hybrids), is quick and easy, and should result in healthy growth if you use the correct size of pot and the right kind of potting mixture.

Requirements for healthy plants

The plants we grow in our homes come from temperate, sub-tropical and tropical areas where widely differing growing conditions exist. For example, some are exposed to direct sunlight, others are protected from the fierce rays of the tropical sun by neighbouring plants or are given some shade from overhanging trees, while still more grow on the forest floor in considerable shade. This diversity of natural habitat explains why different plants require different conditions when grown indoors.

Having said this, however, the ability to adapt to unfamiliar conditions is a major reason for the popularity of many common house plants. Most generally dislike widely fluctuating temperatures, although a drop of temperature at night is natural and preferred by most plants in the home. Cool conditions during the day (when heating may be turned off) followed by much warmer conditions during the evening (when heating may be turned on) are therefore against the natural pattern, but house plants have proved to be very adaptable to conditions in the home. Of course, some are inevitably more resilient than others.

There is much pleasure and fulfillment to be derived from growing and looking after house plants. Maintaining healthy and attractive plants does not involve complicated or time-consuming procedures but just sensible and sensitive attention to the plants' basic needs. To thrive, plants need adequate light at the preferred intensity and for the right duration, a comfortable temperature, and the right level of atmospheric humidity. They have to be watered when they start to dry out a little, and some need a dormant period during the winter when the water supply needs to be curtailed—allowing the plant to rest and often encouraging flower-bud production. Food must be provided, the right kind of growing medium made available and, as the roots fill the pots, plants will need potting on. These and other needs are described in the sections that follow.

Basic tools and equipment for the indoor gardener

Fork

Trowel

Wooden stakes

Wooden plant supports

Secateurs

Anvil pruner

Bamboo stakes

Scissors

Knife

Twine

Photosynthesis

This is the process undertaken by the parts of plants containing the green pigment chlorophyll, in which light energy is used to produce carbohydrates from water and carbon dioxide. During daylight hours, carbon dioxide is taken from the air through the pores (stomata) of the leaves—situated mainly on the leaf undersides. Photosynthesis occurs through the action of light on the chlorophyll in the leaves. The light energy is used to split water molecules into oxygen and hydrogen. The hydrogen is then combined with the carbon dioxide taken in through the stomata to form carbohydrates, such as glucose, which provide the plant with food. Certain minerals are required for these complex chemical reactions to occur, and these are taken up, with water, by the roots.

The essential processes
Photosynthesis occurs during the day, or whenever light is available to the green parts of a plant. This diagram shows the movements of carbon dioxide, oxygen, water and minerals during this process. Photosynthesis cannot take place in the dark and the flow of oxygen and carbon dioxide is reversed as the plant respires or "breathes".

Light

Carbon dioxide and light enter the plant through the upper and lower leaf surfaces.

Oxygen

Water vapour

Carbon dioxide

Oxygen and water vapour are expelled into the air as by-products of photosynthesis.

Water and minerals from the potting mixture are absorbed by the roots and used to produce sugars by photosynthesis.

Water

Minerals

Terracotta pots

Powdered fertilizer

Drip saucers

Long wire ties

Fertilizer spikes

Liquid fertilizer

Hormone rooting powder

Mist-sprayer

Paintbrush

Stub wires

Short wire ties

Pesticide dusting powder

Plastic plant ties

Liquid fungicide

Pesticide aerosol spray

Watering can

Signs of ill-health

Slow or sluggish growth
If symptom occurs during summer months:—
Are you overwatering? (see p.251)
Are you underfeeding? (see p.252)
Does the plant need repotting? (see p.257)
If symptom occurs during winter months:—
Is this a natural rest period?

Wilting
Is the potting mixture very dry? (see p.251)
Are you overwatering? (see p.251)
Is there adequate drainage? (see p.255)
Is the location too sunny? (see p.245)
Is the temperature too high? (see p.246)

Drooping leaves and wet soil
Are you overwatering? (see p.251)
Is there adequate drainage? (see p.255)

Brown leaf tips/spots on leaves
Are you overwatering? (see p.251)
Is the plant too close to the sun or another source of heat? (see p.246)
Is the humidity level too low? (see p.247)
Is the plant standing in a draught? (see p.246)
Are you overfeeding? (see p.252)
Have you splashed water on the leaves? (see p.249)

Falling flowers, leaves and buds
Are you overwatering? (see p.251)
Are you underwatering? (see p.251)
Is the temperature inconsistent? (see p.246)
Is the light inconsistent? (see p.245)
Is the humidity level too low? (see p.247)

Variegated leaves turning green
Is the plant getting enough light? (see p.245)

Rotting at the leaf axils
Has water lodged in the axil? (see p.249)

Leaves turn yellow
If growth is straggly:—
Are you overwatering? (see p.251)
Is the plant getting enough light? (see p.245)
Is the temperature too high? (see p.246)
Are you underfeeding? (see p.252)
Does the plant need repotting? (see p.257)
If leaves fall off the plant:—
Are you overwatering? (see p.251)
Is the plant standing in a draught? (see p.246)
Is the humidity level too low? (see p.247)
Is the temperature too low? (see p.246)

Plant adaptations

Thin, delicate-looking leaves
These usually indicate that plants come from tropical regions where they are protected from the extremes of great heat or cold.

Leathery or waxy leaves
These usually indicate that plants come from hot, dry areas, since such plants store water more effectively, reducing the amount of water lost through transpiration.

Spines or fuzzy hair
These usually indicate that plants come from desert areas as they help to baffle hot desert sunshine—the spines take the place of leaves and the stem becomes thick and succulent.

Light

Light is essential to all plants. Without enough light, growth suffers, and leaves become small and pale. Healthy growth depends on the process of photosynthesis, triggered off by the action of light on the green pigment chlorophyll. This pigment is present in red, bronze, purple and grey leaves as well as green ones; the other colour is just an overlay to the green beneath. Variegated-leaved plants, however, are at a disadvantage as the yellow, cream or white sections on their leaves contain no chlorophyll. For this reason, variegated-leaved plants generally need brighter light if their strong leaf colour contrast is to be maintained.

Indoor light levels

Plants in their native habitats have adapted to a wide range of different light levels. Indoors, you should try to provide the light intensity preferred by each plant as far as possible. To do this, you need to assess the amount of light present in various parts of any particular room. This can be difficult, because the human eye is not a good judge of light intensity; it compensates for different light levels to give the impression of even overall lighting. The only really accurate way of measuring light intensity is to use a small hand-held photographic light-meter, or a camera with a built-in meter, which both give a good indication of light levels. You will probably be surprised at how low the levels of light are indoors: on a south-facing windowsill your plants will only get about half as much light as they would if they were growing outside, due to reflection from the glass. And as little as one metre into the room there is only about three-quarters as much light as at the window. Having said this, however, most popular house plants are extremely tolerant, their adaptability being the main reason for their popularity.

Day length

In addition to intensity, light duration or day length is an important factor in determining how much light a plant receives. Most plants need about 12 to 16 hours of daylight to sustain active growth. Foliage house plants fall into two main groups: those that stop growing in the late autumn and need resting during the winter, and those that will continue to grow throughout the winter and remain attractive. Foliage plants from the tropics which, in the wild, receive around 12 hours of sunlight each day throughout the year, will only continue to grow all the year round in temperate regions if they are given as much light as possible in winter, by using supplementary artificial light, and when kept in a warm room. Plants from more temperate regions stop growing (or slow down their growth very considerably) with the onset of winter and a shorter day.

In general, flowering plants need more light than foliage plants in order to initiate flower bud production and to allow the buds to develop properly. In many plants, flower production is triggered off by day length. These plants fall into two groups: long-day plants and short-day plants. Long-day plants flower when they have received more than 12 hours of light a day over a certain period. (It does not matter whether the light is natural or artificial—African violets (*Saintpaulia* hybrids) can be induced to flower at any time of year under artificial light.) Short-day plants flower

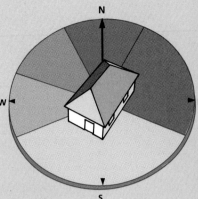

Light intensity and orientation
Levels of light intensity striking a house from all points of the compass. The lighter area corresponds to the strongest light, and the darkest area to the weakest, (assuming the sun is shining from the south). By finding out the orientation of your house, you will be able to place plants in appropriately lit positions.

Daylight levels
In northern regions (B) plants receive more but less intense daylight in summer and less adequate light in winter than those further south (A).

when they receive less than 12 hours light a day over a certain period. Poinsettias (*Euphorbia pulcherrima*), chrysanthemums (*Chrysanthemum* hybrids), azaleas (*Rhododendron simsii*) and Christmas cacti (*Schlumbergera* sp.) are short-day plants which flower naturally in the autumn, but chrysanthemums can now be bought all through the year because growers can simulate the short day and initiate flower production by covering the plants in black polythene for the requisite number of hours each day. Many plants appear to have no strong preference with regard to day length, and flower through most or all of the year. These are known as day-neutral plants.

How plants seek light
All plants turn their leaves towards the source of light, apart from stiff-leaved species such as mother-in-law's tongue (*Sansevieria* sp.), many palms and dracaenas, and rosette-shaped bromeliads. Rooms with white or pale-coloured walls will reflect light back on to plants, whereas those decorated in darker colours absorb light and will cause plants to turn towards the window. To counteract this natural tendency, and to promote balanced, upright growth, you should turn your plants frequently.

Suitable light levels for different plants
In *The Plant Finder's Guide*, the light preference of each featured plant is indicated by one of three symbols. These stand for sunny, filtered sun and shady, and are described in detail on the following page.

Sunny

A sunny position is one that gets direct sunlight for all, or part of, the day. South-facing windows will receive sunlight for most of the day, east-facing windows receive sunlight for several hours in the morning, and west-facing ones for several hours in the afternoon. The strength of the sunlight will depend on latitude and on the orientation of the room. South-facing rooms receive more intense light, but in summer it reaches less far into the room than in east- or west-facing rooms. In lower latitudes, or at the coast where light is brighter due to reflection from the sea, some form of shading may be necessary at a large south-facing window in summer, to prevent possible leaf scorching and too-frequent drying out of the potting mixture. This type of bright light is for plants such as desert cacti, succulents from open bush or savanna, hard-leaved bromeliads from the tree-tops and certain sun-loving flowering plants.

Filtered sun

Filtered sun is direct sun that has been filtered through a translucent curtain or blind, or baffled by a tree or building outside. This level of light is also found between 1 and 1.5 metres from a window which receives sun for all, or part of, the day. Although no direct sun falls here, the general level of brightness is high. Filtered sun is about a half to three-quarters as intense as direct sunlight. If you are in any doubt about the amount of light your plant needs, place it in filtered light, as few plants like direct, hot summer sunlight. In general, too little light is less harmful than too much light. Palms, tropical rain forest plants, and shrubs, including dracaenas, ti plants (*Cordyline terminalis*), and finger aralias (*Dizygotheca elegantissima*), and soft-leaved bromeliads, such as scarlet stars (*Guzmania lingulata*) and flaming swords (*Vriesea splendens*), prefer this kind of light, as it is similar to the dappled light they receive in their native forest.

Shady

This position is one that receives no direct or indirect sunlight, yet does not have poor light. This level of light is found in, or just a little distance from, a well-lit north-facing window. It is also found in shaded areas within sunny rooms—for instance, along side walls—where the plant is well out of reach of direct sunlight, yet no more than 1.5-2 metres from a sunny window. Shady positions receive about a quarter as much light as sunny ones. This amount of light suits plants from low-down in the jungle canopy where they are shielded from the rays of direct sun. However, day length in tropical jungles is considerably greater than that in northern hemispheres in winter, and you may need to move shade-loving plants nearer to the source of light during our winter. No flowering plants, or foliage plants with variegated leaves, will be happy in a shady position. Without sunlight, they will lose most of their leaves, and those that remain will lose their variegation.

Levels of light intensity in a room

Different levels of light in a typical room, in the northern hemisphere, on a summer day when direct sunlight is not obscured by clouds. In lower latitudes the light would be brighter, but would extend less far into the room. Obviously, the amount of light entering a room will be affected by local factors such as the number and size of the windows, and the presence of nearby buildings and trees.

Curtains absorb light, reducing the levels on either side of the windows.

Blind for shading plants on the windowsill from hot summer sun.

East- or west-facing windows get good light all day and direct light for a few hours.

South-facing windows receive direct sun for much of the day.

Bird's nest fern
Asplenium nidus

Belgian evergreen
Dracaena sanderana

Stick yucca
Yucca elephantipes

Poor light	Shady	Filtered sun	Sunny
An area more than 2m away from the source of light. No plant will thrive here, even though the area seems bright to the human eye.	A moderately-lit area 1.5-2m away from a sunny window, usually along a side wall, or near a well-lit north-facing window.	A well-lit position 1-1.5m inside a south-, east- or west-facing window, or one receiving direct sun-light filtered by a tree or curtain.	A position which receives direct sunlight for most, or part of, the day. The strength of the sunlight will depend on latitude.

Temperature and humidity

Temperature

House plants have a preferred temperature range in which they thrive, and usually another that they will tolerate. Most popular house plants are from tropical and sub-tropical areas and do best in a temperature range of 15°-21°C. (Seeds usually germinate best when temperatures reach 18°C or more; and tip-cuttings and divided sections root well at 18°-24°C.) Other types of plants—mainly temperate evergreens and flowering species—prefer cooler conditions in the range of 10°-15°C. These are the two temperature ranges described by the mini-climates in *The Plant Finder's Guide* as "warm" and "cool". Although these are the conditions to which the plants are best suited, they will almost certainly be tolerant of slightly higher or lower temperatures for at least part of the time.

Plants that grow naturally in cool places will grow faster when given higher temperatures. Some may adapt and thrive, perhaps growing more quickly than is convenient indoors, although the blooming period of certain short-term flowering plants is greatly reduced if they are given higher temperatures than they need. It is rare that plants from a warm place do well in much cooler conditions.

In general, a fall in temperature of 2°-5°C at night is natural in the wild and advisable indoors. Some plants, such as cacti, can tolerate a much sharper fall, but fluctuations of more than 8°-10°C between daytime and night-time temperatures should be avoided in the home.

Winter- and spring-flowering bulbs must have their "wintering" at around 7°-10°C—a period when root growth is encouraged and active top growth discouraged. In addition, many house plants, especially evergreen species, require a winter rest period, away from the steady winter warmth of most domestic rooms. If possible, it is best to set aside a specific room which can be kept reasonably cool for several months.

Radiator
Rising heat is harmful if plants are not protected by a shelf.

Door
Opening doors causes temperatures to drop sharply, as cool air rushes in.

Cooker
A great deal of heat is generated by cookers, but only for short periods.

Window
Strong sunlight raises the temperature and may scorch some plants.

Variable temperatures
above
This typical kitchen does not have a uniform temperature, and this factor should be borne in mind when positioning plants.

Monitoring temperatures *left*
It is always a good idea to monitor temperatures. The photograph shows a simple thermometer and a minimum/maximum thermometer which measures the daily fluctuation in temperature by recording the highest and lowest levels reached.

Temperature chart Suitable ranges for plants featured in *The Plant Finder's Guide*

Legend:
- ▬ Winter rest period
- ▬ Ideal range for active growth
- ● Minimum tolerated in winter rest period
- ● Minimum tolerated by most tropical house plants
- ● Maximum tolerated by most house plants without additional humidity

Plant	0	5	10	15	20	25	30
Seeds					18–32		
Cuttings					18–24		
Succulents				15–21			
Ferns				15–21			
Jungle cacti				15–21			
Palms			13–21				
Most other house plants		7–21					
Desert cacti		7–15					
Hardy bulbs before flowering	0–10						

°Centigrade

Humidity

Humidity is the amount of water vapour contained in the air. It is affected by changes in temperature: warm air is capable of carrying more moisture than cold air, and it will cause water to evaporate from all available sources, including the leaves of plants. The amount of water in the air is measured on a scale of "relative" humidity—that is, the amount of water in the air compared to saturation point at a given temperature. 0 per cent equals absolutely dry air and 100 per cent equals absolutely saturated air. A relative humidity of at least 40 per cent is a requirement for most plants. To maintain this degree of humidity, a greater amount of water will need to be present in warm air than in colder air.

Cacti and succulents are used to a level of around 30-40 per cent, but the average tolerant house plant does best with a level of around 60 per cent. The thin-leaved jungle plants, such as maidenhair ferns (*Adiantum raddianum*) and painted nettles (*Coleus blumei*), however, enjoy a level nearer 80 per cent. These three figures correspond to the "low", "medium" and "high" humidity categories given in *The Plant Finder's Guide*. The relative humidity level of the average living room with the heating switched on, but with no humidifying device, is only around 15 per cent so the air in bathrooms and steamy kitchens makes them better homes for most plants than living rooms.

Signs of humidity deficiency

There are a number of signs which indicate that a plant is suffering from a lack of humidity: its leaves may begin to shrivel or show signs of scorching—watch out for the drying out of leaf tips on plants with long, narrow leaves, such as spider plants (*Chlorophytum comosum*) and palms; buds may fall off; or flowers may wither prematurely.

Plants lose moisture from the tiny pores (stomata) of the leaves. These open during the day to take in carbon dioxide from the air but, at the same time, water from the tissues of the leaves escapes; this process is known as transpiration. Low levels of humidity mean that plants lose more moisture through transpiration. House plants grown in warm rooms, therefore, suffer all the disadvantages: the warm air encourages them to grow, but "sucks" moisture from their leaves and causes water in the potting mixture to be taken up more quickly, making more frequent watering necessary. You can alleviate this condition by increasing the humidity.

How to increase humidity

Portable humidifiers powered by electricity can be bought to increase the level of humidity throughout the room. These are effective—keeping humidity levels between 30 and 60 per cent in heated homes—benefiting people and furniture as well as plants. Growing several plants in proximity helps to make the air around them more humid, as moisture transpired by one plant increases the humidity for its neighbour. Arrangements of plants in bowls and large containers therefore offer good growing conditions. Other methods of increasing humidity include mist-spraying and standing plants on trays filled with moist pebbles.

The ultimate solution for those plants which must have a very high level of humidity is to grow them in closed or almost-closed containers such as bottle gardens and terraria.

Ways of increasing humidity

Mist-spraying *left*
A hand-spray fitted with a fine mist nozzle, used once or twice a day, temporarily places a thin film of moisture over the leaf and stem surfaces. Spraying also washes off room dust and discourages certain insect pests.

Pebble-filled trays *right*
Stand pots on a tray lined with moist pebbles. The water evaporates into the surrounding air.

Burying pots in peat *below*
Bury pots up to their rims in a larger outer container filled with moist peat or vermiculite (see pp.48-9).

Lining baskets *right*
Line hanging baskets with sphagnum moss and wet it thoroughly by regular spraying (see pp.54-5). Periodically dunk the whole basket base in a bowl of water.

Temperature/humidity ratio
Water in grams

The higher the temperature the greater the amount of water the air can hold. If this water is not supplied artificially, moisture is "sucked" out of plants. Therefore, if the temperature is high, additional humidity must be supplied.

Watering 1

In the wild, water appears as rain, mist or fog and is taken up mainly by the root system. Plants in the home are reliant on us to meet all their watering needs. Water is essential to all plants; without it they will die. The length of time this takes may vary from one day for young seedlings to several months in the case of a succulent plant, but death will always occur eventually. Water acts as a transport medium, in the way blood does for animals, and it is also essential for the process of photosynthesis, which supplies the plant's food. Water from the potting mixture is passed by the roots to all parts of the plant, carrying with it the nutrients vital for the food-manufacturing process. It charges stems and leaves and makes them sturdy and plump (turgid); without it they cannot stay erect. Any shortage of water results in stems and leaves going limp and drooping, flowers fading quickly, and buds falling before they can open. A temporary drought often means that leaves shrivel and go brown at the edges and the tips, making the plants look unattractive.

When to water

Knowing when to water can be difficult but, as a general rule, you should water potted plants when they need it. This may seem to be an over-simplification, but it is accurate. The real problem is to judge when that is. Drooping leaves and limp stems are obvious signs that more water is needed, but you should not wait for such an advanced stage to be reached. There are more subtle signs: some plants' leaves take on a paler, translucent look when water is needed; on others, the flower buds dry and shrivel. Each plant has its own watering needs, dependent on its size, its natural environment and, most importantly, the time of year; actively growing plants need a lot of water, the same plants can manage with much less during the winter rest period. Never water routinely just because someone tells you to water every so many days. It is far better to test the potting mixture first, as this will indicate whether or not the plant needs watering. "Weighing" the pot in your hand regularly can also give an indication of the amount of water in the potting

mixture; a mixture that is saturated with water weighs more than one that is dry. This method is reliable, but it takes a little practice to gauge whether or not the plant needs water, and is not always practical with larger plants in bigger pots. Moisture gauges are available which record on a dial the exact moisture content of the potting mixture. Readings such as "wet", "moist" or "dry" can be seen at a glance and allow you to act accordingly. Quite simple small indicator "sticks" or probes can be bought which are pushed into the mixture and change colour according to the moisture content. Generally, play safe and, if in doubt whether to water, wait a day or two before taking the decision.

How to water

Most plants prefer to be given a really thorough drink, and like the dose to be repeated only when a given amount of the potting mixture has dried out. To water frequently in dribbles is bad practice. To give too little often means that the water never reaches the lower layers of the mixture which become compacted around the roots; and to give too much often results in a waterlogged potting mixture. Waterlogging forces air out of the potting mixture and provides ideal conditions for the action of root-rotting bacteria and fungi.

Type of water to use

Tap water is safe to use on most plants, even though it can have a high lime content. It is always best to apply it when it is tepid, or at least at room temperature; stand a can filled with water overnight in the same room as the plant, to allow the water to reach room temperature and some of the chlorine to dissipate. Ideally, the water should be as lime-free as possible. Rain water is good if you live in the country but, if collected in towns, it is liable to be polluted by chemicals. Water can be boiled (and allowed to cool) for the real lime-haters such as azaleas (*Rhododendron simsii*); distilled water is also lime-free, but rather expensive for use on anything but the most precious of plants. Do not use water from an ordinary domestic water-softener, as this is full of chemicals and can cause serious damage.

Watering checklist
Plants needing plenty of water

- Plants which are actively growing.
- Plants with delicate-looking, thin leaves, e.g., angel wings (*Caladium hortulanum* hybrids).
- Plants in very warm rooms, especially those near windows in summer.
- Plants with many large leaves that clearly transpire a lot of water.
- Plants that have filled their pots with a mass of healthy roots.
- Plants that are grown in relatively small pots, e.g., African violets (*Saintpaulia* hybrids).
- Plants grown in dry air.
- Plants from bogs and marshy areas, e.g., umbrella plants (*Cyperus* sp.).
- Plants grown in free-draining potting mixes, including peat-based mixtures.
- Plants in clay pots.
- Plants with budding leaves and flower blossoms.

Plants needing less water

- Plants which are resting and those without buds or flowers.
- Plants with thick, leathery leaves, e.g., rubber plants (*Ficus elastica*).
- Plants grown in cooler rooms, especially in winter.
- Plants which are succulent and therefore naturally adapted to store water for future use, e.g., cacti; they transpire much less than leafy plants.
- Plants that have recently been repotted and whose roots have not yet penetrated all of the mixture.
- Plants that are given a high level of humidity, e.g., ferns, and those grown in a shady position or in bottle gardens and terraria.
- Plants grown in water-retentive potting mixtures, including soil-based mixtures.
- Plants grown in plastic and glazed clay pots.
- Plants that have thick, fleshy roots or water-storing sections on their roots, e.g., spider plants (*Chlorophytum comosum*) and asparagus ferns (*Asparagus setaceus*).

Methods of applying water

Topwatering *left*
Pour water on to the surface of the potting mixture; this gives more control over the amount of water the plant receives and flushes away any excess mineral salts which may have accumulated.

Watering from below *right*
Stand the pots in saucers filled with water. This method forces mineral salts to the upper layer of the potting mixture, but these can be flushed away with an occasional topwatering.

Bromeliad watering
Pour the water into the "cup" with a narrow-spouted watering can.

How much water to give

It is very important to choose the right amount of water, since damage to plants can occur by both underwatering and overwatering. Overwatering is probably more fatal to plants than underwatering (see also pp.250-1). In *The Plant Finder's Guide*, three symbols have been used to indicate the correct amount of water to give each plant shown; these recommend watering plentifully, moderately or sparingly. A detailed explanation of the three main instructions is given below. Although the illustrations show topwatering, details of how to water from below are also given.

Watering sparingly
Give enough water at each watering to barely moisten the potting mixture throughout. Do this in several stages, adding a little water each time. Never give so much water that it appears in any quantity through the drainage hole in the bottom of the pot. When watering from below, put no more than 1cm in the saucer at a time. Repeat if necessary.

1 Test the potting mixture with a stake. It is time to water when approximately two-thirds of the mixture has dried out.

2 Add just enough water to the surface of the potting mixture to allow percolation without water appearing in the saucer.

3 Test again with the stake. Add a little more water if you find any dry patches. Never leave water in the saucer.

Watering moderately
This involves moistening the mixture all the way through, but allowing the top 1-3cm to dry out between applications. When watering from below, stand pots in 1cm of water and repeat until the surface of the potting mixture becomes moist.

1 When the potting mixture feels dry to the touch, give the plant a moderate amount of water.

2 Pour on enough water to moisten, but not saturate, all of the potting mixture.

3 Stop adding water when drops start appearing from the drainage hole. Pour away any excess water from the saucer.

Watering plentifully
This involves keeping all of the potting mixture moist and not letting even the surface of the mixture dry out. Give enough water at each watering to let some flow through the drainage holes at the bottom of the container. If watering from below, keep re-filling the saucer until no more water is taken up. Half an hour is usually sufficient.

1 When the potting mixture feels dry to the touch, give the plant plenty of water.

2 Flood the surface of the potting mixture with water until it flows through the drainage hole.

3 Empty the saucer once the excess water has drained through the potting mixture.

Watering 2

Going away on holiday can present problems if you have a collection of healthy house plants and no-one to look after them. An absence of just a few days should not cause any harm to your plants; if they are given a thorough watering and moved into a cool room, they should quite happily survive. Increasing the humidity can also help at this time (see p.247). For longer periods, some form of self-watering system is required so that your plants do not suffer.

Certain of the methods shown below are better suited to plants in plastic pots; others are suited to plants in clay pots, as they need a larger, more constant supply of water. Automatic methods of watering are not suitable for plants in containers without drainage holes because of the risk of waterlogging the potting mixture. Happily, such containers are usually glazed and, therefore, water loss is much less than with porous clay pots. Plants in these kinds of containers should be well watered before departure on holiday, placed out of direct sun or strong light and stood on trays filled with moist pebbles or even a thick wad of wet newspaper—either of which will improve the humidity and allow a plant to survive a drought period.

Capillary mats
Place the capillary mat on a draining board or a shelf next to the bath and let at least half of it trail into the sink, or bath, which should be filled with water. As the mats are made of thick felt or felt rubber, the water will be carried up to the plants. The plants then take up what water they need by capillary action. Use capillary mats for plants in plastic pots; the thinness of a plastic pot and the many holes in its base allow the easy passage of water. Clay pots are too thick—the pot tends to absorb the water, rather than passing it to the plant.

Covering with transparent material *right*
Plants can be put into large plastic bags or into purpose-made domes. The processes of respiration and photosynthesis produce water vapour which condenses on to the sides of the bag or container. Do not use this method for long periods, as the plant may begin to rot.

Temporary wicks *left*
Simple wicks for short-term use can be made using water-absorbent materials such as oil-lamp wicks, cotton shoe-laces or old tights. Place one end in a reservoir of water and the other firmly in the potting mixture. Capillary action should do the rest.

Making a "self-watering" wick

This type of wick, made in a similar way to a temporary wick, is actually embedded in the potting mixture and is suitable for permanent or long-term use. It enables the plants to take up their water needs automatically, by capillary action, and saves the grower time and effort. Some growers "wick" their plants throughout the year. However, regular checks should be made to ensure that the plant is not being overwatered or underwatered by the wick. If this happens, remove the wick immediately.

These wicks are suitable for plants in either clay or plastic pots. The reservoir can be any container which will safely support the plant pot and should be covered by a lid (pierce a hole for the wick) to prevent the water from evaporating.

1 Carefully remove the plant from its pot, taking care not to damage the root ball in any way as you do so.

2 Make a wick using a strip of cotton or nylon material. Push it through one of the holes in the bottom of the pot.

3 Carefully push one end of the wick up into the root ball using a thin cane or a pencil.

4 Lower the plant back into the pot. Stand the pot over a reservoir, ensuring that the "tail" extends into the water.

Possible watering problems

If the watering instructions given in *The Plant Finder's Guide* are followed, your plants should receive the right amount of water for healthy growth. However, there are problems which arise if plants are underwatered, or overwatered—particularly during the winter rest period.

Watering in winter

At some time during the twelve month season, most plants need a period of rest. Many should be fed and watered more sparingly than during the rest of the year, others need no food or water at all. The rest period is brought on naturally by the reduced amount of light available to plants (so it coincides with winter in the northern hemisphere), and to give too much water at this time stimulates growth which is not supported by adequate light. This results in poor, and often mouldy growth, browning of leaves and early leaf fall.

Underwatering

Underwatering can still occur if you apply water "little and often", as the plant may need a large dose of water to thoroughly soak its roots. Should the potting mixture get over-dry (this happens particularly readily with peat-based potting mixtures), it can shrink appreciably, leaving a gap between root ball and pot sides. Any water applied to the plant just runs quickly away. The only solution is to soak the pot in a bowl or bucket of water until the mixture has swollen up again and the gap closed. The symptoms of underwatering are easily recognized and can often be arrested in time to save the plant. Plants particularly susceptible to problems if underwatered are those with succulent-looking stems, such as painted nettles (*Coleus blumei*), busy Lizzies (*Impatiens* sp.), and all primulas and selaginellas.

Overwatering

The symptoms of overwatering can take much longer to show themselves than those of underwatering. Again, watering "little and often" can lead to overwatering. Many plants need to start to dry out before they are re-watered and, if the potting mixture is kept permanently wet, the mixture soon becomes waterlogged. A warning sign that your mixture is waterlogged is the presence of green moss on the surface, since it will only grow in a constantly wet medium. Waterlogging leads eventually to plant death. The first indication that something is wrong with the plant is when a few leaves fall or become yellow, or when the plant makes poor growth. The lack of air and excess of water in the potting mixture cause the roots to become rotten, and cut off the supply of water and food to the plant. To save an overwatered plant, carefully remove it from the pot and check the roots; if they feel soft and come away easily, they are rotten and best removed. Replace the plant in the pot with some fresh potting mixture containing at least 25 per cent sand to aid drainage. Plants particularly susceptible to problems if overwatered include many of the cacti or succulents, whose bodies or leaves are adapted to store water.

Some plants, however, thrive on plenty of water. Their natural habitat is the swamp or bog and, consequently, their potting mixture should always be kept saturated.

Reviving a parched plant

If a plant does become parched and dried-out, it is often best to cut back the top growth and wait for next year's growth. If, however, you rescue it just in time, you could try the following emergency treatment.

Dried-out root ball

Root ball problems

Often, the root ball has shrunk away from the sides of the pot so that any water given runs away. Alternatively, the potting mixture often becomes compacted so that water cannot penetrate it.

Compacted root ball

1 This plant has clearly wilted, as the drooping leaf and flower stalks can no longer support themselves.

2 Begin reviving the plant by using a fork to break up the dried-out potting mixture. Do not injure the roots.

3 Immerse the pot in a bucket filled with water until the air bubbles cease to rise from the potting mixture. Use a mist-sprayer on the leaves.

4 Allow any excess water to drain away, and put the plant in a cool place. Within a few hours the plant should begin to revive.

Danger signs

Too little water

- Leaves rapidly become wilted and limp.
- Leaf growth slows.
- Lower leaves become curled or yellow in colour.
- Lower leaves fall prematurely.
- Leaf edges become brown and dried-out.
- Flowers fade and fall quickly.

Too much water

- Leaves develop soft, rotten patches on their surface.
- Leaf growth is poor.
- Leaf tips become brown.
- Leaves become curled or yellow in colour.
- Flowers become mouldy.
- Young and old leaves fall at the same time.
- Roots rot away.

Feeding

Plants are capable of manufacturing their own food but, in order to do so, they must have a supply of light, minerals and water. Minerals are present in garden soil and in most potting mixtures, and manufactured fertilizers are made up of a mixture of the minerals that plants need to carry out the essential processes in photosynthesis. The plant does all the work of converting the raw materials to form the food it needs for healthy growth (see p.242). When plants are bought ready potted, sufficient minerals should already be in the potting mixture to last the plant several weeks. Soil-based potting mixtures contain loam, which is normally rich in nutrients. Their main advantage is that they release minerals over a period of several months, so plants grown in these mixtures will last longer without supplementary feeding than those grown in peat-based potting mixtures. However, the loam content of soil-based mixtures may vary considerably in its nutrient value.

Peat-based potting mixtures were introduced because of the high cost and difficulty of obtaining reliable loam. They contain a mixture of peat moss and sand to which is added perlite and vermiculite. The mixture has no food value, but some manufacturers add nutrients to the base and, by looking at the list of ingredients on the packet, you can check whether or not they are present. The nutrients that are added are of the slow-release kind and should feed plants for around eight weeks. However, some nutrients are soon leached away from the mixture by regular watering, or are used up quickly by the plants, so it is advisable to start giving supplementary feeds to plants grown in peat-based potting mixture about six weeks after purchase, or eight weeks after repotting.

Signs of a hungry plant

A hungry plant has an unhealthy "washed-out" look. Hunger signs are very slow—or a lack of—growth; weak stems; small, pale or yellowing leaves; lower leaves falling before they should, and few or no flowers. Ideally, plants should not be allowed to reach these extremes before you notice that they need feeding.

How often to feed

The Plant Finder's Guide recommends the feeding frequency for each featured plant. Fertilizer should only be applied during the active growth period, since feeding during the rest period will result in pale, spindly growth.

Feeding checklist

Too little fertilizer

- Slow growth, with little resistance to disease or attack by pests.
- Pale leaves, sometimes with yellow spotting.
- Flowers may be small, poorly coloured or absent.
- Weak stems.
- Lower leaves dropped early.

Too much fertilizer

- Wilted or malformed leaves.
- White crust on clay pots and over the surface of the potting mixture.
- Winter growth is lanky while summer growth may be stunted.
- Leaves may have brown spots and scorched edges.

"Each-time feeding" is practised by many specialist growers. It involves feeding at every watering with a considerably reduced strength of feed (half or quarter strength). This is a way of keeping a constant but weak supply of food always available—which is particularly important to plants that are grown in relatively small pots, and in peat-based potting mixture. It also prevents an unnecessary and harmful reserve of nutrients building up. New plants or recently repotted plants will not need feeding for some time: those in soil-based potting mixture should not need feeding for about three months; plants in soilless mixture (peat-based etc.) will need feeding after about six weeks.

The feeding tips given in *The Plant Finder's Guide* assume that you are looking for the maximum of strong and vigorous growth. In some cases, you may feel that you would like to keep a plant at about its present size, but in a healthy state. Three feeds of standard liquid fertilizer spread over the active growth period (roughly, mid-March, mid-June and mid-September) would keep most plants healthy without encouraging rampant growth.

Feeding guidelines

- Fertilizer is not medicine for an ailing plant; feeding will often only make matters worse. If a plant looks unhealthy, examine it for possible causes, including pests and disease, before dosing it with fertilizer.

- Overfeeding can do as much damage as underfeeding. Feed only at the strength (or much less) given in the instructions on the label.

- Feed no more frequently than recommended on the label or in *The Plant Finder's Guide*.

Effects of fertilizers

Fertilizer	Supplied as	Effect	Use
N Nitrogen	Nitrates N	Manufacture of chlorophyll. Active leaf and shoot growth.	All foliage house plants, especially at start of growing season.
P Phosphorus	Phosphate P_2O_5	Healthy root production. Flower bud production.	All house plants, especially those grown for their flowers.
K Potassium	Potash K_2O	Healthy formation of leaves; flower and fruit production.	All flowering house plants, bulbs and plants grown for their berries.
Trace elements	Iron, zinc, copper, manganese, magnesium	Essential processes such as photosynthesis and respiration.	All house plants.

Types of fertilizer

Fertilizers can be bought in many different forms: as liquids, soluble powders and crystals, pills or tablets and "spikes" or "pins". Liquid fertilizers, bought in concentrated form, are very convenient, as the bottles are easy to store and the contents need only to be diluted with water. Water soluble powders and crystals are also easy to handle and only need a thorough stirring in the prescribed amount of water to be dissolved completely. "Spikes" and "pins" are cards impregnated with chemicals that release foods when watered. These are often called slow-release fertilizers, as they work over a period of three to six months, slowly giving up their stored minerals. Their disadvantage is that they tend to produce "hot-spots"—concentrations of food around the pill or "spike"—which can burn nearby roots. In addition to fertilizers applied to the potting mixture, there are foliar feeds: fertilizers that are diluted with water and then sprayed on to the leaves of plants which do not readily absorb minerals through their roots. Foliar feeds also have an immediate tonic effect on any plant which looks starved. Always follow the instructions given on the packet, as an excessive amount of fertilizer can damage roots and leaves.

What fertilizers contain

Balanced growth relies on three essential minerals. Nitrogen (supplied as nitrates) is vital for producing energy-forming chlorophyll, and healthy leaf and stem growth. Phosphorus (supplied as phosphates) allows healthy roots to develop.

Potassium (supplied as potash) is essential for fruiting and flowering and the general sturdiness of the plant. The packaging of fertilizers always indicates the relative chemical contents (shown as percentages) of the three main foods and may mention other ingredients, such as iron, copper and manganese, often under the general heading of "trace elements". The three most important minerals may be spelled out fully, as nitrogen, phosphorus and potassium, or be given the codes N, P and K. Sometimes, only the percentage numbers appear, but the coding is always arranged in the same order to avoid confusion.

What to feed

Fertilizers suitable for use with house plants are usually ones with an even balance of the essential nutrients. These are known as standard or balanced fertilizers and will promote generally good growth in most plants. There are, however, specialist fertilizers for more specific purposes. High-nitrate fertilizers encourage healthy leaf growth and are suitable for foliage plants. High-potash fertilizers are often called "tomato-type" fertilizers because they are used for tomatoes when they start to flower and fruit; these are useful for encouraging flowering and fruiting house plants that have reached a similar stage. High-phosphate fertilizers build up a strong, healthy root system and encourage the formation of flower buds, although foliage growth is slower. It is good practice to use a different fertilizer when the plant is flowering from the one used when it is not.

Methods of feeding

The method of feeding depends upon the type of plant you have and the form of fertilizer you have chosen to use. If you are using liquid fertilizer, or powders and crystals which have to be mixed with water, apply when watering the plant in the normal way. Before giving any type of food, ensure the potting mixture is already moist—to add food to dry soil is to risk root damage by "burning" with high concentrations of minerals. Foliar sprays are best applied with a mist-sprayer, used outside or in the bathtub to avoid inhalation and marking furnishings.

This type of food is rapidly absorbed, and will act very quickly on a plant with unhealthy foliage. Fertilizer pills are a very convenient form of feeding, as they can be inserted into the mixture and left to release their food gradually. Spikes, on the other hand, can be easily removed if you feel that a plant would benefit from a period without the stimulus of the fertilizer. Feeding mats are also now available; these are placed underneath the pot and the nutrients they contain are absorbed into the potting mixture.

Slow-release fertilizer spikes
As they tend to produce "hot-spots" of concentrated fertilizer, push the spike in at the edge of the potting mixture. Water well to help dissolve the food.

Foliar sprays
Always dilute to the correct concentration before spraying over both sides of the foliage with a mist-sprayer.

Liquid fertilizers
Add to the water you would give the plant at its normal watering time. These can be applied either from above or from below.

Slow-release fertilizer pills
These should be pushed deep into the potting mixture with the blunt end of a pencil. Try to avoid damaging the roots when pushing the pill in.

Pots and potting mixtures

Types of pot

Most house plants are sold in plastic pots, as this is the cheapest way of packaging them, but many other kinds are available including traditional, unglazed clay pots, and purpose-made ceramic and china pots. Almost any domestic container can be used to display plants effectively (see pp.28-31), but they may not all provide ideal conditions for healthy growth. All purpose-made containers will have one or more drainage holes to allow any excess water to drain away. It is possible to grow plants directly in bowls and other containers without drainage holes, but they need to be lined with drainage material and greater care is required when watering to prevent roots from rotting.

Pot shape *left*
In all pots, from the smallest available, with a diameter of 3cm, to the largest, with a diameter of 30cm, the depth is equal to the diameter of the rim.

Shards and gravel
These increase the drainage of a pot, and a layer is especially important in pots without drainage holes.

Gravel

Shards

Plastic pots
Plants grown in plastic pots need less frequent watering; all plastic pots have several holes in their base.

Clay pots
Plants grown in clay pots dry out more quickly; the smaller sized clay pots have only one drainage hole in the base.

The depth of the pot
Measured from the top of the lip to the base, this is equal to the diameter.

The diameter of the pot
Measured at the rim, this is equal to the depth.

Standard pot dimensions
Always wider at its rim than at its base, and as deep as it is wide. Pots are usually round in shape, although square pots are also available and are useful for grouping several plants together.

5cm

7cm

10cm

Half-pots *below*
Half-pots are less deep than broad, and come in a range of sizes up to 30cm in diameter. Use them for seed sowing, rooting cuttings, and for plants with a shallow root system.

Drip saucers *right*
Made in a similar material, and a little larger than the base of the pot.

Pots with a built-in saucer base *below*
Made of a decorative plastic, these pots are supplied as hanging pots with a built-in drip tray.

Potting mixtures

Garden soil is totally unsuitable for use in pots in the home. It is full of bugs, disease spores and weed seeds and its chemical content and physical make-up are uncertain. House plants should be grown in ready-prepared potting mixtures or a do-it-yourself mixture based on one of the standard prepared mixes. The contents of these have been very carefully tested as to their suitability to particular plants, and the ingredients have been sterilized to kill off unwanted visitors. The range of potting mixtures may seem large but a few basic potting mixtures will provide for the different needs of all the house plants featured in this book; details are given in *The Plant Finder's Guide*. There are two main mixtures, soil-based and peat-based. Soil-based mixtures have a heavy texture suitable for large plants; although sterilized, the soil contains some micro-organisms which break down organic matter into essential minerals, thus maintaining soil fertility. Peat-based mixtures are lighter and cleaner to handle but they often contain no built-in nutrients, so regular feeding is necessary.

Types of potting mixture

Potting mixtures are usually packaged in plastic bags of various sizes; the larger they are the more economical they become. The basic mixes are loam (soil) or peat. Specialized mixtures contain added ingredients. Additives for the mixes can be bought separately for home-made potting mixtures.

Bromeliad potting mixture *right*
Spongy and very porous, which suits the shallow root system of the bromeliads.

Bulb fibre *below*
Clean, light and drains well. Good drainage is essential to prevent the bulbs from rotting.

Soil-based potting mixture *left*
A heavy mixture. Suitable for large, top-heavy plants.

Charcoal *below*
Absorbs excess minerals and waste, keeping the mixture "sweet".

Peat-based potting mixture *right*
A lightweight, standardized mixture, containing very few nutrients.

Fern potting mixture *above*
Contains perlite or sand, and charcoal to keep it well drained.

Perlite *below*
Gives potting mixture an open texture for aeration and drainage.

Vermiculite *left*
Absorbs and retains nutrients and water.

Aggregate
Made of clay pellets, it has excellent water-retentive properties and is used for hydroculture and to provide drainage.

Sphagnum moss
Has excellent water-retaining properties.

Potting mixture recipes

Soil-based potting mixture
Best for large, established plants. A suitable home-made mixture consists of one-third sterilized fibrous loam, one-third medium-grade peat moss, leaf mould or tree bark and one-third coarse sand or fine perlite. A balanced fertilizer should also be added.

Peat-based potting mixture
A suitable mixture consists of one-third peat moss, one-third medium-grade vermiculite, and one-third coarse sand or medium-grade perlite. Add two tablespoonfuls of dolomite limestone powder to every half-litre of the mixture to counteract the acidity of the peat.

Bromeliad potting mixture
A very open mixture, high in humus and almost lime free. A suitable mixture consists of half coarse sand or perlite and half peat moss. Specialist growers add other ingredients to the above mixture, including chunky pieces of partly composted tree bark (available in small bags) and pine needles (sometimes available locally)—all ensure that excess moisture drains away swiftly.

Fern potting mixture
A high-humus mixture which should have good drainage. A suitable mixture consists of three-fifths peat-based potting mixture and two-fifths coarse sand or medium-grade perlite. Add one cup of charcoal granules to every litre of the mixture (to help sweeten it) and add a balanced granular or powdered fertilizer (according to the instructions on the pack).

Bulb fibre
Use only for indoor bulbs; it does not contain enough nutrients for other pot plants. A suitable mixture consists of six parts peat moss, two parts crushed oyster shell and one part charcoal.

Useful additives

Humus (leaf mould)
Retains nutrients and gives an open texture.

Manure
Used as a dried powder, cow manure is nutrient rich.

Peat moss
Holds water and added fertilizer very well.

Tree bark
Holds water and added fertilizer very well.

Dolomite limestone powder
Acts to reduce the acidity of potting mixtures.

Eggshell/oystershell
Reduces the acidity and assists drainage of potting mixtures.

Limestone chips
Reduces the acidity and assists drainage of potting mixtures.

Coarse sand
Opens up potting mixtures for better aeration and drainage.

Rockwool
Holds moisture and allows air to penetrate.

Repotting and potting on

Plants in gardens have a free root run. Their roots spread as far as they need to in search of water and food. With a few exceptions (bromeliads and other epiphytic plants), most wild plants have roots that run under the surface of the soil, where some moisture and food is usually present and where the soil temperature (which is cool) stays fairly constant. By contrast, the roots of house plants are confined within a relatively small container. Young, healthy plants quickly fill their pots with roots, and then find that there is nowhere else for them to go but through the hole in the bottom of the pot, or over the surface of the potting mixture. When this happens, the mixture dries out quickly and needs very frequent watering and feeding. "Potting on", or planting in a larger pot, is then necessary.

Sometimes it is not obvious just by looking at plants that they need potting on, so you must take them out of their pots and examine the root ball and root system. Look to see whether the roots have penetrated all the available potting mixture; if they have, it is time to move the plant into a larger pot—usually the next size up; if not, return the plant to its original container. Some plants thrive in small pots, in which case the roots of the plants should be checked and the plant put back in the same pot with some fresh potting mixture. This is known as "repotting", but the same term is often used to describe moving a plant to a larger pot.

When the maximum pot size has been reached, or if the plant is very large, the potting mixture can be revitalized by removing the top few centimetres and replacing it with fresh mixture containing added fertilizer. This is called "topdressing".

As repotting and potting on can be a messy business, it is best to deal with several plants at the same time, protecting furniture and the floor with newspaper. Have ready all the materials you will need—potting mixtures, pots, fertilizers and drainage materials. Make sure all the pots are clean, and soak any new clay pots until the air bubbles stop rising; this will ensure the pot will not absorb water from the potting mixture.

Removing plants from their pots

This can be an awkward business if plants are large, an unusual shape, or have sharp spines. Cover the area where you are working with newspaper, and water the plant an hour before the operation; this will help it slide out of the pot more easily, avoiding root damage and spilling of dry potting mixture. Repot the plant as quickly as possible to avoid drying of the roots.

Removing a plant from a small pot

1 Place the palm of one hand on the surface of the mixture with the main stem between your fingers.

2 Turn the pot upside-down and gently tap the pot edge on the side of a table.

3 The plant and its root ball should then slide out easily into your hand.

Removing a plant from a large pot

1 Gently run the blade of a blunt knife or spatula around the edge of the potting mixture.

2 Lay the pot on its side and tap it with a block of wood to loosen the potting mixture. Rotate the pot slowly, tapping it on all sides. Support the plant with one hand whilst doing this.

3 Make sure the plant is completely loose before attempting to remove it. If the plant is very large, two pairs of hands may be necessary—one to hold the plant steady, the other to pull the pot away.

Removing a cactus from a pot

1 With a prickly plant, such as a cactus, use a rolled up piece of paper to protect your hand.

2 Place the paper round the cactus, making sure the paper is long enough to make a "handle".

3 Holding the paper "handle" in one hand, gently pull the pot away with the other.

Potting on

The term "potting" refers specifically to the transfer of cuttings and seedlings to their first pot, while "potting on" is used to describe transferring a plant to a larger pot. It should be done at the beginning of the growing season. Do not pot on during, or just prior to, a rest period as no new root growth will be produced to penetrate the extra potting mixture; this will then become waterlogged and cause the existing roots to rot. Never pot on if the plant is unhealthy in any way (apart from being potbound), as this can cause unnecessary shock. Do not feed plants which have just been potted on for the first four to six weeks; instead let them send out new roots into the potting mixture in search of food.

A potbound plant
The earliest recognizable stage of a plant becoming potbound is when new roots start to cover the root ball. The roots will eventually become densely matted and form a thick spiral in the base of the pot. Potting on at this stage is essential.

Mass of new roots visible on surface of the root ball.

Roots begin to spiral at base.

Roots in a mass at the base of the pot, as they grow out of the drainage hole.

1 Remove any moss or other green surface growth from the top of the root ball.

2 Line the new pot with drainage material and ensure the plant will sit at the same level.

3 Prepare a mould by filling the space between the new pot and the old with potting mixture.

4 Insert the plant, fill in any gaps round the sides of the root ball and firm in gently to ensure it is supported.

Repotting

Plants do not always need potting on. If they are not potbound, or thrive better in a smaller pot, they may simply need repotting—taking them out of their pots and returning them to clean pots of the same size with some fresh potting mixture. Often, it is enough to gently tease away some of the old potting mixture and to supply the plant with a little fresh mixture which is high in nutrients. If the plant is growing too fast, or is already too big, the roots may need pruning to allow room for the new potting mixture.

1 Remove the plant from the pot gently. Watering about an hour before will help the plant to slide out.

2 To allow room for the new potting mixture, you may need to prune the roots by cutting slices off the root ball.

3 Place the plant in a clean pot of the same size. Fill in round the edges with new potting mixture and firm down.

Topdressing

Eventually, with well-established plants that have been potted on several times, it will not be practical to move them into larger pots. You must then find a way of providing them with extra nourishment. Topdressing each spring is the best way of doing this. The method also suits house plants, such as the amaryllis (*Hippeastrum* hybrids), which resent root disturbance and flower best when thoroughly potbound. Always use new potting mixture to which a slow-release fertilizer high in nutrients has been added.

1 Gently scrape away the top few centimetres of the potting mixture, with an old kitchen fork or similar implement, taking care not to damage the roots.

2 Refill the pot to its original level using fresh potting mixture of a suitable type. Firm this down to ensure the plant is properly anchored in the pot.

Growing plants in artificial light

The use of artificial light is becoming more widespread among indoor gardeners, either as a substitute or supplement for natural light, or to allow plants to be grown in places where the light level is otherwise too low for healthy plant growth or regular flower production.

Incandescent bulbs can scorch plants if placed too close to them, and do not produce enough light for a plant's growing needs if placed the right distance away to avoid scorch. Incandescent floodlights are more effective, as they concentrate a beam of light by means of built-in reflectors, but this is still only sufficient for display purposes.

Fluorescent tubes are the most satisfactory and economical way of providing artificial light for plants in the home. They are available in several different colours; the coating on the outside of the tube determines the colour of the light. If you are using a fitting with two tubes, a combination of "natural white" and "daylight" gives the closest approximation to natural light. Plants require the violet/blue and red wavelengths: "daylight" bulbs are high in blue but low in red; "warm white" and "natural white" are high in red, but low in blue. The simplest units consist of a reflector which holds one or two tubes and is supported on legs, enabling plants to be positioned underneath the lights. Multi-layered units are also available which have lights under each shelf to illuminate the plants immediately below. Alternatively, you can provide lights for plants in a bookcase or shelf-unit, or in the space between a kitchen countertop and wall-hung cabinets. It is important that any home-constructed units be fitted by a competent electrician.

Plants vary in their light needs (see pp.244-5) in natural conditions, and equally so under artificial light tubes. If they are too close, the foliage will be scorched, if too distant they will become etiolated and flowering species will produce fewer blooms than they should. Plants grown for their flowers, such as African violets (*Saintpaulia* hybrids), need to be 20-30cm from the tubes, but most foliage plants are better placed 30-40cm away. Pots can be lifted nearer to the tubes by standing them on blocks of wood or upturned empty pots, and those that prefer least light should be stood at the ends of the tubes. Cuttings can be raised very well under artificial lights, as long as they are positioned the right distance away from them.

To grow plants exclusively under lights, the tubes must be kept on for around 12-14 hours per day for foliage plants and 16-18 hours per day for flowering plants, unless they are short-day types—such as poinsettias (*Euphorbia pulcherrima*)—which require less light. Electric timer switches can be installed so that the lights will come on when it is most convenient. When using units to provide additional light in winter, plants should have as much normal daylight as possible, and then the tubes should be illuminated for around 5 or 6 hours in the evening.

Decorative and functional lighting *left*
This small light fixture is equipped with a special bulb which should provide the light needed to keep this Boston fern (*Nephrolepis exaltata* "Bostoniensis") healthy in a position which would otherwise be too dark for it. The light also serves a decorative purpose, casting an interesting shadow on to the wall behind.

Types of bulbs *below*
Fluorescent light tubes, in a range of lengths and wattages, are the most efficient means of artificially lighting your plants. Incandescent bulbs provide effective display lighting and have the advantage of manoeuvrability.

Simple but effective strip lighting *right*
A single, 2m long fluorescent bulb suspended from the ceiling provides uncomplicated artificial lighting for the plants below. This type of bulb generates more light per watt than any other form of lighting and wastes less of its energy as heat. The attractive foliage of the plants is shown off to full advantage under the fluorescent light, which also fulfills their light needs.

Providing extra light *right*
A simple unit, like this one suspended from a wooden beam, is quick and easy to install. It can light a large number of plants in places which would otherwise be too dark for healthy plant growth.

Self-contained unit *below*
An illuminated unit filled with flowering plants can be a source of great pleasure through the dark months of winter. African violets (*Saint-paulia* hybrids), which naturally come into bloom in September, can be encouraged to flower all through the winter in this way.

Hydroculture

Hydroculture is the practice of growing plants in containers filled with water to which nutrients are added. Traditionally, the method was called hydroponics and can still be seen in its simplest form when hyacinth bulbs (*Hyacinthus orientalis* hybrids) are placed in bulb glasses filled with water; the bulbs sense the water is there and root down into it.

During the 1970s, growers started to market house plants growing in purpose-made, watertight containers filled with a special aggregate to support the roots of the plant, and chemically charged water to meet the plant's food needs. The special containers ranged in size from those suitable for housing a single plant to large, floor-standing models popular with establishments such as banks, libraries, hospitals and municipal offices, who liked the idea of bold, low-maintenance displays of plants. The beauty of hydroculture is that the plants need very little attention and virtually no expertise is required to cultivate them successfully (see also pp.72-3). Other advantages include vigorous and healthy growth, and freedom from soil-borne diseases and pests.

The basic materials for hydroculture are the aggregate, usually packed in plastic bags, and the container, which may be used on its own or have a liner. The aggregate must be clean and inert and can be grit, pea-gravel, perlite or, more commonly, a purpose-made granule composed of expanded clay. One name given to a particular aggregate is hydroleca—"hydro" meaning water, and "leca" standing for "lightweight expanded clay aggregate". This consists of lightweight pellets of varying sizes and fairly random shape that have been fired in a rotary kiln at extremely high temperatures. As a result, most of the clay has been forced to the outside wall of the pellet, leaving a honeycombed centre. The great advantage of the pellets is that their outside cases conduct water from the reservoir sitting at the bottom of the container, thus moistening all the pellets. Another important feature is that there is plenty of air circulating between the upper pellets, where most of the plant's roots are.

Feeding methods

To feed plants grown in hydroculture, fertilizer is put into the water, but it can be put there in several different ways. The simplest way is to use a standard liquid fertilizer in the water used for filling the reservoir. The danger with this method is that nutrients which are not used immediately by the plants tend to crystallize out of the liquid on to the pellets and roots of the plant, and ought really to be washed out of the base periodically, which is rather a messy business. It is much simpler to use a specially designed hydroculture fertilizer bonded into a pad or disc, or packed in a sachet which is placed in the water. The advantage of these pads or discs is that they do not release multi-chemical fertilizer all the time, but only when the water lacks the particular element, and so no harmful build-up of chemicals is possible.

Containers for hydroculture

There are two main types of container that can be used— the single container and the double container. The single container may be made of any kind of watertight material (other than untreated metal that would affect the chemicals

Types of hydroculture

Hydroculture is easy to do and containers range from the simple bulb glass, to the more complex double container. Most plants can be grown in hydroculture and growth is usually vigorous.

Using a single container *above*
The plant is grown in the aggregate. Water is poured directly onto the aggregate.

Using a double container *below*
The plant is grown in the aggregate, but its roots may grow out of the inner container and come into direct contact with the reservoir of water.

Using a bulb glass *left*
This is a very old method of hydroculture. The bulb glass is specially designed to hold a column of water underneath the base of the bulb. Use a bulb that is large enough to support itself in the bowl of the glass; this prevents it toppling over when the top growth appears.

put into the water and would probably rust), ideally with a broad base to give stability. Glass is probably the best material to use. Apart from looking attractive, a glass container allows you to keep a check on the water level and the amount of roots in the container.

The double container has a similar watertight outer container into which fits a smaller container. The small container hangs on the rim of the larger container and holds the aggregate and plant. The inner container is usually made of plastic and has holes or large slits in its sides and base to allow air and water to circulate around the pellets and the roots of the plant.

In both cases, the water should only be in the lower regions, never in the upper ones. With the single container, the bottom quarter or third of the aggregate should be submerged; with the double container, it is normally enough that the inner container, filled with the aggregate, be in direct contact with the reservoir of water. A water gauge will indicate when more water is needed.

Potting up rooted cuttings in hydroculture

Cuttings that have made roots in water can be planted in hydroculture containers in much the same way as cuttings are planted in potting mixture. Hold the cuttings upright and gently trickle the aggregate around the roots, then tap the container gently to settle the aggregate. Never bury the cuttings deeper than you would if planting them in a potting mixture, and shade the planted cuttings for a few days until they have settled down in their new home. When they have made strong root growth, carefully transfer the pots to their permanent position.

Rooting cuttings in hydroculture *right*
Cuttings of such plants as ivies (*Hedera* sp.), tradescantias (*Tradescantia* sp.), and wandering Jews (*Zebrina pendula*) can be rooted in "nursery beds"—small pots, filled with aggregate, which stand in deep saucers of water to which a little ordinary fertilizer at quarter strength has been added.

Potting on in hydroculture

A plant grown in hydroculture grows quickly but produces a much more compact root system than a plant grown in a potting mixture, so annual potting on is unnecessary. However, the plant will eventually need potting on as the roots grow to fill the container. Potting on in aggregate is a similar process to potting on in potting mixture, but much less messy and time-consuming. Always remember to pot on in a similar type of container—either single or double. If potting on in a double container, the size of the outer container needs to be increased as well as the size of the inner container to maintain the size ratio.

1. Cover the bottom of the new container with a layer of clean aggregate. Remove the plant from the old container. Do not pull the plant out as this will tear the roots.

2. Hold the plant over the new container of aggregate, making sure it is at the same level as before. Spread the roots out and trickle in the new aggregate.

3. Once the plant is properly anchored, fill with enough water to cover the bottom third of the new container, or until the water gauge indicates that it is "full".

Transferring a plant from potting mixture to hydroculture

It is not normally recommended that you transfer a well-developed or mature plant out of potting mixture into hydroculture because of the trauma it would suffer. However, it is possible. Because of the shock, it will be necessary to give the plant warmth and high humidity for 10-12 weeks to aid its recovery. A heated propagator provides the best conditions, but a warm greenhouse is also suitable, provided that the air around the plant is made very humid by the use of a plastic, tentlike cover and the temperature maintained at a constant level. During this time, all of the old, soil-adapted roots will die and new, succulent ones adapted to the semi-aquatic life will be made.

1. Using both hands, remove the mature plant from its pot, taking care not to damage the root ball. It is not advisable to use a rare or treasured specimen.

2. Supporting the plant with one hand, carefully tease apart the root ball, removing as much of the potting mixture as is possible without tearing the roots.

3. To remove the final traces of the potting mixture, wash the roots thoroughly under a gently running tap. Make sure the water is not too cold, as this will cause further trauma to the plant.

Pruning and training

House plants may need to be pruned periodically, or trained to the shape you wish them either to maintain or take on. They may become too big for the space available, or odd branches can start to grow in places where you do not want them, giving the plant an unbalanced look. Messy, tangled growth needs to be thinned out, and branches and stems induced to grow in a particular direction. Some plants need their growing points nipped out frequently to avoid unwanted leggy shoots and encourage a close, bushy shape. New growth on certain climbing plants will need to be supported as it is not capable of supporting itself.

The correct way to prune

Always cut just above the bud where you want the new shoot to form. Slope the cut downwards, away from the bud, and do not leave a long "snag", as this will be liable to rot.

Too far from bud

Correct way to prune

Too close to bud

Angled in wrong direction

When to prune

Spring is the best time for pruning nearly all plants, as it is the season when new, active growth begins, but overlong stems can normally be cut back in the autumn if they get in the way or overcrowd the plant.

Some plants only make flower buds on the new season's growth and you can therefore cut away a lot of old growth in the spring, confident that you are not harming the prospect of flowers in the coming season. However, when cutting back woody-stemmed plants, it is usually safest to cut back into the previous year's growth and not beyond.

Whatever tool you use for pruning, it is important that it is sharp, to avoid bruising or otherwise damaging the remaining stem. A razor blade, scalpel or scalpel-like knife is excellent for soft-stemmed plants, and a finely pointed pair of scissors will allow you to get into the leaf axils of really bushy plants. For woody stems, secateurs are essential.

Deadheading

Deadheading involves cutting away any dead or faded flowers on the plant. This encourages the plant to put more effort into producing new flowers rather than producing seeds, as would happen naturally.

Flowers on long stalks

Deadhead plants such as African violets (*Saintpaulia* hybrids), whose flower stalks arise from the base of the plant, by pulling and twisting out the whole stalk.

Flowers on short stalks

Deadhead flowers in clusters, or on short stalks arising from a main stem, by pinching them off between your thumb and index finger.

Cutting back

Cutting back is probably the most drastic form of pruning, but usually improves the attractiveness of a plant. It allows you to get rid of totally unwanted growth and lets you keep favourite plants that would otherwise become too big to be grown in the home. A drastic cutting back often improves growth by ridding the plant of old, weak sections and encouraging new, strong shoots with short gaps between the leaves.

Cutting back straggly growth

Fast-growing plants which climb, or are trained round hoops and canes, can lose their shape after one, two or three seasons' growth. Jasmine (*Jasminum* sp.) is a climber which needs particularly drastic cutting back. Do not be afraid to cut out all but the newest growth; if the plant is cut back in early spring, it will be covered with new growth by the summer.

1 If growth round the hoop becomes very straggly, cutting back will provide attractive, bushier new growth.

Cutting back to create close growth

Plants with long stems, such as ivies (*Hedera* sp.) or philodendrons, may develop large gaps between the leaves in winter. This may be due to insufficient light or overcrowding. To correct the condition, the stems affected must be cut back to allow new, close growth (the tips can be used as cuttings). The initial cause of the problem must then be identified and put right.

1 Stems with large gaps between leaves, particularly those of trailing plants, will look better if cut back.

Cutting back a tall plant

Cutting back usually encourages new growth, so merely snipping away the top 10-15cm of a large plant will only prove a temporary solution. When a rubber plant (*Ficus elastica*) or rainbow plant (*Dracaena marginata*) almost reaches the ceiling, it needs shortening by about a metre if you want to keep it indoors for a few more years. The plant may look odd for several weeks but once the new leaves appear the cutting back will have been worthwhile.

1 A favourite plant which has grown too tall can be cut back drastically and kept in the home for a few more years.

Pinching out

Growing tips should be pinched out frequently on plants that would naturally grow long unbranched stems, but which look better when growth is more compact. Pinching out also prevents climbers and trailers becoming too straggly.

How to pinch out *right*
Nip out the growing tip or point with your index finger and thumb.

2 Unwind the stems from the hoop and cut them off, using sharp scissors, until only two of the youngest stems remain.

3 Wind the remaining stems round the wire hoop and secure with wire plant ties.

2 Using sharp scissors, cut the stem back to the point (node) where tight growth exists, taking out the elongated, leggy growth.

3 If the plant is then given the correct growing conditions, the new growth will have short gaps between the leaves.

2 Use secateurs to remove the head of a woody-stemmed plant. Cut down by as much as half its original height.

3 Staunch any flow of latex with a dusting of powdered charcoal. Give the plant the kind of growing conditions it needs to grow at its best and new leaves will be produced in four to six weeks.

Training plants

Many house plants can be trained to grow in a variety of shapes, by appropriate pruning or pinching out to obtain a bushy plant or a tall plant with a bare stem, known as a standard, or by training the plant to grow round a support. Most plants attain a rewarding shape within a few years.

Growing a standard

1 Remove all the side shoots that form on the main stem, but leave the foliage.

2 At the desired height, pinch out the growing tip. Remove foliage from the stem.

Growing a bushy plant

1 Pinch out the growing tips to encourage the development of side shoots.

2 Maintain the bushy shape by pinching out the growing points of new side shoots.

Training plants around a support

Support can be provided by fastening the stem of the plant to thin canes, bamboo, wire hoops or trellises pushed into the potting mixture. Ties made of twine, raffia, soft wire rings or wire-and-paper twists can be used. Fasten them so that they secure the stems, but not so tight that they will bite into the stems as they thicken.

Circular

Rectangular

Fan-shaped

Propagation 1

All plants eventually reach the stage when they cease to be as attractive as they once were and need replacing with younger, more vigorous specimens. Propagating your own plants is a cheap and satisfying way of rejuvenating your house plant stock.

There are two main ways in which new plants can be produced—they may either be grown from seed (see p.269) or propagated vegetatively.

Vegetative propagation

This method of propagation involves taking a specific part of a plant and encouraging it to make roots of its own, so that it can establish itself and become a plant in its own right. Generally, but not always, plants propagated vegetatively look just like the original plant the section was taken from. Virtually any part of a plant can be used: plantlets that develop on leaf surfaces or on trailing stolons, offsets and stem or leaf cuttings. Alternatively, clumps may be divided (see p.267), or stems layered or air-layered (see p.268). You can propagate some plants by more than one of the methods mentioned, others can only be propagated in one particular way. Quick rooting and establishment is, in all cases, vital. The faster the section can make roots of its own and become established as a separate plant the safer it is; unrooted sections are at risk from wilting, rot and a number of other hazards. Special rooting mixture are available for the propagation of cuttings—these hold plenty of air and water, but have few nutrients, which would scorch the new roots.

With practically all types of vegetative propagation, the best season to choose is the spring, just as new growth is starting.

Equipment for propagating plants

Scissors

Widger

Sharp knife

Watering can

Jam jar propagator

Paintbrush

Plastic bag propagator

Plant labels

Hormone rooting powder

Labelling pencil

Peat pots

Peat tray

Peat pellets

Seed tray

Electric heat propagator

Cold propagator

Propagating from stem cuttings

Most house plants can be propagated from stem cuttings of one kind or another. Cuts should be made with a really sharp knife or razor blade, as bruised or split stems are liable to rot. If possible, water the plant about two hours before taking the cutting, as this ensures that the stems and leaves are fully charged with moisture. If you have to use a flowering stem, gently pinch off the flowers first. Coating the cut end of the stem with hormone rooting powder will hasten the rooting process.

Rooting a soft-stemmed cutting in water

1 Make a clean cut just above a leaf axil or node; the parent plant can then make new shoots from the top or upper leaf axils.

2 Make another cut immediately below the lowest node or leaf axil of the cutting and gently remove the lower leaves.

3 After approximately four weeks, 2-4cm of new root will have formed, and the cutting can then be transferred to potting mixture.

Rooting a soft-stemmed cutting in potting mixture

1 Select a healthy stem, with about three nodes spaced fairly close together, and make a clean cut, giving a 10-15cm "tip" cutting.

2 Trim the cutting just below the lowest leaf node and remove the lower leaves to prevent them rotting in the rooting mixture.

3 Make some holes with a stick and plant several cuttings in the same pot, gently firming the mixture with your fingers.

Taking a woody-stemmed cutting

1 To propagate a woody-stemmed plant, remove any lower leaves that remain and cut the stem into short pieces, each of which should include at least one node. The rooting process may take several weeks longer than with a soft-stemmed plant.

2 Place the cuttings, horizontally or vertically, in rooting mixture. Roots will develop from buried nodes and new top growth from the nodes exposed to the air.

Propagation 2

Propagating from leaf cuttings

Some plants can be propagated from leaf cuttings. A complete leaf, with its leaf stalk attached, is pulled or cut from the parent plant and then grown in barely moist rooting mixture, or, in certain cases, water. The leaves should be inserted into the mixture at a 45 degree angle, and may be rested against the pot edge to give them maximum support; the cut end should not be buried too deeply. The new roots and shoots will develop from the cut end of the leaf stalk, or along the leaf edges (veins). Leaf cuttings may be planted singly in small pots, or a number may be planted together in larger pots or shallow trays. Enclosing the container in a plastic bag creates a humid atmosphere and usually eliminates the need for further watering. African violets (*Saintpaulia* hybrids) and rhizomatous begonias are examples of popular house plants which can be reproduced in this way. The leaves chosen should be neither too old nor too young, so—in the case of an African violet, for example—the extreme inner and outer leaves of the rosette should not be used. Large-leaved begonias should not have their leaves cut into sections, as they are then liable to rot, but the leaves can be used whole if their outer edges are trimmed off to reduce leaf area and loss of water by transpiration.

Rooting leaf cuttings in potting mixture

1 Remove one complete leaf with a sharp knife or razor blade, and trim the stalk to a length of 4-5cm.

2 Plant the leaf in barely moist rooting mixture and cover the pot with a plastic bag to increase humidity.

3 When new plantlets appear at the base of each leaf, cut away the parent leaf.

Rooting leaf cuttings in water

1 Remove a healthy leaf with a leaf stalk attached, and trim the stalk to a length of 4-5cm.

2 Cover a water-filled jar with plastic and insert leaves through holes punched in the plastic.

3 Roots and small plantlets will form underwater. These can then be separated and planted in potting mixture.

Rooting leaf sections in potting mixture

The leaves of certain plants, including the mother-in-law's tongue (*Sansevieria* sp.), Cape primrose (*Streptocarpus* hybrids) and emerald ripple peperomia (*Peperomia caperata*), can be cut into pieces, which are rooted separately to produce many new plants. A cluster of plantlets will push up through the mixture from a section of Cape primrose leaf and, most probably, just a single plantlet from the cut base of each piece of mother-in-law's tongue leaf. The segments of leaf must be inserted base downwards in the rooting mixture—otherwise no roots will develop.

Mother-in-law's tongue and Cape primrose leaves should be cut crosswise at 5-8cm intervals and then planted almost vertically in a sandy rooting mixture, with between a quarter and a half of the section buried. Emerald ripple peperomia leaves should be cut into four sections (one cut down the leaf, one cut across it) and planted with a cut edge just in contact with a barely moist rooting mixture. If leaves from a variegated mother-in-law's tongue plant are used (as shown here), the new foliage which is produced will revert to plain green.

1 Remove the parent plant from its pot and select a healthy, mature leaf which is unblemished. Cut or break off the leaf at the base.

2 Cut the leaf crosswise, with a sharp knife, at 5-8cm intervals. Each large leaf will provide several segments from which new plants can be propagated.

3 Plant the leaf cuttings together at a slight angle in the rooting mixture. They may be supported by plant labels or rested against the pot side, if required.

4 New roots will develop from the buried cut edge of each leaf section. When the plantlets are well-developed, pot them up and treat them as mature plants.

Propagating from plantlets

A number of house plants make "plantlets" —small replicas of themselves—on their leaves or at the ends of stolons or arching stems. Pickaback plants (*Tolmeia menziesii*) produce plantlets on their leaves, while strawberry geraniums (*Saxifraga stolonifera*) produce plantlets on stolons. If plantlets are left on the parent plant until they are well developed, they can usually be detached and potted up to develop roots of their own in a rooting mixture. Alternatively, strawberry geraniums and spider plants (*Chlorophytum comosum*) can be layered (see p.268), although plantlets may be less inclined to make roots of their own while they continue to be sustained by the parent through the linking stem.

1 Cut off a leaf or stolon (shown above) which bears a well-developed plantlet. Leave about 3cm of the leaf stalk or stolon attached to the plantlet. Bury this stalk in a pot of rooting mixture with the plantlet resting on the surface.

2 Cover with a plastic bag to provide extra humidity. Roots should develop in three weeks.

Propagating from offsets

These are small plants which appear around the base of mature plants. Most grow directly from the stem but some may be produced on long stalks or stolons. Bromeliads and succulents often produce offsets at the base, and many of the spherical cacti make clusters of them. If offsets are to survive on their own, they should not be detached until they are well established and have developed the normal shape and characteristics of the parent. Well-developed offsets often have some roots of their own already formed, and this inevitably makes subsequent establishment easier and quicker.

1 Choose an offset, ideally one which already has some roots attached, and gently break it off the main stem. This may be done at the same time as you repot the parent plant.

2 Plant the offsets in barely moist rooting mixture in separate pots. Place the pot in a plastic bag until active growth indicates that the offset is well rooted.

Propagating by division

Plants such as African violets (*Saintpaulia* hybrids), most ferns and some cacti can usually be divided by taking them out of their pots and firmly but gently pulling apart obviously separate sections, each comprising a single or small cluster of plants and a healthy root system. It may be necessary to tease or wash away some of the potting mixture so that you can see the separate sections. Sometimes these are joined together with tough thickened roots, and you may need a sharp knife to make the division. In addition, ferns often have densely packed fine roots that make pulling the sections apart difficult.

1 You may need to use a knife to start a division so that you can get your thumbs into the cut area and successfully lever the sections apart, dividing the root ball equally.

2 Pot up the divisions at the same level as previously, in a pot slightly larger than the root spread. Water sparingly until sections get established and new growth appears.

Propagation times

Soft-stemmed cutting in water: four to six weeks for adequate roots to form; then transfer to potting mixture.

Soft-stemmed cutting in potting mixture: three to four weeks for adequate roots to form.

Woody-stemmed cutting in potting mixture: eight to ten weeks for adequate roots to form.

Whole leaf in potting mixture: three to four weeks for adequate roots to form; then a further two to five weeks before new topgrowth appears.

Whole leaf in water: three to four weeks for adequate roots to form; then transfer to potting mixture.

Leaf section in potting mixture: four to six weeks for adequate roots to form; then a further four to eight weeks before new topgrowth appears.

Plantlet in potting mixture: three to four weeks for adequate roots to form; then a further two to five weeks before an attractive-looking new plant develops.

Offset in potting mixture: three to four weeks for adequate roots to form; then a further two to three weeks for a plant of a useful size to develop.

Division in potting mixture: two to three weeks for a plant of a useful size to develop.

Propagation 3

Layering

This is the process by which roots are encouraged to form on a trailing stem while it is still in contact with the rest of the plant. Layering is practised in the garden when semi-woody stemmed shrubs have their stems bent down and held in contact with the soil to encourage them to make roots. It is not often practised indoors, except with sweetheart plants (*Philodendron scandens*) and ivies (*Hedera* sp.)—both of which make aerial roots at the nodes or leaf joints. As with the propagation of plantlets (see p.267), the stems are brought into contact with a suitable rooting mixture in a nearby pot. Many creeping plants are constantly sending roots down into the potting mixture over which they grow. The new growths can be cut from the parent plants and potted up separately at virtually any time.

1 Bring the stem into contact with a pot containing suitable rooting mixture, securing it firmly in place with a hairpin or a piece of bent wire. Heap a little rooting mixture over the point of contact to further encourage rooting.

2 New roots form within three to four weeks at the node, and a young plant will begin to grow. When this happens, cut the new plant free, taking care not to spoil the shape of the parent. Several plants can be propagated in this way simultaneously.

Air layering

Air layering is a way of propagating a prized plant that has grown too big for convenience or one that has lost some of its lower leaves and is starting to look untidy. It is often used for woody-stemmed plants that do not root quickly from cuttings and are so stiff that their stems cannot be bent down for layering.

The woody stem is "injured" to encourage it to put forth roots at the point of injury; the top section is then cut off and potted up. One method involves making a single upward-slanting cut in the stem, but this puts it in danger of being broken off. A somewhat safer way of air layering is described here.

Before
After

1 Score out two rings, 1-2cm apart, just below the lowest healthy leaf on the stem. Peel off the bark between them, leaving the stem tissue undisturbed.

2 Brush the stripped area of stem with a thin layer of hormone rooting powder to encourage the rapid production of new roots.

3 Using insulating tape or strong thread, secure the end of an oblong piece of plastic around the stem, just below the point at which the stem is cut.

4 Pack the cuplike plastic sheath with moistened sphagnum moss. This is the most effective rooting medium for air-layering.

5 Lash the top of the plastic around the stem to ensure that the moisture cannot escape. The cut section of stem should now be completely covered.

6 After several weeks, roots will appear through the moss. Remove the plastic cover and cut the stem cleanly, just below where the roots are growing.

7 Plant the new root ball in a pot large enough to allow a 5cm space around it. Fill with a suitable potting mixture, and water sparingly until well established.

Growing from seeds

Very reliable strains of seeds are available for such popular house plants as wax begonias (*Begonia semperflorens-cultorum*) and busy Lizzies (*Impatiens* sp.), and the best hybrid forms can often be raised in this way.

Seeds are best sown in a suitable peat-based rooting mixture (see p.264). Use half-pots, pans or seed trays depending on the quantity of seed being sown. Very small seed, such as that of begonias (*Begonia* sp.) and African violets (*Saintpaulia* hybrids), resembles dust, and is best sprinkled over the surface of the rooting mixture. Slightly larger seeds can have a shallow layer of finely sieved mixture placed over them, and sizeable seeds should be buried at one and a half times their own depth. Once water has penetrated the outer coating of the seed, growth begins and, from that point onwards, a constant supply of moisture is needed. Any drying out is fatal, but too much water will result in rotting, so a balance must be struck.

Temperatures above 15°C are needed for swift germination and some of the sub-tropical and tropical plants need much higher levels. Some seed germinates best in the dark, other types need light to grow—so always follow the instructions on the packet. It is very important to give small seedlings the quantity of bright light they need from the very earliest stages of growth. If a seedling starts to make elongated growth, due to insufficient light, it will never develop into a really satisfactory plant. Containers should be placed near to a source of bright light as soon as the first seedlings start to appear. However, it is important to avoid hot direct sunlight that could cause scorch and certainly dries up the surface of the mixture. It is a good idea to check trays, pots and pans every day.

Clear plastic tops are available for the standard sizes of pots and seed trays. These create a humid atmosphere conducive to rapid germination.

Sowing seeds

1 Spread a thin layer of gravel in the bottom of a tray—this provides good drainage and prevents waterlogging. Cover the gravel with a layer of suitable rooting mixture.

2 Mark out shallow furrows as a guide for sowing. Scattering seed indiscriminately over the whole surface will often result in overcrowding of seedlings.

3 Take small pinches of fine seed from a hand-held container and sprinkle them along the furrows. Larger seeds can be individually spaced at regular intervals in the furrows.

4 Cover the seeds, if appropriate, and thoroughly moisten the mixture with a fine mist-sprayer. Then place a sheet of glass or clear plastic on top and put the tray in a warm place.

Thinning out

1 At an early stage, carefully thin out seedlings growing very close together. This gives those that remain a better chance of thriving.

2 The spaces between remaining seedlings should be roughly equal to their height. Use your fingertips to carefully firm the mixture around each one.

3 When a seedling has developed at least two true leaves, gently remove it from the mixture using a plant marker, or something similar, to ease out the young roots.

4 Transfer each seedling to a pot containing mixture suitable for the adult plant. Ensure that the lower leaves are not buried and avoid handling the stem.

Problems, pests and diseases 1

Healthy, well-maintained house plants grow sturdily, look good and are less likely to develop problems or be attacked by pests or disease. Unhealthy plants are usually the result of poor cultivation, neglect or wrong treatment—actual pests or diseases are, in fact, rarely to blame.

The first step to ensuring that your plants remain in peak condition is to choose them carefully, bearing in mind the amount of time and effort you can devote to them and the conditions you have to offer. Buy a specimen which looks healthy and protect it on the journey home. A plant will also need a period of acclimatization to its new surroundings; try to ensure it is placed in a suitable position and not moved for a few days. It is unwise to introduce a new plant into an existing collection until it has been carefully examined; ideally, it should be isolated from your other house plants until it can be given a clean bill of health.

Preventive action

The successful way to care for any plant is to give it neither too much nor too little of the essential growth factors: water, food, light, warmth and humidity. Apart from meeting your plants' specific growing needs, though, it is well worth devoting a few minutes, every week or two, to cleaning them and generally looking them over. Turn over the leaves and examine the undersides carefully—this will help you to spot any problems at an early stage. Should signs of ill health or pest infestation be apparent, immediate action must be taken if the plant is to be saved. Also pay close attention to the growing points; these, being soft and succulent, are more liable to attack by aphids than older, leathery leaves. In several flowering plants, such as the Cape primrose (*Streptocarpus* hybrids), the leaves are rarely attacked—it is the flower stalks and flower buds that are the susceptible parts. Some pests are a little choosy about their host plants, appearing only on certain species. Others are less discriminating and will attack any plant.

Routine maintenance

The action of cleaning a plant often dislodges the odd pest and may even prevent a real infestation. Household dust spoils the look of leaves and, to some extent, clogs the pores through which they breathe—it also reduces the amount of light which can be used for photosynthesis. See that plants are not crowded together so closely that air cannot circulate freely between them, or that some fail to get enough light because others are shading them. Remove any yellowing or damaged leaves and take off all flowers as they fade. Flower stalks should be taken off right to the base when all the individual blooms on the stalk are finished. Leaving sections of stalk behind can cause rotting in the centre of the plant.

Keeping plants clean

Plants which are kept in the home are bound to get dusty, so a regular cleaning programme is essential. Clean leaves look more attractive and they allow a plant to function more efficiently. Various methods of cleaning are given below, depending on the size and texture of the plant's leaves. By far the most effective method of cleaning a plant of any shape or size is to stand it outside in a gentle shower, in a sheltered position, during the milder months. Rain water leaves no nasty white deposit behind and the leaves are thoroughly freshened by the experience.

Wiping with a damp cloth
Plants with large, smooth leaves can be cleaned with a damp sponge or soft cloth. Use a weak solution of soapy water and give a clear rinse afterwards. A shower will also benefit these plants, but ensure that the water pressure is not high enough to damage the leaves.

Removing faded leaves and flowers
Remove any faded flowers or yellowing leaves that are due to old age, taking them right off to the base. Snip off brown leaf tips with sharp scissors. As these are usually due to dry air, increase the level of humidity provided.

Routine checklist for ensuring healthy plants

In the majority of cases, ailments that affect house plants are not due to actual disease or infestation by pests. It may just be that one or more of the plant's growing needs are not being met. The following checklist will help you to determine the likely reason behind any symptoms of ill health displayed by your plants. If more than one of the plant's growing needs are not being met, it will be necessary to correct them all, to ensure healthy plant growth. If any symptoms persist, examine for any likely pests or diseases.

- Are you overwatering?
- Are you underwatering?
- Is the plant getting the sort of light it prefers?
- Is the temperature too high or too low for proper growth?
- Is the level of humidity conducive to the plant's needs?
- Have you remembered to cater for any winter rest the plant may need?

- Does the plant stand in a draught?
- Is the pot size correct?
- Are the roots of the plant completely filling the pot?
- Is the plant growing in the right sort of potting mixture?
- Would the plant benefit from being grouped with others?
- Is the plant dusty and in need of a clean?

Cleaning a plant with hairy leaves
Hairy-leaved plants will be damaged if you attempt to clean them with a damp cloth, as the hairs trap the water, causing rotting. You can, however, "sweep" away any dust which may have accumulated by using a soft, dry 1-2cm paintbrush.

Immersing a small plant
On warm days it is possible to wash leaves clean of dust by inverting a small plant and submerging it in a bowl of lukewarm water to which a little soap has been added. Swirl the plant around gently for a few seconds, remove it from the water and allow it to drain.

Examining for pests
It is a good idea to inspect your plants carefully at regular intervals. Pay particular attention to tender growing tips and the undersides of the leaves; scale insects and aphids are especially likely to congregate there. Watch out for the sticky honeydew that these pests exude, as this may encourage sooty mould.

Physiological problems

The most common problems met with in house plants are caused by overwatering, underwatering, fluctuating temperatures, draughts, strong sunlight causing leaves to scorch, cold water causing spotting on the foliage, and low levels of humidity.

Too much or too little water
Overwatering is a very common problem and can be a killer. The dangers of underwatering are less, but the signs of both faults are very similar: in each case the plant droops or wilts because it is not absorbing enough water. Consistent overwatering, when water is frequently given to an already moist potting mixture, means that air cannot reach the roots, so they stop growing and start to break down and die. With little or no roots, a plant cannot take up enough water to sustain it. To prevent overwatering, only water when the potting mixture starts to dry out, and wait until this happens again before giving more water. If a plant prefers a moist potting mixture, keep it moist all the time, but never sodden wet (see p.251).

If a plant is underwatered, it will be obvious that there is little or no water left in the mixture; there may also be a considerable gap between the root ball and the inside of the pot where the potting mixture has shrunk and, in the case of a soil-based potting mixture, the surface may become caked hard or even cracked.

Fluctuating temperatures
When temperatures fluctuate by more than 8°-10°C, leaf drop may occur. Aim at keeping the temperature fairly even, with only a slight fall at night. Avoid the opposite—cool days when the heating is turned off and warm evenings when the heating is turned on. It is better to keep all but the most warmth-loving plants at a lower temperature all the time, moving them to a room that is not directly heated at night.

When temperatures soar, African violets (*Saintpaulia* hybrids) and many other gesneriads will drop most or all of their flower buds; during a heatwave try to keep temperatures down and increase the level of humidity.

Draughts
Plants abhor draughts: the thin and more delicate fern fronds will be blackened by them, the leaves of angel wings (*Caladium hortulanum* hybrids) and painted-leaf begonias (*Begonia rex-cultorum*) will droop, and crotons (*Codiaeum variegatum pictum*) will drop their leaves. Avoid sites next to draughty or open windows and, at night, do not leave plants behind drawn curtains.

Sun scorch
The leaves of plants that prefer to grow in some shade can easily develop brown dehydrated patches if exposed to really strong sunlight. Those plants that can tolerate direct sun, but which are not used to it, can be scalded by sudden exposure. Always acclimatize plants gradually to brighter light.

Insufficient light
If a plant is not receiving enough light, its growth will be generally sluggish. Flowering plants will not bloom as they should, and flower buds may drop off. The new leaves of plants with variegated foliage will revert to a uniform green. To ensure that all parts of the plant receive sufficient light, turn plants regularly, or place them where a reflective surface can throw light on to the side facing away from the light source.

Cold water spots
African violets (*Saintpaulia* hybrids), gloxinias (*Sinningia speciosa*) and a number of other gesneriads can have their leaves marked with lighter coloured patches if they are watered with cold water, or if water is allowed to collect on the leaves at the time of watering. Use tepid water and avoid wetting the foliage.

Incorrect humidity
Low levels of humidity can cause browning of leaf tips and leaf edges; this is particularly obvious on plants with thin leaves, such as peacock plants (*Calathea makoyana*), spider plants (*Chlorophytum comosum*) and many ferns. Increase humidity by regular mist-spraying and by standing plants on trays filled with moist pebbles.

Problems, pests and diseases 2

Pests

House plants are sometimes attacked by insects and other pests which eat their leaves, stems and roots or suck their sap. A minor infestation is hardly noticeable and often does little damage but, if left unchecked, numbers quickly build up and then serious harm can be done. The ways in which pests arrive on plants vary, but new plants should always be thoroughly checked and infested plants should be moved away from healthy ones. Some pests prefer to feed on particular plants and will leave others alone, whilst others are less discriminating. A few types, such as aphids and whiteflies, are very common—they thrive throughout the world, adapting to very different conditions, and are extremely difficult to get rid of—others need special conditions to do well and are therefore easily discouraged.

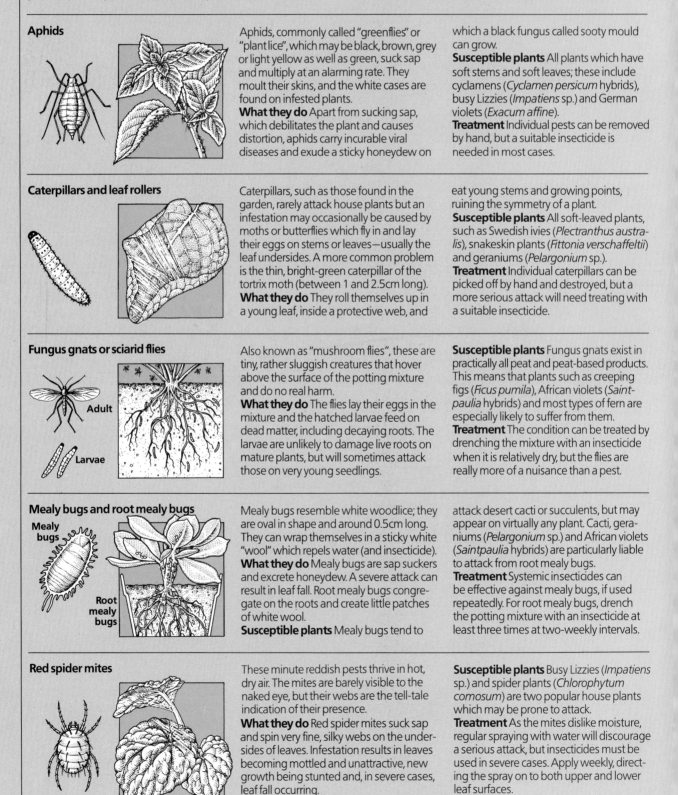

Aphids

Aphids, commonly called "greenflies" or "plant lice", which may be black, brown, grey or light yellow as well as green, suck sap and multiply at an alarming rate. They moult their skins, and the white cases are found on infested plants.

What they do Apart from sucking sap, which debilitates the plant and causes distortion, aphids carry incurable viral diseases and exude a sticky honeydew on which a black fungus called sooty mould can grow.

Susceptible plants All plants which have soft stems and soft leaves; these include cyclamens (*Cyclamen persicum* hybrids), busy Lizzies (*Impatiens* sp.) and German violets (*Exacum affine*).

Treatment Individual pests can be removed by hand, but a suitable insecticide is needed in most cases.

Caterpillars and leaf rollers

Caterpillars, such as those found in the garden, rarely attack house plants but an infestation may occasionally be caused by moths or butterflies which fly in and lay their eggs on stems or leaves—usually the leaf undersides. A more common problem is the thin, bright-green caterpillar of the tortrix moth (between 1 and 2.5cm long).

What they do They roll themselves up in a young leaf, inside a protective web, and eat young stems and growing points, ruining the symmetry of a plant.

Susceptible plants All soft-leaved plants, such as Swedish ivies (*Plectranthus australis*), snakeskin plants (*Fittonia verschaffeltii*) and geraniums (*Pelargonium* sp.).

Treatment Individual caterpillars can be picked off by hand and destroyed, but a more serious attack will need treating with a suitable insecticide.

Fungus gnats or sciarid flies

Also known as "mushroom flies", these are tiny, rather sluggish creatures that hover above the surface of the potting mixture and do no real harm.

What they do The flies lay their eggs in the mixture and the hatched larvae feed on dead matter, including decaying roots. The larvae are unlikely to damage live roots on mature plants, but will sometimes attack those on very young seedlings.

Susceptible plants Fungus gnats exist in practically all peat and peat-based products. This means that plants such as creeping figs (*Ficus pumila*), African violets (*Saintpaulia* hybrids) and most types of fern are especially likely to suffer from them.

Treatment The condition can be treated by drenching the mixture with an insecticide when it is relatively dry, but the flies are really more of a nuisance than a pest.

Adult

Larvae

Mealy bugs and root mealy bugs

Mealy bugs

Root mealy bugs

Mealy bugs resemble white woodlice; they are oval in shape and around 0.5cm long. They can wrap themselves in a sticky white "wool" which repels water (and insecticide).

What they do Mealy bugs are sap suckers and excrete honeydew. A severe attack can result in leaf fall. Root mealy bugs congregate on the roots and create little patches of white wool.

Susceptible plants Mealy bugs tend to attack desert cacti or succulents, but may appear on virtually any plant. Cacti, geraniums (*Pelargonium* sp.) and African violets (*Saintpaulia* hybrids) are particularly liable to attack from root mealy bugs.

Treatment Systemic insecticides can be effective against mealy bugs, if used repeatedly. For root mealy bugs, drench the potting mixture with an insecticide at least three times at two-weekly intervals.

Red spider mites

These minute reddish pests thrive in hot, dry air. The mites are barely visible to the naked eye, but their webs are the tell-tale indication of their presence.

What they do Red spider mites suck sap and spin very fine, silky webs on the undersides of leaves. Infestation results in leaves becoming mottled and unattractive, new growth being stunted and, in severe cases, leaf fall occurring.

Susceptible plants Busy Lizzies (*Impatiens* sp.) and spider plants (*Chlorophytum comosum*) are two popular house plants which may be prone to attack.

Treatment As the mites dislike moisture, regular spraying with water will discourage a serious attack, but insecticides must be used in severe cases. Apply weekly, directing the spray on to both upper and lower leaf surfaces.

Scale insects

Adult

Most scale insects are brown or yellowish in colour; they appear mainly on the undersides of leaves and are particularly partial to crevices. The young insects are very active and move about over the plant, but mature pests remain stationary, enclosed in their waxy cover, and appear as circular or oval raised discs.

What they do Both suck sap and excrete sticky honeydew—often the first sign that they are present is when this sticky residue is noticed on leaves or furniture. Honeydew may lead to infection by sooty mould.

Susceptible plants All plants are vulnerable to attack, but some types of scale insects prefer particular plants. The citrus family and ferns—especially bird's nest ferns (*Asplenium nidus*)—are most susceptible.

Treatment Spraying is not very effective, due to the hard protective coating of the adult insects, and systemic pesticides should be used.

Vine weevils

These pests are increasing in numbers and an attack can be disastrous. Adult weevils are large and almost black in colour; their grubs are cream-coloured.

What they do Adult pests bite pieces out of the foliage, leaving a permanent scar. The grubs eat roots, tubers and corms. Often, the first sign of their presence is when a plant droops and an inspection may reveal that it has no roots left at all!

Susceptible plants The most commonly affected plants include the mother-in-law's tongue (*Sansevieria* sp.), African violet (*Saintpaulia* hybrids) and all types of rosette-shaped succulents.

Treatment Adult pests can be removed by hand and destroyed, and the potting mixture should be drenched with a suitable insecticide. A plant without a root system cannot usually be saved.

Whiteflies

These tiny, white, mothlike creatures are sometimes found in the home, but are more common in greenhouses or conservatories. When whiteflies appear indoors, they have usually been brought in with temporary flowering pot plants.

What they do They settle mainly on the undersides of the leaves, sucking sap and depositing sticky honeydew. Their almost translucent larvae are often present in large numbers on the undersides of leaves.

Susceptible plants Whiteflies tend to attack certain flowering plants, such as geraniums (*Pelargonium* sp.), grown during the summer in the garden.

Treatment These are persistent pests which may prove difficult to eradicate. Repeated applications of a spray insecticide for the larvae and a systemic kind for the adults will eliminate them in time.

Leaf miners

Leaf miners are the slim, sap-sucking maggots of a small fly. They can sometimes be seen if the leaves are examined closely.

What they do The grubs tunnel between the surfaces of the leaves of certain plants, causing a mosaic of irregular white lines. The progress of leaf miners is usually rapid and the appearance of a plant will quickly be spoiled if no action is taken.

Susceptible plants Chrysanthemums (*Chrysanthemum* sp.) and cinerarias (*Senecio cruentus* hybrids) are the most popular house plants likely to be attacked by these pests. Plants that are purchased are unlikely to be affected, but cinerarias grown by the amateur from seed can be at risk.

Treatment Damaged leaves should be picked off and a spray insecticide used on the leaves. Alternatively, a systemic insecticide can be applied to the potting mixture.

Earthworms

Although they are to be encouraged in the garden, where their feeding enriches the soil and their movements serve to aerate it, earthworms that get into the potting mixture of house plants can be a nuisance.

What they do Constant burrowing among the roots causes disturbance and loosens the potting mixture. Their presence is usually noticed when heaps of their casts appear on the surface of the mixture and plants seem loose in their pots.

Susceptible plants Worms may infest any plant which is left in the garden during a shower of rain. They enter the mixture through the drainage holes in the pot.

Treatment Water affected plants with permanganate of potash solution and pick off any worms that surface. Tapping the pot will cause them to surface.

Slugs and snails

Slug

Snail

Slugs and snails will not survive in the home for long, as their presence is soon noticed and they can be easily picked off by hand and destroyed. They can, however, be troublesome in greenhouses and conservatories.

What they do Both are very fond of juicy stems, and can eat away large sections of them rapidly. They are most active at night and during prolonged wet spells.

Susceptible plants Plants that are left outside in summer and autumn can be seriously damaged by these pests. Christmas and Easter cacti (*Schlumbergera* and *Rhipsalidopsis* sp.) are especially at risk because of their succulent stems.

Treatment Protect all indoor plants while they are outdoors by sprinkling slug pellets around them. Renew pellets frequently as rain washes out the chemicals.

Problems, pests and diseases 3

Diseases

House plants are not prone to many air-borne diseases and, of those that are found, most gain a foothold because the plant has been overwatered, or because water has lodged in leaf axils causing conditions in which fungi and bacteria can thrive. Damaged leaves and bruised stems may spark off one of several bacterial diseases, and overcrowding, resulting in a lack of adequate air circulation, can also spell trouble. Many pests transmit diseases, and an infestation will, in any case, weaken a plant and make it more susceptible to disease. Always remove diseased sections as soon as you see them, and isolate an affected plant from the rest of your collection whilst treatment is being given.

Blackleg

This disease, also known as "black rot" and "black stem rot", strikes plants just where the stem meets the potting mixture, but spreads both upwards and downwards to the roots. An attack rarely occurs unless the potting mixture is kept too wet for too long, but stem cuttings are liable to be affected during propagation.
Susceptible plants This disease is most common on geraniums (*Pelargonium* sp.).

Treatment Always use free-draining potting mixtures and be particularly sparing with water during the period that geranium cuttings are rooting. Avoid damaging stems and always remove faded leaves. There is no cure for this disease but cuttings taken from the tops of stems that are unaffected can be rooted—dip the cut ends into hormone rooting powder containing fungicide.

Grey mould

This fungus, which is also called "botrytis", usually starts growing on fallen leaves and flowers, but can also start when water lodges in the axils of the leaves. It strikes quickly when temperatures are low and the air is moist, and rarely in warmer weather and in dry air. Whole leaves or stems can be affected, assuming an unpleasant, fluffy-grey, mouldy appearance.
Susceptible plants Grey mould affects plants with soft stems and leaves, such as African violets (*Saintpaulia* hybrids), cinerarias (*Senecio cruentus* hybrids), angel wings (*Caladium hortulanum* hybrids) and purple velvet plants (*Gynura aurantiaca*).
Treatment Fading leaves should be removed, and plants should be watered and mist-sprayed less frequently. A suitable fungicide may have to be used in severe cases, and to prevent further attacks.

Sooty mould

Sooty mould grows on the sticky honeydew secreted by pests such as aphids and scale insects. As such, it is a sure sign that a plant is infested with some sort of sap-sucker. The mould itself looks just like a thick layer of soot and feels sticky. Although sooty mould does not directly attack the leaves, its presence spoils the appearance of the plant, clogs the breathing pores of the leaves, and reduces photosynthesis by obscuring light.
Susceptible plants Citrus plants are particularly liable to be affected.
Treatment Regular washing of the leaves with soapy water avoids the possibility of an attack, and is the only way of washing off the objectionable mould once it appears. The best means of treatment is to attack the sap-sucking pests which deposit the sticky honeydew.

Mildew

Mildew appears as powdery white patches on leaves, stems and, occasionally, flowers. These patches can be distinguished from grey mould by the absence of fluffy growths. Stricken leaves become distorted and fall from the plant. Low temperatures combined with high humidity, poor air circulation and overwatering provide ideal conditions for mildew.
Susceptible plants Soft-leaved and succulent-stemmed plants, including some begonias, are particularly susceptible; other kinds of begonia, even when growing alongside affected plants, are not attacked.
Treatment To treat plants affected by mildew, pick off all affected leaves and spray the rest of the plant with a fungicide.

Stem and crown rot

If the stem of a plant starts to go soft and slimy, the reason may be stem rot. Low temperatures and soggy potting mixture may cause plants to become infected. An attack of crown rot will cause the leaves to be eaten away from the centre outwards.
Susceptible plants Plants with soft stems, such as busy Lizzies (*Impatiens* sp.) and German violets (*Exacum affine*), are prone to stem rot. Other susceptible plants are cacti; when soft, dark-brown or black patches appear near to potting mixture level, it is likely to be stem rot. Rosette-shaped plants, such as echeverias (*Echeveria* sp.) and African violets (*Saintpaulia* hybrids), are liable to attack from crown rot.
Treatment An attack is usually fatal but unaffected sections may be dusted with sulphur and re-rooted if their shape justifies their being retained.

Diagnosis chart

The diagnosis chart below should enable you to determine what is wrong with your plant. Most problems occur because of incorrect growing conditions but, if the symptoms continue, check the plant for any likely pests and diseases, and treat accordingly.

Signs of pests

● Distorted stems and leaves ● Damaged flowers ● General air of lack-lustre ● Sticky "honeydew" substance on leaves and stems *Occurs mainly in spring, summer and autumn*	Aphids (plant lice or greenfly)
● Mottled or finely pitted leaves ● Curled up leaf edges ● Fine silky webbing on leaf undersides and leaf axils *Occurs mainly in spring, summer and autumn*	Red spider mites
● Sticky substance on leaves which may turn black ● Waxy brown or yellow encrustations on leaf undersides *Occurs throughout the year*	Scale insects
● Yellowing leaves ● General air of debility ● Tufts of waxy, white wool in leaf axils and around areoles of cacti ● "Honeydew" on leaves or on cactus stems *Occurs throughout the year*	Mealy bugs
● Poor growth and yellowing leaves ● Clumps of white, waxy bugs on roots *Occurs throughout the year*	Root mealy bugs
● Crescent-shaped sections eaten out of leaf edges of plants with thick, succulent leaves *Occurs in spring and summer*	Vine weevils (adults)
● Wilting of the whole plant when potting mixture is still moist ● Roots or tubers eaten away *Occurs in spring, summer and autumn*	Vine weevils (larvae)
● Sticky "honeydew" on leaves ●·Pure white insects resembling moths on leaf undersides *Occurs in summer and autumn*	Whitefly
● Minute, sluggish, brown flies circling above potting mixture ● Piles of "soil" made by tiny larvae appear under the pot *Occurs throughout the year*	Fungus gnats
● Nibbled leaves and stems ● Rolled up leaves with fine sticky webbing holding them together ● Distorted growth caused by leaves or shoots being "stuck" to their neighbour *Occurs throughout the year*	Leaf rolling caterpillars

Signs of disease

● Fluffy grey mould on half-rotted leaves *Occurs from autumn to spring*	Grey mould (botrytis)
● Soft, slimy stems ● Black or brown decayed areas *Occurs in autumn and winter*	Crown or stem rot
● Thin, black, sootlike deposit on leaves and stems growing on the "honeydew" secreted by sap-sucking insects *Occurs in summer and autumn*	Sooty mould
● Powdery white patches on leaves and stems ● Twisted leaves ● Leaf fall and possible total defoliation *Occurs in spring and autumn*	Powdery mildew
● Black shrivelled sections of stem just above the potting mixture *Occurs in late autumn and winter*	Blackleg

Other danger signs

● Pale elongated growth with large gaps between the leaves ● Small new leaves, small or few flowers ● Variegated leaves lose colour contrast ● New shoots that should be variegated appear plain green	Lack of sufficient light
● Large, irregularly shaped, light-brown patches on leaves ● Drooping leaves and stems ● Stunted flowers and unduly short or misshapen flower stalks	Too much sun or unaccustomed sun. Light too bright for those that prefer some shade
● Brown leaf tips and leaf edges ● Some leaf curl	Air too dry and/or potting mixture allowed to dry out too much between each watering
● Blackening or shrivelling of small leaf sections ● Serious leaf drop of large-leaved plants	Draughts or too cold a position
● Green slime on clay pots ● Algae, moss and other plant growth on the surface of the potting mixture ● Yellowing leaves and leaf drop	Overwatering

Problems, pests and diseases 4

Pesticides

All types of pesticide are labelled as to their contents and the pests or diseases they should be used against. Always follow strictly any specific instructions, such as the dilution ratio and the method of application.

Contact insecticides

Insecticides are most commonly applied in liquid form as a fine spray, so that they hit the pest directly and, with luck, kill it quickly before it has time to multiply. These "knock-out" sprays work on contact, affecting the insect's respiratory system or otherwise destroying it.

Most sprays have an unpleasant smell and should not be inhaled. Take plants to be treated out into the garden or on to a balcony, as good ventilation while spraying is essential.

Some insecticides are poisonous to animals, birds and fish, and need careful handling. Others may not be suitable for particular plants, or broad families of plants, since their chemical content could burn the leaves and possibly do more harm than the pests. The label should warn you of this.

Systemic insecticides

Systemic insecticides work in another way. They are taken up by the sap—either from the potting mixture or through the leaves—and the sap-sucking or leaf-chewing insect is poisoned. Some stay as a thin film on the surface of the leaves, killing the insects that eat them; these are often called "stomach insecticides". Systemics can be applied in a number of ways: they can be watered on to the mix, sprinkled over it in the form of granules or pushed into it as a "pin" or "spike". They can also be sprayed on to the foliage of plants; the active ingredients work their way into the sap and circulatory system of the plant and poison pests taking them in. All systemics are relatively long-lasting and they can kill "newcomers" (pests that arrive on the plants some time after the application of the chemicals), whereas contact sprays only affect insects that they make direct contact with.

Some insecticides combine both the knock-out effect and the long-term systemic coverage. New products are regularly appearing, which is just as well since some pests eventually develop a resistance to one chemical. Vary your insecticide from time to time to avoid the possibility of resistance build-up.

Fungicides and bactericides

The best way to prevent disease is to ensure that your plants are grown in the conditions they prefer. Because disease is less frequently met with than attack by pests, it can be controlled by a much smaller range of chemicals. These are known as fungicides, which combat fungal diseases, and bactericides, which combat bacterial diseases. Most of these act systemically and are therefore capable of combating disease which occurs in any part of a plant. They are also unlikely to harm healthy plants, as can unsuitable insecticides, and are not usually harmful to people.

Fungicides and bactericides are most effective when applied in advance of attack, and it does no harm to use them purely as a precautionary device.

Application methods

Insecticides, fungicides and bactericides are packaged in various forms and can be applied in a number of ways. In addition to the normal sprays, aerosols, dusts, granules and spikes, diluted chemicals can be used as a bath into which small plants can be dipped. When it is necessary to treat sub-soil pests by soaking the potting mixture, a watering can may be used to apply the insecticide. In all instances, great care should be taken to follow the manufacturer's instructions and to ensure adequate ventilation is provided when applying the chemicals.

Spraying
Coat all parts of the plant evenly, paying particular attention to the undersides of leaves. If possible, use sprays and aerosols outside so that the spray is not breathed in.

Soaking
Chemical solutions can be applied to the potting mixture using an ordinary watering can—but avoid splashing the leaves. Always use at the recommended strength.

Dusting
Dusting powders are especially useful on cut or bruised leaves. Give upper and lower surfaces a thorough coating. The potting mixture can also be dusted.

Sprinkling
Sprinkle granules evenly on to the potting mixture. The chemical is gradually released with each successive watering.

Inserting a spike
Push the spike into the potting mixture using a pencil or your finger. This method is quick and convenient.

How to apply pesticides

Key

- Soaking — black droplet
- Spraying — white droplet
- Dusting — black square
- Spike — small black square
- Granules — black triangle
- Pellets — black circle

	Benomyl	Bupirmate and Triforine	Butoxycarboxim	Dimethoate	Gamma HCH dust	Green sulphur dust	Formothion	Malathion	Metaldehyde	Perimicarb	Permanganate of potash	Permethrin	Pirimiphos-methyl with synergized pyrethrins	Pyrethrum with Resmethrin	Comments
Aphids			Soaking / Spraying	Spraying			Spraying	Soaking / Spraying		Spraying			Spraying	Soaking / Spraying	
Blackleg															No known cure
Caterpillars				Soaking / Spraying								Soaking / Spraying			
Earthworms											Soaking				
Fungus gnats										Soaking					
Grey mould (botrytis)	Spraying														
Leaf miners				Spraying											
Leaf rollers				Spraying											
Mealy bugs and root mealy bugs				Spraying				Soaking / Spraying				Soaking / Spraying	Soaking / Spraying		
Powdery mildew	Spraying	Spraying				Dusting									
Red spider mites			Spike	Soaking / Spraying				Soaking / Spraying				Soaking / Spraying	Soaking / Spraying		
Scale insects				Soaking / Spraying				Soaking / Spraying							
Slugs and snails									Pellets						
Sooty mould															Remove with a damp sponge
Stem and crown rot	Dusting					Dusting									
Vine weevils				Soaking / Spraying	Granules, Dusting										
White flies				Soaking / Spraying				Soaking / Spraying				Soaking / Spraying	Soaking / Spraying	Soaking / Spraying	

Glossary 1

Adventitious roots Roots appearing in an unusual place, such as on stems or leaves, e.g., on the stems of cuttings placed in water or on the leaves of some succulent plants.

Aerial roots Roots that appear at nodes. They are mainly used for climbing but are also capable of absorbing moisture from the air. Many only develop properly if they can grasp a suitable rooting medium such as sphagnum moss, e.g., the philodendrons and their relatives the Swiss cheese plant, pothos vine, devil's ivy and arrowhead plant.

Annual A plant grown from seed that completes its life cycle in one season. Annuals must be thrown away once this cycle is complete. A number of perennial plants are treated as annuals (a recommendation is made in *The Plant Finder's Guide*), because of the difficulty of overwintering them or because they seldom look attractive in subsequent years, e.g., German violet. See also *biennial, perennial.*

Anther The male part of the flower which produces pollen.

Areole An organ unique to the cacti, consisting of a cushion or hump from which the spines and flowers arise.

Areole

Axil The angle between the leaf or leaf stalk and stem from which new leaf or side-shoot growth and flower buds arise. Buds found here are known as axillary buds. Side-shoot growth is prevented if they are pinched out.

Axil

Berry A succulent fruit in which the usually small but hard seeds are embedded in the fleshy pulp. This pulp is usually brightly coloured to attract animals and birds.

Biennial A plant grown from seed which takes two growing seasons to complete its life cycle. A rosette of leaves is produced in the first year, the flowers in the second. Biennials should be thrown away once this cycle is complete as it is difficult to make them flower again, e.g., foxglove. See also *annual, perennial.*

Bleeding When sap flows freely from a damaged stem. This is particularly obvious in such plants as the crown-of-thorns and rubber plant which bleed a milky-white latex. The flow can be staunched by applying powdered sulphur or charcoal. See also *latex.*

Bract A modified leaf, often colourful, which backs relatively insignificant flowers and acts as a method of attracting pollinating insects and birds, e.g., the petal-like red bracts of the poinsettia and the bell-shaped bracts of the paper flower.

Bracts

Flowers

Bud An embryo shoot, leaf or an immature flower. A terminal growth bud is situated at the tip of a stem or side shoot, an axillary bud is one found in the axil of a leaf stalk. Growth buds are normally protected from damage and cold by closely overlapping scales or sheaths. See also *sheath, axil.*

Axillary bud   Terminal bud

Bulb An underground storage organ containing a young plant. The organ stores food during the rest period and usually a complete embryo flower, e.g., tulip, daffodil. See also *corm, tuber.*

Bulb

Bulbil A small immature bulb attached to a parent bulb, it can also appear on the stems or leaves of the parent plant, e.g., some lilies.

Calyx The collective name for the ring of green sepals which surrounds the petals in most flowers. The calyx protects the developing flower buds. See also *sepal.*

Capillary action Also known as capillary attraction, this is the drawing up of water by a thread or hair. The term is also used to describe the way potting mixture draws up water when the pot and mixture are placed in direct contact with a dish or bowl of water.

Cereal Plants of the grass family cultivated for their seed as food, e.g., wheat, barley. See also *grass.*

Chlorophyll The green pigment found in the stems and leaves of plants.

Compound leaf A leaf divided into two or more segments, e.g., umbrella plant. See also *pinnate, palmate.*

Corm An underground storage organ made up of a thickened stem covered with a thin papery skin. At the top of the corm a bud produces both roots and shoots, e.g., crocus, sword lily. See also *bulb, tuber.*

Corm

Corolla The collective name for the ring of petals. The corolla may be made up of separate petals or the petals may be fused into one unit. See also *flower, petal.*

Crown The growing point of a plant, particularly of a rosette-shaped plant, e.g., African violet. The crown can also be the basal part of an herbaceous plant where the root and shoots meet. See also *root crown.*

Cultivar A type of plant or flower that has been developed in cultivation and named by the plant breeder. Cultivar names are enclosed by quotation marks to distinguish them from the scientific names. See also *variety.*

Cutting A term usually applied to a stem cutting. This is a section of stem, 7-10cm long, (usually the growing tip), which is used in propagation to root and develop into a new plant.

Deciduous A plant that loses its leaves at the end of the growing season. These plants do not make good house plants as they are not decorative through the resting period. New leaves appear in the spring to replace those lost in the autumn. See also *evergreen.*

Dieback The death of a section of stem. This is often caused by faulty pruning.

Double flower Flowers having at least two layers of petals. Often the stamens and pistils at the centre of the flower are replaced by more petals. Double-flowered forms are usually cultivars, e.g., modern roses. See also *single flower, semi-double flower.*

Double flower

Epiphyte A plant that grows on another plant but is not a parasite. Epiphytes use the host plant purely as an anchor and take no direct nourishment from it. Many bromeliads and ferns are epiphytes, producing strong, wiry roots which cling to tree trunks and branches, and other plants.

Etiolation The technical name for pale, sickly growth. The gaps between the leaves become greater and the flowers fewer. Insufficient light and overcrowding cause the condition.

Evergreen A plant which retains its leaves throughout the year. See also *deciduous*.

Exotic A plant introduced from abroad. The term is often applied to plants that have their origins in tropical and sub-tropical regions. Most house plants, therefore, are exotic.

Eye The centre of a flower, which is often a different colour to the rest of the bloom, e.g., black-eyed Susan, primula.

Family A term used to describe a large association of plants in which certain characteristics are constant. Many genera make up one family, e.g., *Compositae* is the family name for all the plants with daisylike flowers. See also *genus, species*.

Filament The stalk supporting the anther. These two parts make up the stamen. Normally, many filaments are clustered together in the middle of the flower, e.g., passion flower. See also *stamen, anther*.

Floret A small flower among many others making up a flower head, e.g., most daisy flowers are made up of many florets.

Floret

Flower Usually the most striking feature of a plant, this is an organ of very specialized parts concerned with sexual reproduction. Some plants produce flowers that carry only male parts (stamens), or female parts (pistils). These parts are usually surrounded by a ring of coloured petals and green sepals, although there are many variations of this pattern. Some plants have both male and female flower heads on the same plant but, in most plants, both male and female parts are enclosed in the same flower head. Begonias are an example of a flower which is either male, when it is a collection of bright petals with pollen-filled stamens, or female, when it has a large winged seed sac backing the petals.

Pistil
Stigma
Style
Ovary
Stamen
Anther
Filament
Corolla
Petals

Forcing The technique of bringing a flower into growth ahead of its natural season. Usually a term applied to spring bulbs when they are encouraged to flower early. Azaleas and cyclamens are also "forced".

Frond Botanically, a term used to describe the deeply dissected "leaves" of ferns which bear spores and arise from a rhizome. It is also loosely applied to palm leaves.

Fruit A widely used term that describes any mature ovary bearing ripe seeds. The outer covering may be soft and fleshy, such as the berries of the Christmas cherry, or a dry pod with hard seeds inside, such as the seed pod of the Cape primrose. See also *nut, berry*.

Genus (pl. genera) A group of allied species. Usually a group of plants (though sometimes only one) which are similar in structure and which most probably evolved from a common ancestor. The genus name always begins with an upper case letter, e.g., all ivies belong to the genus *Hedera*. See also *species, family*.

Germination The first stage of a seed's development into a plant. The first visible stage is the sprouting of the new seedling. Germination can be swift (four to six days), or take many weeks or even months. It is a dangerous period as the seed is no longer protected by the hard outer casing, and strong roots and leaves have not yet developed.

Gourd The large, fleshy fruit of climbing and trailing annual plants native to tropical America. The dried fruits can be used in decoration.

Grass Annual or perennial plants of the family *Gramineae*. In the home, their decorative seed heads and threadlike stalks can be used in flower arrangements or dried for winter decoration. See also *cereal*.

Growing tip Also known as growing point, this is the tip of a shoot from which vigorous new growth emerges.

Hardy A plant capable of surviving outside throughout the year, even in areas where there is the possibility of a winter frost. Spotted laurel and Japanese fatsia are examples of hardy house plants.

Herbaceous A word usually associated with perennial plants whose growth dies down in the late autumn and is replaced with fresh growth the following spring. Plant material is stored as a bulb, corm, rhizome or tuber, e.g., begonia, daffodil. Herbaceous plants never have woody stems. See also *woody*.

Hip A fleshy type of fruit, especially common in the rose family.

Hybrid A plant derived from two genetically different parents. Cross fertilization is common between plants of different species within the same genus. Plants arising from such crossings are known as primary hybrids; they usually have some of the characteristics of both parents, but may favour one more than the other. Cross fertilization is possible, but rare, between plants of different genera, e.g., *Fatshedera* is a hybrid of *Fatsia* and *Hedera*. These crossings are known as bigeneric or intergeneric hybrids. Many naturally occurring hybrids are sterile.

Inflorescence A group of two or more flowers on one stem. An inflorescence may vary considerably in shape from the narrow and spikelike lavenders and sword lilies to the broad round heads of hydrangeas and Egyptian star clusters. See also *raceme, panicle, spike, umbel*.

Juvenile Usually applied to the leaves of a young plant that are different in shape from those of a more mature plant, e.g., eucalyptus foliage, which is round when taken from young plants and thin and pointed when taken from older trees. The leaves of young philodendrons may also be a different shape to those of older plants.

Latex A free-flowing, milky-white fluid which exudes from plants such as crown-of-thorns and rubber plants if stems are cut or damaged. See also *bleeding*.

Leaf The energy-producing organ of the plant. Light striking the green part of the leaf starts the process of photosynthesis. Sepals, petals, tendrils and bracts are thought to be modified leaves. In most cacti, the stems take over the function of leaves.

Leaflet A part of a compound, pinnate leaf, properly known as a pinna. See also *compound leaf, pinna, pinnate*.

Leaflet (pinna)

Leaf mould Partially decayed leaves used in potting mixtures to provide nutrients, bacterial activity and an open, free-draining consistency. More correctly known as humus, it may be difficult to buy but can be found under deciduous trees (leaf litter) or made by composting fallen leaves.

Margin The border of a leaf or flower petal. This may be lobed or toothed, or of a different colour to the main body of the leaf.

Node A stem joint at which the leaves are borne. The node may be notched or swollen and is a point from which the new roots of such plants as ivies and philodendrons are commonly made.

Node

Nut A type of fruit consisting of a hard or leathery shell enclosing a seed that is often edible. See also *fruit*.

Glossary 2

Offset Also known as an offshoot, this is a new plant produced by the parent at its base, or on short stolons, and is normally detachable from the parent. See also *stolon*.

Ovary The basal part of the flower in which the seeds are formed. The ovary wall becomes the fruit wall. See also *flower, fruit*.

Palmate A term applied to compound leaves with several leaflets arranged fanwise from a common point, shaped like a hand, e.g., finger aralia. See also *compound leaf*.

Palmate

Panicle A type of inflorescence consisting of a large branched cluster of flowers, each with a number of stalked flowers, e.g., lilac, most grasses. See also *inflorescence*.

Perennial A plant that lives for an indefinite period, e.g., African lily. Perennials can be herbaceous or woody. See also *annual, biennial*.

Petal Usually the showy part of the flower. Petals protect the centre of the flower and, when coloured, are intended to attract pollinating insects to the stamens and pistils. Sepals are often confused with petals. Petals may be few (three in many tradescantias) or many (as in a double-flowered rose). They are collectively known as the corolla. See also *sepal, stamen, pistil, flower, corolla*.

Photosynthesis The process by which carbon dioxide is converted into carbohydrates within the leaf. It is sparked off by light striking the green pigment in leaves and stems. See also *chlorophyll, leaf*.

Pinching out Also known as stopping. A form of pruning practised by gently pulling off, with forefinger and thumb, the soft growing tips of shoots to induce bushiness.

Pinna An individual section of a much divided leaf or frond, commonly known as a leaflet. Used when describing fern fronds. See also *frond, leaflet*.

Pinnate A term used to describe a compound leaf that is divided into several or many pairs of oppositely arranged pinnae (leaflets), e.g., parlour palm. See also *compound leaf, leaflet, pinna*.

Pistil The female part of a flower, comprising stigma, style and ovary. See also *stigma, style, ovary, flower*.

Plantlet A young plant. The stage beyond that of a seedling, but also used to describe "offspring" that are produced on leaves or stolons, e.g., pickaback plant. See also *seedling*.

Raceme A type of inflorescence. An elongated, unbranched flower head, each flower having a short stalk. The flowers normally develop and open from the bottom of the raceme, higher ones opening as the lower ones fade, e.g., hyacinth. See also *inflorescence*.

Raceme

Rest period A period within the 12-month season in which the plant should be allowed to become inactive, producing little or no leaf or root growth.

Rhizome A creeping stem, usually horizontal and often underground, from which leaves, side shoots and roots appear. It often acts as a storage organ to enable plants to survive through a short period of drought, e.g., painted-leaf begonia.

Rib A main or prominent vein of a leaf.

Root The lower part of a plant, normally in the potting mixture, which serves to hold it firm and pass nourishment and water to it from the potting mixture. There are two types of root: fine, fibrous roots and the larger, single tap roots. Most plants have one type of root or the other; few have both.

Root ball The mass of potting mixture interspersed with roots seen when a plant is taken from its pot. Examination of the root ball is a way of establishing whether a plant needs repotting or potting on.

Root crown The basal part of a plant, where the stem meets the roots.

Root hair The fine feeding hairs covering the surface of the roots. These are microscopic and cannot be seen with the naked eye.

Rosette An arrangement of leaves radiating from a distinct centre, e.g., African violet.

Runner A creeping stem, running along the surface of the potting mixture, which takes root at its nodes and produces a new plant at that point. See also *stolon*.

Scurf Fine, scalelike particles on leaves or stems giving them a grey or silvered appearance, e.g., silver crown.

Seed The fertilized and ripened part of a flowering plant (ovule), capable of germinating and producing a new plant. Seeds range in size from under 1mm to around 20cm in diameter; most seeds are pea-sized.

Seedling A young plant raised from seed which still possesses a single unbranched stem.

Semi-double flower A flower with more than one layer of petals but with fewer than a

fully double bloom, e.g., some African violets. See also *single flower, double flower*.

Semi-double flower

Sepal The outer part of a flower, often green, which protects the middle of the flower and the more delicate petals. Flowers such as the anemone are actually made up of sepals rather than petals. See also *calyx, petal*.

Sheath A protective wrapping for a growing point, e.g., rubber plant.

Shrub A woody-stemmed bushy plant, smaller than a tree and usually with many stems which branch near the ground. It is often difficult to define the difference between a large shrub and a small tree. Most house plants are shrubs rather than trees. See also *tree, woody*.

Single flower A flower with the normal number of petals, e.g., Marguerite daisy. See also *double flower, semi-double flower*.

Single flower

Spadix A small spike with minute flowers embedded in it, usually surrounded by a spathe, e.g., the centre part of a flamingo flower. See also *spathe*.

Spadix

Spathe

Spathe A prominent modified leaf or bract surrounding the spadix. Usually fleshy and white, sometimes coloured, e.g., flamingo flower. See also *spadix*.

Species The members of a genus are called species. From its seed each persistently breeds true to type in its main characteristics. A plant's name is made up of at least two parts: the name of the genus and the name of the species, e.g., *Coleus* (genus) *blumei* (species). See also *genus, family*.

Spike A type of inflorescence, in the form of a long unbranched flower head. Very similar in appearance to a raceme except that the individual flowers of a spike have no stalks, e.g., sword lily.

Spike

Spore Minute reproductive bodies produced by ferns and mosses—the equivalent of seeds in a flowering plant. Spores are held in spore cases on the underside of some fronds (some fronds are sterile and do not bear spore cases) and may be arranged in a number of patterns—herringbone, marginal or scattered.

Stalk The organ supporting the flower (flower stalk), the leaf (leaf stalk) or the anther (filament). See also *filament*.

Stamen The pollen-bearing male organ of a flower, comprising a filament and two anther lobes containing pollen. See also *filament, anther, flower*.

Stigma The tip of the female reproductive organ (pistil) on which the pollen settles. See also *flower, pistil*.

Stolon A creeping stem that produces a new plantlet at its tip or wherever it touches the potting mixture. See also *runner*.

Stomata The pores through which gases enter and leave the plant. They are usually situated on the underside of the leaves.

Style The style supports the stigma, holding it in an effective place for pollination. See also *stigma, pistil, flower*.

Succulent A plant which has fleshy leaves or stems capable of storing water. Usually plants from arid areas, e.g., Chinese jade.

Sucker A shoot arising from below the surface of the potting mixture, usually from the roots of a plant.

Tendril A wiry projection from the stem that twines around a support and enables a plant to climb. The tendrils may be spiralled, e.g., passion flower, or forked.

Tendril

Topdressing The process of replacing the top few centimetres of potting mixture with fresh mixture as an alternative to repotting. Topdressing is most useful for plants which have grown too large for moving into bigger pots. It involves carefully scraping away some of the old potting mixture in spring, doing as little damage as possible to the roots, and firming in fresh mixture.

Transpiration The continual, natural water loss from leaves. This may be heavy or hardly noticeable, depending on the time of day or time of year—factors which affect the relative humidity. Heavy transpiration in warm weather causes wilting which is damaging to the plant.

Tree A woody-stemmed plant with an obvious trunk topped with branches. See also *woody, shrub*.

Tuber A thick, fleshy stem or root which acts as a storage organ. Some tuberous-rooted plants lose their leaves and stem in the autumn and the tuber stores food for renewed growth the following spring, e.g., begonia. Occasionally tubers are produced on stems, e.g., rosary vine. See also *corm, bulb*.

Tuber

Turgid A term applied to plants that are "crisp" and healthy as their cells are full of water. Also applied to cuttings that have obviously produced roots of their own and are taking up sufficient water for their needs.

Umbel A type of inflorescence. A flower head in which the individual flower stalks arise from a common point. Commonly known as a cluster, e.g., regal geranium, hydrangea. See also *inflorescence*.

Umbel

Undulate A leaf margin or petal that has a wavy edge. Undulate does not refer to toothed or serrated edges.

Variegated A term applied to leaves streaked or spotted with another colour (usually cream or yellow). Variegation is usually the result of a mutation and is sometimes due to a virus infection; rarely is it natural or built-in. Variegated-leaved plants are popularly cultivated and need good light to maintain variegation. Cuttings from certain variegated-leaved plants produce plants with plain green leaves.

Variety A word used to refer to variations of the plant that have occured in the wild, but sometimes incorrectly used to describe a form developed in horticulture. Cultivar is a more accurate term for the latter. Varietal names are printed in italics. See also *cultivar*.

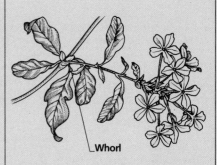

Whorl

Whorl A circle of three or more leaves or flowers produced at the nodes on a stem or stalk, e.g., Cape leadwort.

Wintering A term used to describe the simulation of winter conditions indoors to encourage winter- and spring-flowering bulbs to make good roots before top growth starts.

Woody Refers to plants which have hard stems which persist above ground all year, e.g., paper flower. See also *herbaceous*.

Index

Acknowledgments

Author's acknowledgments

I should like to thank the following for their help:
Elizabeth Eyres who has edited the book and Jane Owen who has laid it out so delightfully.
Priscilla Ritchie who has given invaluable help in creating studio
shots in my absence, together with the photographer, Dave King.
Richard Gilbert who has performed monumental work on the horticultural
wants of plants—not my forté.
And lastly, Hilary Bryan-Brown, my secretary, who has coped amazingly
with both a new set of plant names and my handwriting!

Dorling Kindersley's acknowledgments

Richard Gilbert for all his tireless work and efficiency; Chris Thody for finding
plants; Helen Claire Young and Tina Vaughan for design assistance; Caroline
Ollard and Sophie Galleymore-Bird for editorial assistance;
Vickie Walters for picture research; Sue Brown and Sarah Hayes Fisher for styling;
Judy Sandeman for production; Richard Bird for the index;
Adrian Ensor for black and white prints; Sebastian von Mybourg at
The Flowersmith; Anmore Exotics; The Vernon Geranium Nursery; The Royal
Horticultural Society; Holly Gate Cactus Nursery; Syon Park Garden Centre; Clifton
Nurseries Ltd; Coolings Nursery; Bourne Bridge Nurseries; Inca (Peruvian Art and
Craft Ltd), 15 Elizabeth St, London SW1; The General Trading Company, 144
Sloane St, London SW1; Zeitgeist, 17 The Pavement, London SW4; Ceramic Tile
Design, 56 Dawes Rd, London SW6; Chris Frankham of Glass House Studios; Neal
Street East, London; and Habitat.

Illustrators

David Ashby Will Giles Tony Graham Nicholas Hall Coral Mula Sandra Pond James Robins Lorna Turpin

Photographic credits

EWA Elizabeth Whiting and Associates CP Camera Press SG Susan Griggs Agency DK Dorling Kindersley **T** = top, **B** = bottom, **L** = left, **R** = right, **C** = centre

1, 2, 3, 4, 5 Philip Dowell/DK; **6L** Ken Kirkwood/English Style (courtesy of Margot Johnson); **6C** Michael Boys; **6R, 7L & R;** Michael Dunne/EWA; **7C** Lucinda Lambton/Arcaid; **8L** Andreas Einsiedel/EWA; **8C** Richard Bryant/Arcaid; **8R** Michael Boys; **9L** Richard Bryant/Arcaid; **9C** John Hollingshead; **9R** Michael Dunne; **10, 11** Linda Burgess; **12, 13, 14, 15, 16, 17, 18, 19, 20, 21, 22, 23, 24, 25** Philip Dowell/DK; **26, 27** Linda Burgess; **28, 29** Dave King/DK; **30CL** Fuer Sie/CP; **30T, CR & B** Dave King/DK; **31T** Mon Jardin et Ma Maison/CP; **31BL** Schöner Wohnen/CP; **31BR** Michael Boys/SG; **32TL & TR** Dave King/DK; **32B** Michael Nicholson/EWA; **33** Jean Durand/The World of Interiors; **34T** Tom Dobbie/DK; **34B** Dave King/DK; **35T** Tom Dobbie/DK; **35B** Dave King/DK; **36T** Michael Boys/SG; **36B** John Vere Brown/The World of Interiors; **37L** Dave King/DK; **37TR** Michael Nicholson/EWA; **37BL & BR, 38T & B** Tom Dobbie/DK; **39T** Dave King/DK; **39B** IMS/CP; **40T** Fuer Sie/CP; **40B** Dave King/DK; **41TL & TR** Linda Burgess; **41B** Dave King/DK; **42TL** Michael Boys/SG; **42TR** Linda Burgess; **42B** Dave King/DK; **43L** Tom Dobbie/DK; **43R** Michael Boys/SG; **43B** Dave King/DK; **44TR** Linda Burgess; **44TL** Richard Bryant/Arcaid; **44B** Dave King/DK; **45TL** IMS/CP; **45TR** Schöner Wohnen/CP; **45B, 46, 47T & C** Dave King/DK; **47B** Geoff Dann/DK; **48, 49, 50** Dave King/DK; **51L** Michael Dunne/EWA; **51TR** Jessica Strang; **51B, 52, 53T & BR** Dave King/DK; **53BL** Hus Modern/CP; **54** Spike Powell/EWA; **55** Dave King/DK; **56, 57, 58** Trevor Melton/DK; **59T** Linda Burgess; **59B** Schöner Wohnen/CP; **60** Dave King/DK; **61BL** Pamla Toler/Impact Photos; **61BR** K-D Buhler/EWA; **62TL** John Moss/Colorific; **62TR & B** Pamla Toler/Impact Photos; **63, 64** Dave King/DK; **65T & B** Linda Burgess; **66, 67, 68T** Dave King/DK; **68BL** Michael Boys/DK; **68BR** Geoff Dann/DK; **69, 70, 71TL & R** Dave King/DK; **71BL & R** Tom Dobbie/DK; **72, 73T & BL** Dave King/DK; **73BR** Michael Boys; **74T & BR** Dave King/DK; **74BL** Schöner Wohnen/CP; **75** Dave King/DK; **76, 77**

Linda Burgess; **78, 79** Philip Dowell/DK; **80, 81, 82, 83, 84, 85, 86, 87, 88, 89, 90, 91, 92, 93** Dave King/DK; **94, 95** Linda Burgess; **96, 97, 98, 99T** Dave King/DK; **99B** Linda Burgess; **100, 101, 102** Trevor Melton/DK; **103TL** Jessica Strang; **103TR & B** Linda Burgess; **104, 105T & BL** Dave King/DK; **105 BR** Tom Dobbie/DK; **106, 107, 108T** Dave King/DK; **108B** Zuhause/CP; **109, 110, 111** Dave King/DK; **112, 113** Schöner Wohnen/CP; **114TL** Michael Dunne; **114TR** Bill McLaughlin; **114BL** Ron Sutherland; **114BR** Schöner Wohnen/CP; **115TL** Jessica Strang; **115BL** John Vaughan/The World of Interiors; **115C** Jacques Dirand/The World of Interiors; **115TR** Dave King/DK; **115BR** Femina/CP; **116** John Hollingshead; **117T** Schöner Wohnen/CP; **117B** Tim Street-Porter/The World of Interiors; **118T** Ken Kirkwood/English Style (courtesy of Tricia Foley); **118B** John Vaughan/The World of Interiors; **119TL** Michael Boys; **119TR** Schöner Wohnen/CP; **119B** Michael Boys; **120L** Schöner Wohnen/CP; **120R** Clive Helm/EWA; **120B** IMS/CP; **121** Dave King/DK; **122T** IMS/CP; **122C** Michael Boys; **122BL** Michael Dunne; **122BR** Ken Kirkwood/English Style (courtesy of Michael Baumgarten); **123** John Vaughan/The World of Interiors; **124TL** Ken Kirkwood/English Style (courtesy of Lesley Astaire); **124TR** Michael Boys; **124CL** Ken Kirkwood/English Style (courtesy of Lesley Astaire); **124CR & B** Michael Boys; **125** John Vaughan/The World of Interiors; **126TL** Ken Kirkwood/ English Style (courtesy of Stephen Long); **126TR** Schöner Wohnen/CP; **126B** Peter Woloszynski/The World of Interiors; **127** Dave King/DK; **128TL & TR** Michael Boys; **128TR** Michael Boys/SG; **128B** Jessica Strang; **129** Schöner Wohnen/CP; **130** Peter Woloszynski/The World of Interiors; **131TL** Michael Boys; **131TR** Ken Kirkwood/English Style; **131B** Schöner Wohnen/CP; **132T** M Deneux/Agence Top; **132B** Neil Lorimer/EWA; **133T** Hussenot/Agence Top; **133B** Schöner Wohnen/CP; **134T** Michael Boys; **134B** Kent Billequist/CP; **135** Tim Street-Porter/The World of Interiors; **136T** Richard Bryant/Arcaid; **136CL** Michael Dunne; **136C** Jessica Strang; **136B** Ken Kirkwood/English Style (courtesy of Lesley Astaire); **137T** Schöner Wohnen/CP; **137B** Bill McLaughlin; **138TL** Suomen/CP **138R** Schöner Wohnen/CP; **138BL** Michael Dunne; **139** Dave King/DK; **140T** Spike Powell/EWA; **140B** Femina/CP

141T Lucinda Lambton/Arcaid (courtesy of Virginia Antiques, London W11); **141R** Schöner Wohnen/CP; **142TL** Lucinda Lambton/Arcaid; **142TR** Mon Jardin et Ma Maison/CP; **142C** Linda Burgess; **142B** Lucinda Lambton/Arcaid; **143** James Wedge/The World of Interiors; **144T** Jessica Strang; **144BL & BR** Schöner Wohnen/CP; **145TL** Lucinda Lambton/Arcaid (courtesy of Tessa Kennedy); **145TR** Bill McLaughlin; **145B** Clive Frost/The World of Interiors; **146TL** Lucinda Lambton/Arcaid (courtesy of Lyn le Grice Stencil Design, Bread St, Penzance, Cornwall); **146TR** Michael Boys/SG; **146BL & BR** Lucinda Lambton/Arcaid; **147** Dave King/DK; **148T & B** Michael Boys; **149** John Vaughan/The World of Interiors; **150TL** Bill McLaughlin; **150TR** Ken Kirkwood/English Style (courtesy of Philip Hooper); **150B** Jessica Strang; **151** Dave King/DK; **152T** Ken Kirkwood/English Style (courtesy of The Victorian Society); **152BL** Richard Bryant/Arcaid; **152BC** Michael Dunne; **152BR** Spike Powell/EWA; **153** Jacques Dirand/The World of Interiors; **154** Ron Sutherland; **155TL** Tim Soar/Arcaid; **155TR** Bill McLaughlin; **155B, 156TL** Linda Burgess; **156TR** Jessica Strang; **156B** Ken Kirkwood/English Style (courtesy of Matyelok Gibbs); **157TL** Linda Burgess; **157TR** Michael Boys; **157B** IMS/CP; **158, 159** Andreas Einsiedel/DK; **162, 163, 164, 165, 166, 167, 168, 169, 170, 171, 172, 173** Tom Dobbie/DK; **173TL** Dave King/DK; **174, 175, 176, 177** Tom Dobbie/DK; **177TL** Dave King/DK; **178, 179, 180, 181, 182, 183, 184, 185, 186, 187, 188, 198, 190, 191, 192, 193** Tom Dobbie/DK; **194, 195** Dave King/DK; **196, 197, 198, 199, 200, 201L** Tom Dobbie/DK; **201R** Dave King/DK; **202, 203, 204, 205, 206, 207** Ian O'Leary/DK; **209** Dave King/DK; **210, 211, 212, 213, 214, 215, 216, 217, 218, 219, 220, 221, 222, 223, 224, 225, 226, 227, 228** Trevor Melton/DK; **229** Dave King/DK; **230, 231, 232, 233, 234, 235, 236, 237, 238, 239** Philip Dowell/DK; **240, 241** The Design Group; **242, 246, 254, 255** Dave King/DK; **258L** IMS/CP; **258R, 259L** Dave King/DK; **259R & B** Femina/CP; **264** Dave King/DK.

Front cover photograph Dave King
Photograph of John Brookes Tom Dobbie